821.3 Kay
Kay, Dennis.
William Shakespeare
   sonnets and poems
                    $ 34.00

D0206391

William Shakespeare
Sonnets and Poems

Twayne's English Authors Series

Arthur F. Kinney, Editor

University of Massachusetts, Amherst

TEAS 547

**PORTRAIT OF WILLIAM SHAKESPEARE
(NO ARTIST ATTRIBUTED)**

From the Art Collection of the Folger Shakespeare Library.

William Shakespeare
Sonnets and Poems

Dennis Kay

University of North Carolina at Charlotte

Twayne Publishers
An Imprint of Simon & Schuster Macmillan
New York

Prentice Hall International
London • Mexico City • New Delhi • Singapore • Sydney • Toronto

Twayne's English Authors Series No. 547

William Shakespeare: Sonnets and Poems
Dennis Kay

Copyright © 1998 by Twayne Publishers

All rights reserved. No part of this book may be reproduced or transmitted in any form or by any means, electronic or mechanical, including photocopying, recording, or by any information storage and retrieval system, without permission in writing from the Publisher.

Twayne Publishers
An Imprint of Simon & Schuster Macmillan
1633 Broadway
New York, NY 10019

Library of Congress Cataloging-in-Publication Data

Kay Dennis.
    William Shakespeare : sonnets and poems / Dennis Kay.
       p.   cm. — (Twayne's English authors series ; TEAS 547)
    Includes bibliographical references and index.
    ISBN 0-8057-1649-1
    1. Shakespeare, William, 1564–1616—Poetic works. 2. Sonnets,
English—History and criticism. I. Shakespeare, William,
1564–1616. II. Title. III. Series.
PR2984.K34 1998
821'.3—dc21   97-36462
                                                       CIP

This paper meets the requirements of ANSI/NISO Z3948–1992 (Permanence of Paper).

10 9 8 7 6 5 4 3

Printed in the United States of America

For my sons,
James, William, and Thomas

Contents

Editor's Note

During his lifetime, William Shakespeare was much better known and much more admired as a poet than a playwright; his narrative poems, *Venus and Adonis* and *Lucrece*, unlike his sonnets or any of his plays, were always in print and widely read. In this new general introduction to Shakespeare's poetry, Dennis Kay shows why this is so. By examining the manuscript tradition and the practice of publishing as quite separate functions in Elizabethan England, he is able to shed important new light on the form and ideas in Shakespeare's poetry. The detailed analyses of his narrative poems, placing them in the traditions of literature to which Shakespeare was responding, will be useful to readers. Even more useful, perhaps, is Kay's long discussion of Shakespeare's sonnets, examining them as part of a tradition that began with introspective verse and narrative in the medieval period and seeing them as particular responses to the work of Samuel Daniel and Edmund Spenser, and most frequently and importantly, the work of Sir Philip Sidney. Questions of the authenticity of recent attributions of poems to Shakespeare, the place of biography in his sonnets, and the attention given to homosexuality in his work are treated here at some length. This is a highly accessible study of the most popular English poet of all time.

Arthur F. Kinney

Preface

The justification for this volume is simple. It springs from the conviction that, while the poems and sonnets are often relegated to a marginal position in Shakespeare criticism and in the classroom, the study of these works ought to be regarded as central to an attempt to understand Shakespeare's work, career, and subsequent reputation.

Shakespeare's poems *Venus and Adonis* (1593) and *Lucrece* (1594) were published with dedications signed by the young writer himself when he was not yet thirty years old. With these works, he announced himself as a writer with serious literary ambitions, as someone who aspired to be regarded not just as the writer of commercially successful theatrical scripts, but as a poet. In Shakespeare's England, these poems were best-sellers for more than a generation, enjoying a degree of popularity none of Shakespeare's plays could match. When in 1609, close to the end of his theatrical career, his sonnets were published, they were marketed as *Shake-speare's Sonnets: Never Before Imprinted,* thereby declaring their connection with a writer who by then had outstripped his contemporaries and acquired considerable fame and status. And four centuries later, even though (perhaps because) they are rarely formally studied in school, the *Sonnets* still speak to a wide readership. They are today by far Shakespeare's single best-selling work.

This book devotes separate chapters to each of these three texts. There are two additional chapters. In chapter 4, I discuss other poems written by, or attributed to Shakespeare. Inevitably, the study of such texts raises questions of attribution and authenticity, issues that are inseparable from the image, reputation, and cultural value attached to Shakespeare and his name both in the past and today. Recent discussion of the Shakespeare canon, therefore, has directed attention to the sort of writer he was, to the ways the idea and practice of authorship were understood in Elizabethan and Jacobean England, and also to the place Shakespeare has in modern culture. The first chapter is contextual. Since Shakespeare's verse was mostly written in the years from about 1592 to about 1603, I have tried in those pages to sketch what seem to me some of the more relevant features of English literary culture at that time.

This book is intended to be a companion and complement to other volumes in the Shakespeare series and has in particular been conceived in relation to my own *William Shakespeare: His Life and Times* (1995). Although the present volume contains plenty of dates, names, and facts, it is intended to be more a resource for its readers than a final work of reference. In other words, I hope it will raise questions as well as provide basic information. It seeks to make some connections and suggest many more between Shakespeare's poems and the social, cultural, and literary environment in which they were written, and also seeks to discuss these poems in ways that link them with the plays.

Shakespeare continues to attract considerable scholarly and critical attention, and my notes are designed to reflect some of that interest and to encourage the reader to explore some of the more exciting areas investigated by recent research. Although this book has an academic origin in my graduate seminar on Shakespeare's sonnets and poems at Oxford University in 1994, I have tried also to bear in mind that the sonnets in particular are widely read, quite independently of academic study. It is also to those independent readers, as well as to students, that this book is directed. I have therefore tried to raise many of the issues that academic scholarship and criticism have explored and debated over the last twenty years, but in a language that I hope will be accessible and clear, while doing justice to the complexity of the matters involved.

Dennis Kay

Abbreviations

Abbreviations used for works frequently cited are as follows:

Riverside: *The Riverside Shakespeare.* 2nd edition. Edited by G. Blakemore Evans, with the assistance of J. J. M. Tobin. Boston: Houghton Mifflin, 1997. Quotations from Shakespeare's works, unless specified otherwise, are taken from this edition.

Arden: *Shakespeare's Sonnets.* Edited by Katherine Duncan-Jones. The Arden Shakespeare. Third Series. New York: Thomas Nelson and Sons Ltd., 1997.

Booth: *Shakespeare's Sonnets.* Edited with analytic commentary by Stephen Booth. New Haven: Yale University Press, 1977.

Chambers: Chambers, E. K. *William Shakespeare: A Study of Facts and Problems.* 2 vols. Oxford: Oxford University Press, 1930.

Evans: *The Narrative Poems.* Edited by Maurice Evans. The New Penguin Shakespeare. London: Penguin, 1989.

G. B. Evans: *The Sonnets.* Edited by G. Blakemore Evans, with an introduction by Anthony Hecht, The New Cambridge Shakespeare. Cambridge: Cambridge University Press, 1996.

Ingram and Redpath: *Shakespeare's Sonnets.* Edited by W. G. Ingram and Theodore Redpath. London: University of London Press, 1964.

Kerrigan: *The Sonnets and A Lover's Complaint.* Edited by John Kerrigan. New Penguin Shakespeare. London: Penguin, 1986.

Prince: *The Poems.* Edited by F. T. Prince. The Arden Shakespeare. London: Methuen, 1960.

Roe: *The Poems.* Edited by John Roe. The New Cambridge Shakespeare. Cambridge: Cambridge University Press, 1992.

Rollins: *The Sonnets.* Edited by H. E. Rollins. New Variorum Edition, 2 vols. Philadelphia: Lippincott, 1944.

Rollins, *Poems:* *Shakespeare: The Poems.* Edited by H. E. Rollins, New Variorum Edition, 2 vols. Philadelphia: Lippincott, 1938.

Schoenbaum: Schoenbaum, S. *Shakespeare: A Compact Documentary Life.* Oxford: Oxford University Press, 1977.

Wells and Taylor: *Works.* Edited by Stanley Wells and Gary Taylor. Oxford: Oxford University Press, 1986.

Chronology

1564   William Shakespeare born to John and Mary (Arden) Shakespeare.

1565   John Shakespeare is appointed alderman.

1566   Brother Gilbert born.

1568   John Shakespeare elected bailiff.

1569   Sister Joan born.

1571   Sister Anne born.

1574   Brother Richard born.

1577   John Shakespeare suffers financial difficulties.

1579   Anne Shakespeare dies.

1580   Brother Edmund born.

1582   William marries Anne Hathaway.

1583   Daughter Susanna born.

1585   Son Hamnet and daughter Judith born.

1587   John Shakespeare is removed from Stratford Corporation.

1592   Greene attacks Shakespeare in his pamphlet *Groatsworth of Wit*. John Shakespeare fails to attend church. Theaters closed because of plague.

1593   Shakespeare dedicates *Venus and Adonis* to the earl of Southampton.

1594   Shakespeare dedicates *Lucrece* to the earl of Southampton. Lord Chamberlain's Men established.

1596   Is granted coat of arms. Hamnet Shakespeare dies.

1597   Purchases New Place in Stratford.

1598   Recorded as hoarding malt during corn shortage. Francis Meres's *Palladis Tamia* published. Dismantling of the Theatre.

1599   Erection of the Globe. Resides on Bankside. The Globe opens (May/June).

1601   John Shakespeare dies. Essex Rebellion.

1602   Buys 127 acres in Old Stratford and a cottage in Chapel Lane.

1603   King's Men formed. Shakespeare sues Philip Rogers for debt.

1605   Actor Augustine Philips leaves Shakespeare gold 30-shilling piece. Shakespeare buys half-interest in tithes in Stratford area.

1607   Daughter Susanna marries John Hall. Edmund Shakespeare dies.

1608   Mary (Arden) Shakespeare dies. Granddaughter Elizabeth Hall born. Shakespeare sues John Addenbrooke for debt. Shakespeare is a sharer in the second Blackfriars theater.

1610   Probably moves to Stratford.

1611   Defends his tithes in Court of Chancery.

1612   Is witness in the Stephen Belott/Christopher Mountjoy suit. Gilbert Shakespeare dies.

1613   Shakespeare purchases Blackfriars gatehouse. Makes impreso for Lord Rutland, in collaboration with Richard Burbage. Richard Shakespeare dies. Shakespeare is left 5 pounds in the will of John Combe.

1614   Is involved in Welcombe enclosure controversy.

1616   Daughter Judith Shakespeare marries Thomas Quiney. Grandson Shakesper Quiney born. William Shakespeare dies.

1623   Anne Shakespeare dies. Registration of the First Folio.

1626   Granddaughter Elizabeth Hall marries Thomas Nash.

1635   John Hall dies.

1647   Thomas Nash dies.

1649   Elizabeth Nash marries John Bernard. Susanna Hall dies.

1662   Judith Quiney dies.

1670   Elizabeth (Hall) Bernard dies.

Dates of Publication of Shakespeare's Poems

Chapter One
A Poet of the 1590s

Introduction

This chapter, consisting of two parts, sets the stage for the rest of the book. The first part is a brief sketch of the main features of Shakespeare's career during the 10 or 12 years in which most of his poems seem to have been written. The second is a survey of English culture—and in particular the literary, social, and political conditions—in London during that period.[1]

As we will see, most of Shakespeare's poems, with a few exceptions, were productions of the astonishing decade of the 1590s. Even though a few of the sonnets, published in 1609, may be dated to the first years of the new century, the bulk of that collection was written during the preceding decade. By the end of the century, Shakespeare's fame was assured. Between 1598 and 1601 the students of St. John's College in Cambridge University put on plays during the Christmas festivities. In them, they were able to amuse their undergraduate audiences with references to Shakespeare ("sweet Master Shakespeare") as a writer whose works were known to all, and preferred over more conventionally serious poets. Lines and speeches from his plays were part of the common cultural currency, and the actors his scripts had made into celebrities could be imitated in their famous Shakespearean roles (such as Richard Burbage playing the lead in *Richard III*). In *The Return from Parnassus Part I* (4.1), after Ingenioso has just improvised a parody of a passage from *Venus and Adonis,* Gullio responds rapturously:

Ay, marry Sir: these have some life in them! Let this duncified world esteem of Spenser and Chaucer! I'll worship sweet Master Shakespeare, and to honour him will lay his *Venus and Adonis* under my pillow, as we read of one (I do not well remember his name, but I am sure he was a king), slept with Homer under his bed head. (Riverside, 1961–62 [text modernized])

1

This chapter will later explore some of the most striking characteristics of the culture of the 1590s, but this passage gives a vivid picture of some of them. For example, it reveals a self-conscious championing of youth over antiquity, eroticism over probity, pleasure over discipline, life and sweetness over scholastic ("duncified") learning. The scorn of learning expressed in the affected carelessness about history—"I do not well remember his name, but I am sure he was a king"—vividly expresses the cult of the new, the sense that the present was an age that could rank with any in history.

The 1590s was a decade when a generation of exceptional authors in almost all literary genres—drama, prose fiction, history, satire—came to maturity. In the narrower field of poetry, this was a decade that witnessed what Emrys Jones, in the preface to his *New Oxford Book of Sixteenth-Century Verse,* called an "extraordinary explosion of poetic talent."[2] Jones's elaboration of this remark is perhaps a helpful starting point for this chapter:

> The 1590's have a claim to be considered the most remarkable decade in English literary history. This is not simply because they see the arrival of Shakespeare—though that might be thought distinction enough. Shakespeare, however, is only one of many new voices. To put it at its soberest, and avoiding merely inflationary rhetoric: during the 1590's well over thirty poets of at least some talent were known to be writing—and this does not include those anonymous poets who wrote poems of substantial merit. Two or three of these named poets were writers of genius: Spenser, Donne, and—though his writing career had only just started near the end of the decade—Ben Jonson. There are besides Greville, Ralegh, Marlowe, Daniel, Drayton, Chapman, and (not least) Campion—poets who at their best make a unique and irreplaceable contribution to writing in the English language. (P. xxxviii)

Shakespeare in the 1590s

We have some clues about what it meant to be a poet in England in the 1590s. Some come from the life of a celebrated poet of the Elizabethan and Jacobean period who was born (the son of a butcher, according to John Aubrey) in Warwickshire in the early 1560s. He attained prominence and success in London as a playwright, sonneteer, and author of a national epic; and he quarreled with Ben Jonson, before retiring to live out his days in a small Warwickshire village. His name was Michael Drayton, and, writing to a lifelong friend, he recalled in later life how he had known from childhood that he had been born to be a poet:

> For from my cradle (you must know that) I
> Was still inclin'd to noble poesie,
> And when that once Pueriles I had read,
> And newly had my Cato construed,
> In my small selfe I greatly marveil'd then,
> Amongst all other, what strange kinde of men
> These poets were; and pleased with the name,
> To my milde tutor merrily I came,
> (For I was then a proper goodly page,
> Much like a pigmy, scarce ten yeares of age)
> Clasping my slender armes about his thigh.
> O my deare master! cannot you (quoth I)
> Make me a poet, doe it: if you can,
> And you shall see, Ile quickly be a man.[3]

Drayton's literary career, and his reminiscences of its origin, suggests that the story of Shakespeare's life and career in the 1590s may not be unique. Indeed, when studied in context, it will be seen to be in many ways wholly characteristic of its era and culture. In a general sense, the trajectory of Shakespeare's journey—from a rural Warwickshire market town of not much more than a thousand people to London, a metropolis that would be the biggest city in Europe by 1600—was matched by thousands; and these new immigrants to the city could imagine themselves following in the footsteps of some notable and exemplary precursors.

England of this period abounded with stories of country boys who found the streets of London paved with gold. Dick Whittington (died 1423) had established the model—though his cat, the foundation of a fortune in an overseas trade, is an invention of Shakespeare's day, being first recorded in 1605. From Stratford-upon-Avon, Sir Hugh Clopton had risen to be lord mayor of London in 1491. He ended his days as a great benefactor of his hometown and built the bridge that carries the London road over the Avon. He also built the grandest house in Stratford. In 1597, this house, then known as New Place, would become the property of William Shakespeare.

Of course, though it may be typical in its outline, in its specifics, and in the scale of his achievement, Shakespeare's story is remarkable. The decade of the 1590s witnessed Shakespeare's rise from provincial anonymity to metropolitan celebrity; and his success was based in large measure on a totally new commercial enterprise—the first permanent theater had been built in 1576, little more than a decade before his arrival in London. As the 1590s began, Shakespeare was comparatively unknown. Before 1592, there were few traces of him in the records other than his birth in 1564, his marriage at the age of 18 to Anne Hathaway in 1582, and the birth of his children, Susanna (1583) and twins Hamnet and Judith (1585). By the end of the decade, he had become wealthy and, as noted, owned the finest house in Stratford-upon-Avon. His only son, Hamnet, had died in August 1596. His father, having been obliged to step down from public life in the 1570s, returned by the end of the century to a position of trust in the community. The family now bore a coat of arms and owned substantial parcels of land around Stratford. As the new century began, Shakespeare had become an actor and a shareholder in London's leading (and newest) playhouse, the Globe, which opened in 1599. He had also become an important literary figure whose name had acquired considerable market value and whose poems had become a byword for fashionable verse.

How did Shakespeare, competing in a literary marketplace stocked with writers of the highest quality, a few of whom were already well advanced in their careers, attain such rapid and widely recognized prominence? The first phase of Shakespeare's professional career is shrouded in obscurity. What is certain is that by 1592 he was sufficiently well established as a writer of plays—having, as far as we can guess, started out as a player before graduating to work on revisions of scripts in his company's repertoire—to attract a vitriolic attack from the university-educated professional writer Robert Greene. In a public letter addressed to three "University" writers—almost certainly George Peele, Thomas Nashe, and Christopher Marlowe—published at the end of his *Groatsworth of Wit* (1592), Greene complained that a mere actor, one of the "antics garnished in our colours," had lost all sense of his place in the theatrical economy and had stolen the finery of his social and intellectual superiors, the educated writers "that spend their wits in making plays." This "upstart Crow," Greene alleged, had plagiarized the work of poor scholars forced to endure the harsh commercial world of the theater. And having become "beautified with our feathers," Greene continued, he had revealed his "Tiger's heart wrapped in a player's hide." In other words, the savagery of his true nature, hitherto masked by his apparent occupation as an actor, had now been allowed free rein. Greene's remarks mangle the Duke of York's description of Queen Margaret in *3 Henry VI* as a "tiger's heart wrapped in a woman's hide" (1.4.137), so it is clear who is the target of his attack. The barb becomes more pointed as Greene continues with an obvious play on Shakespeare's name, objecting that this hybrid, dishonest, larcenous, shape-shifting monster "supposes he is as well able to bombast out a blank verse as the best of you: and being an absolute *Johannes fac totum* [jack of all trades], is in his own conceit the only Shake-scene in a country" (Riverside, 1959).

What had Shakespeare done to warrant such an attack? At the very least, he had achieved, in Greene's opinion, sufficient prominence to constitute a threat to the livelihood of professional writers. This upstart's versatility, as a "Johannes fac totum," represented a threat to the specialized trade of writers, as did, in Greene's view, his adaptation, recycling, and appropriation of their material.

Perhaps this assault had a personal origin. It has been suggested that a business dispute between the prudent Shakespeare and the profligate Greene, perhaps involving Greene's request for a loan or cash advance, may have been the immediate cause.[4] And not long afterward, following Greene's miserable and impoverished death, the writer Henry Chettle published an apology and retraction, together with character references for Shakespeare, including his own famous testimony:

> . . . myself have seen his demeanour no less civil than he excellent in the quality he professes: besides, divers of worship have reported, his uprightness of dealing, which argues his honesty, and his facetious grace in writing, that approves his art. (Riverside, 1959 – 60)

The implications of Chettle's language are interesting and give some insight into Shakespeare's personality as manifested in his professional life. Shakespeare, Chettle declares on the basis of personal acquaintance, is not rude or rustic; he is "civil"—meaning that he is polite, at home in the city, and not savage (i.e., he does not possess a "tiger's heart"). Second, he is neither a hypocrite nor a social upstart who gives himself airs: rather he is what he appears to be. Being "excellent in the quality he professes" implies that he fits the station in life he has claimed for himself. Third, others, from a higher social class than Chettle—the phrase "divers of worship" implies professional and mercantile bourgeois rather than aristocrats—have found Shakespeare an honorable businessman. In other words, in their business dealings with Shakespeare, they have encountered none of the deceitfulness of which Greene complained in his. In addition, these reliable citizens have been impressed by the speed and eloquence of Shakespeare's writing. This point seems to address the suspicions that successful and prolific artists often face— that there simply is not sufficient time for them to have produced unaided what they claim as their own.

How prolific had Shakespeare been by 1592? Scholars are divided, in almost Swiftian fashion, between the advocates of a "late start" to Shakespeare's career, who speculate that about 4 or 5 plays had been performed by 1592, and the devotees of the "early start," who put that number at 10, or even as many as 14.

What is relevant to the present discussion is that Shakespeare's success on the London stage was evidently rapid and that he was quickly established as a major writer in a commercially profitable business. It is probably the case that he had worked for more than one company during what had been a period of considerable fluidity in their membership (Kay 1992, 144–50).

It is a sobering statistic, though one that illustrates the reality of the theatrical world in Shakespeare's London, that of more than 1,000 plays known to have been performed in the period from 1560 to 1642 (known because their titles are recorded), some textual record (in the form of complete printed scripts, manuscripts, or summaries) survives of only about half.[5] This percentage is not uniform throughout the period. In the 1640s, for example, 169 titles are recorded and 125 texts survive; in the 1570s, there are 79 titles, of which 6 texts remain. For the two decades in which Shakespeare was most active, the figures are as follows: in the 1590s, 266 titles are recorded (by far the busiest decade of those measured), but we have only 78 texts; in the period from 1601 to 1610, there are 183 titles and 103 texts. These figures are based on notoriously incomplete records and rely heavily on documents generated by Court performances and on the invaluable *Diary* kept by Philip Henslowe, proprietor of the Rose Theater, in the 1590s. After surveying such statistics, Andrew Gurr declares that

> The survival in written form of what we now think of as Renaissance drama texts is largely fortuitous. It distorts the social realities from which they came. . . . The total number of playscripts written between 1560 and 1642 was probably at least three times the thousand or so titles that

survive and at least six times the number of surviving texts. (Gurr 1996, 26–27)

Bearing such comments in mind, Shakespeare's survival rate is astonishing. Not only is he associated with very few "lost" plays (the only clear case of which is *Cardenio* [1613], though it is possible there may have been others), but also his extant scripts constitute about 20 percent of the total corpus of dramatic writing that survives from that period of his career.

The vogue for publishing play scripts is a phenomenon of the 1590s and is linked in complex ways with the fluctuating fortunes of the dramatic companies as they consolidated and professionalized their operation. Later in the period, publication might be a means of generating extra income after a script had exhausted its box-office potential. Accordingly, it was more likely to be under the control of the company, or sometimes of the playwright, rather than a sign of dishonesty or of an attempt to realize profits during a financial crisis brought about by plague or some political restriction.

In such a context, it is perhaps more understandable that by 1592 Shakespeare had nothing in print to serve as an obvious target for Greene's published attack and a focus for Chettle's published defense. We can see that these pamphlets were dealing with a novel form of celebrity and wealth, associated with a phenomenal success on the public stage.

As part of a slowly developing series of public health measures designed to limit the spread of infection, London's civic authorities made it a practice to close the theaters at times of plague. The plague that hit London in 1592 and 1593 was severe, but not as deadly as the catastrophes of 1563 and 1603. By the time the disease abated, it had claimed close to 10 percent of the city's population (at least 11,000 lives out of approximately 125,000), with the deaths concentrated in the poorer and more crowded areas, particularly in the northeastern parishes between Bishopsgate and Aldgate. Shakespeare lived close to Bishopsgate, in St. Helen's parish, and his normal walking route to the theater would have taken him through the gate on Gracechurch Street.

On 23 June 1592, in response both to the plague and to riots involving apprentices in the southern suburbs, mainly in Southwark, the playhouses were closed. The initial prohibition was scheduled to last until the law courts reconvened in September. As the plague persisted and concern about unrest continued, the prohibition was extended in January 1593 to include communities within a seven-mile radius of the city of London. The only assemblies to be permitted were for public sermons and church services.

Several of the theater companies, suddenly deprived of their livelihoods, secured licenses to tour the provinces. They traveled with smaller numbers of people and with fewer props and costumes and seem to have enjoyed only limited success. Pembroke's Men, for example, a company with which Shakespeare may well have been involved, was ultimately obliged to return penniless to London, where they were forced to sell off their remaining assets to meet their financial obligations.

Shakespeare's fortunes were not so exclusively tied to those of the theater. It is clear that he used this period to develop his writing in a new direction, which represented in some sense a move from the free-enterprise milieu of the theater back to an earlier form of literary endeavor, the neofeudal system of patronage. No matter how spectacular his success, Shakespeare must have been acutely aware of the novelty and the vulnerability of the theater. In 1593 nobody could have known when, if at all, the theaters would resume their operations. There was always a powerful antitheatrical political lobby, which enjoyed some success in equating the "infection" of seditious ideas and unruly assemblies in the playhouses with the infection of plague. Both disease and dissent, they argued, were nurtured and spread in the godless playhouses.

It is from this milieu that Shakespeare's narrative poems arise. They will be discussed in more detail later, but it is important at this point to note that they seem to show Shakespeare, in dedicating them to the young earl of Southampton, turning from the stage to pursue a more conventional literary career. We cannot know if he imagined the turn would be permanent or if he envisioned a radical departure in his own writing. One of the benefits of aristocratic patronage is the potential for commissions, whether from the patron or his family and allies, to write, translate, or adapt texts that were related to a patron's literary, political, religious, or other interests. A writer accepting such a commission might find he was then able to publish his own original works under the patron's aegis. This was one model. But Shakespeare's decision to dedicate *Venus and Adonis* to Southampton may not have been specifically designed to solicit a commission in this way. Southampton was young and not yet an established patron with an identifiable political-religious-aesthetic agenda as, say, the earl of Leicester had been. What is more, the concept of a literary career was itself in the process of undergoing great change, as will be noted later in this chapter.

What we do know is that while Pembroke's company was collapsing, Shakespeare was occupied writing epyllia, minor epics, for Southampton. *Venus and Adonis* was published in 1593, and *Lucrece* was entered into the Stationers' Register for printing on 9 May 1594. About four weeks later, Henslowe's *Diary* records performances by the reconstituted Lord Chamberlain's Men and the Admiral's Men; and soon after that the two companies were operating full-time with distinct repertoires.

So, by the time the Lord Chamberlain's Men embarked upon a remarkable decade of achievement, Shakespeare had augmented his fame as a scriptwriter with his new status as the author of printed classical poems dedicated to a prominent young nobleman. Shakespeare's identity in the print medium , for the next few years at least, would be shaped by his authorship of these poems.

We have seen, from the vehemence of Greene's attack, the extent to which Shakespeare had gained prominence in the world of the theater by 1592. His appearance in print in 1593, together with changed circumstances in the theater, altered that situation. To get an idea of the extent of Shakespeare's initial visibility in print, one needs to survey chronologically his publications from 1593 to 1600. In the following examination of these, the so-called bad quartos, as well as reprints and new editions, will be included. Two things are likely to be clear immediately. One is the continued prominence of his nondramatic verse. The second is that a transformation of his literary identity seems to have occurred around 1598.

Venus and Adonis was first published in 1593. It was followed in 1594 not only by *Lucrece* but also by *Titus Andronicus* (apparently prepared from the author's papers rather than directly from a document more specifically connected with the stage) and by *The First Part of the Contention betwixt the two Houses of York and Lancaster* (a "bad quarto" of the play published in the First Folio of 1623 as *Henry the Sixth Part Two*). A second quarto of *Venus and Adonis* was also published. In 1595 there was a third quarto of *Venus and Adonis,* as well as *The True Tragedy of Richard Duke of York* (the bad quarto of the play printed in the Folio as *Henry the Sixth Part Three*). Shakespeare's only publication in 1596 was another text of *Venus and Adonis* (fourth quarto). Three plays were published in 1597: the first quarto of *Richard the Third,* and quartos of *Richard the Second* and of *Romeo and Juliet.* In 1598, the first quarto of *Henry the Fourth Part One* and a second quarto of *Lucrece* were published.

In addition, in a striking innovation, texts of three plays also appeared in 1598, with explicit attribution of authorship to William

Shakespeare. They were two additional quartos of *Richard the Second,* a quarto of *Love's Labour's Lost* ("Newly corrected and augmented by W. Shakespere"), and another quarto of *Richard the Third.* In 1599 there were two more quartos (fifth and sixth) of *Venus and Adonis.* William Jaggard, in an apparent effort to capitalize on the increased market value of Shakespeare's name, and to tie his fortunes to those of the new editions of this best-selling erotic poem, compiled *The Passionate Pilgrim,* a later (1612) edition of which would be advertised as "Certaine Amorous Sonnets, betweene Venus and Adonis, newly corrected and augmented, by W. Shakespere." The year also saw the second quarto of *Henry the Fourth Part One* and the "good quarto" ("newly corrected, augmented, and amended") of *Romeo and Juliet.* 1600 saw the publication of the so-called bad quarto of *Henry the Fifth* (*The Chronicle History of Henry the Fifth*), as well as additional quartos of *Titus Andronicus, The First Part of the Contention* (i.e., *Henry the Sixth Part Two*) and *The True Tragedy of Richard Duke of York* (i.e., *Henry the Sixth Part Three*). The spate of texts bearing Shakespeare's name continued, with two more editions of *Lucrece* (third and fourth quartos), as well as quartos, with Shakespeare specifically identified as the author, of *Much Ado About Nothing, Henry the Fourth Part Two, The Merchant of Venice,* and *A Midsummer Night's Dream.*

When this information is presented in such a manner, a couple of striking features become apparent that represent a major contrast with the situation that had irked Greene so much in 1592. First, it is evident that Shakespeare was, as far as the publishing trade and, presumably, the reading and book-buying public were concerned, from 1593 onward, primarily a poet whose works sold extremely well—with market demand requiring reprints and new editions at a frequency and over a period of time unmatched by any of his plays. Second, there is a shift in the way the authorship of the plays is presented. *Titus Andronicus,* to cite only one example, was advertised on its title page in 1594 as being the script of a play "As it was Plaide by the Right Honourable the Earle of Darbie, Earle of Pembrooke, and Earle of Sussex their seruants." This is in obvious contrast with the way Shakespeare's authorship is advertised in *Lucrece,* published in the same year. The appeal of the published theatrical script is to the memory of a theatrical experience, connected specifically with the actors who performed it. The appeal of the published text of the poem includes the memory of the same poet's earlier and very successful *Venus and Adonis.*

The shift in the presentation of scripts occurs in 1598, with the sudden appearance of Shakespeare's name on the title page of *Richard the*

Second, Richard the Third, and *Love's Labour's Lost* and the claim that he was, in some cases, responsible for correcting and improving the text from the version shown in the theaters. Viewed in this way, Shakespeare's trajectory seems simple: from the popular scriptwriter attacked by Greene, to the writer of popular epyllia, to the playwright who aspires to the more elevated status of *auctor* or poet. The picture becomes substantially more complex if we consider Shakespeare's Jacobean career and the role played by publications in his literary endeavors after 1603, but this is a subject outside the concerns of this volume, since it has to do with Shakespeare as a playwright rather than a poet.

In 1592 the idea of published scripts being represented as the revised and polished work of poets would have been inconceivable. Public theaters then were at the opposite end of the literary spectrum from "art." It took another generation before any writer of the upper classes would admit being involved with the public stage.[6] In 1592 the stigma of print, the idea that there was something disreputable about the act of publication, was only beginning to be challenged. Indeed, print was only coming to be thought of as respectable in certain limited circumstances. Shakespeare's career as a writer of poetry, then, unfolded in the context of changes in the way poets were defined and poetry was valued. His poetic endeavors occurred at a time when many literary categories, many kinds of received wisdom, and many long-established practices were undergoing transformation; and it is to those broader circumstances that we now turn.

The 1590s

It would be impossible in a volume of this size to treat adequately the extraordinary decade of the 1590s; but it would also be a mistake, and a distortion, to seek to view Shakespeare the poet in isolation from the culture in which he lived. The discussion that follows is highly selective and designed as much as possible to intersect with the concerns of later chapters.

The Idea of the Poet

One of the most remarkable cultural developments of the 1590s concerned the understanding of what being a poet might mean and what it might be worth. In what follows, the careers and reputations of two of the age's most exalted poets will be touched on briefly in an attempt to illustrate ways in which the status of poetry and of poets was viewed during the most active phase of Shakespeare's career as a poet.

In the latter part of the sixteenth century, the status of poetry and poets was transformed by the value attached to the life and work of Philip Sidney and to the achievement of Edmund Spenser in *The Faerie Queene*. Although the decade began with the appearance in 1590 of the first three books of *The Faerie Queene* and with the revised version of Sidney's *Arcadia,* a movement to exalt contemporary English writers, and to find in them worthy heirs to the greatest writers of antiquity, was already under way. Such a movement—which probably included Spenser's earliest major work, *The Shepheardes Calender* (1579)—had obvious political, religious, and cultural implications. At the time of his death in 1586, Sidney was mourned as a Protestant hero, a chivalric champion who had fallen heroically and virtuously in the Netherlands fighting against Spain. His writings were unknown outside a small group of family and friends.[7]

In 1588, however, Abraham Fraunce published a small volume, a rhetorical manual called *The Arcadian Rhetorike,* in which he sought, among other things, to demonstrate the resources of the English language for eloquence, copiousness, and beauty. He organized the book in an astonishing way. To illustrate each rhetorical figure, he cited a passage of Homer, then one of Virgil, then something from Sidney, and then finally passages from major European writers, such as Tasso and Du Bartas. Immediately and even before its publication, *Arcadia* was declared to be in the first rank of texts produced throughout human history, and Sidney—before anything of his had appeared in print—was considered as the third greatest writer of all time after Homer and Virgil.

As the decade progressed, additional works by Sidney appeared, mainly in unofficial or pirated editions. The work that probably had the most influence on Shakespeare was the 1591 edition of the sonnet sequence *Astrophil and Stella* (with a dazzling and historically self-conscious preface by Thomas Nashe). This influence may be discerned in Shakespeare's sonnets, *Romeo and Juliet,* and elsewhere; and it effectively inaugurated the vogue for printed collections of sonnets. By 1598, however, Sidney's friends and family seem to have decided to take control of the texts, and produced a collected edition of his works—an extraordinary step for an English writer of vernacular fiction. In so doing, they also asserted some control over the management of his image and legend and ensured that Sidney's descent into print was not at too great a cost to his and his family's reputation.[8] Within a short time, Sidney's literary immortality was a certainty, which had acquired the status of a fact. The comparative novelty of the phenomenon is illustrated by an exchange in Ben Jonson's *Epicoene* (1609):

CLERIMONT: A knight live by his verses? He did not make 'em to that end, I hope.

DAUPHINE: And yet the noble Sidney lives by his, and the noble family not asham'd. (2.3.115–18)

Sidney's reputation as a public figure was so generally established, and his posthumous social status as a hero and courtier so secure, that in effect he dignified and authorized the very profession of letters that he seems to have been anxious to avoid when alive.[9]

So Sidney, whose writing was conceived, executed, and circulated in the treacherous, dissembling, and unstable milieu of the court, was transformed by his family after his death into a writer whose texts were available, accessible, and vulnerable to all readers. After his appearance as a published author, the stigma of print diminished rapidly, as the passage from *Epicoene* reflects. In addition, his example bolstered the burgeoning confidence of many writers in the 1590s that they were living in an age that compared favorably with any in the past, and that they rivaled the most revered and authoritative writers of antiquity.

The publication of Sidney's *Works* in 1598 coincides, of course, with the first appearance of Shakespeare's name on the title page of editions of his plays. It is tempting to connect these events and to speculate that the publishers of the plays were, at the very least, capitalizing on a new interest in the authors of vernacular literature. Given the use Shakespeare made of the 1598 Sidney volume, he must have been aware of the implicit and explicit claims made on Sidney's behalf by the very existence and scale of that volume.[10]

Shakespeare would also have been aware of the actions of the self-confident newcomer Ben Jonson. In 1597 and 1598, the young Jonson, who was nominally working for Philip Henslowe at the Rose, acquired an unprecedented degree of control over his scripts. Even though he spent time in prison as a result of his involvement in the banned *Isle of Dogs,* and despite killing one of Henslowe's contracted players in a duel, he was able to sell scripts to rival companies. Thus, *Every Man in His Humour* (in which Shakespeare is known to have acted) was performed by Henslowe's competitors, the Lord Chamberlain's Men on 20 September 1598. When Jonson did publish his scripts, he used his own name unequivocally on the title page, similar to the modern Hollywood practice of placing actors' names "above the title," as in the 1609 quarto of the unambiguously titled *Ben: Ionson, His Case is Alterd*. Jonson's elevated view of his own art and status are well recorded: they receive perhaps their clearest articulation in a scene in *The Poetaster* (1601), in which Augustus relinquishes his throne so that Virgil (a thinly veiled surrogate for Jonson) may sit in it to declaim the latest installment of the *Aeneid* (5.1).

England, of course, had its own Virgil, whose career reached its greatest flowering in the 1590s. Edmund Spenser's literary career was more conventional than Sidney's or Jonson's, partly because it was more explicitly modeled on ancient precedent, beginning, like Virgil's, with pastoral, and proceeding to national epic. Yet Spenser was also an exile, living and working for many years in Ireland. And while he played a significant role in the celebration of Queen Elizabeth through the cult of the Virgin Queen, his relationship to the center of power—the queen and her chief advisers, notably the Cecils—was unsteady and problematic.

The second installment of *The Faerie Queene,* published in 1596, is much more equivocal in its representation of the queen than the first three books (published in 1590) had been; and in Spenser's later shorter poems there is a steady withdrawal from the panegyric mode. The *Prothalamion* exalts the "pleasures chaste" of a virtuous Protestant marriage. In the *Amoretti* and *Epithalamion* he praises his wife, rather than an inaccessible Petrarchan beauty. In Book VI his wife appears as a fourth Grace on a magical mountain top, in a vision from which the queen and her surrogates are notably absent. He ends *The Faerie Queene* by entrusting his life's work, in much the way that Milton would invoke his "fit audience, though few" in *Paradise Lost,* not to the queen or to any of the noble patrons he had invoked at the outset of his enterprise, but instead to his ideal readers, whom he had earlier defined as those who "in their hearts feel kindly flame" (Book IV, Proem). Scholars in recent years have explored the intense and complex relationship between Spenser and his model, Queen Elizabeth. As Louis Montrose pointed out, Spenser may well have been the queen's subject. But in his poem, she was his.[11]

In many of his later works he appears as an exiled, excluded figure—the *Prothalamion* (1595) and the posthumously published *Mutabilitie Cantos* (1609) are good examples—viewing the court and contemporary life with an increasing sense of its falseness and fatuity. As a member of a slightly older generation (he was 12 years older than Shake-speare), he had defined through his life and work what it might mean to be a laureate poet, and his precedent influenced all who followed him. Younger poets, even if they could not match the scale or profundity of the epic, could aspire to follow his example, ambition, and scope.[12]

Spenser returned from Ireland in the last days of 1598, driven out by the uprising of Tyrone. His estates had been destroyed, and it is possible that members of his immediate family had been killed in the bloody conflict. Within a few weeks he too was dead. William Camden reported that the poet ("of the English poets of our age easily the chief") had been buried in Westminster Abbey, next to Chaucer. In the *Annales* Camden went into more detail:

> . . . he surpassed all our Poets, euen *Chawcer* himselfe his fellow citizen, But labouring with the peculiar destiny of Poets, pouerty; . . . for there [in Ireland] hauing scarse time or leisure to write or pen any thing, he was cast forth of doores by the rebels, and robbed of his goods, and sent ouer very poore into *England,* where presently after hee dyed; and was buried at Westminster neer Chawcer, at the charges of the Earle of Essex, all Poets carrying his body to Church, and casting their dolefull Verses, and Pens too into his graue.[13]

Although other writers tried to imitate him, something of the laure-ate idea with which Spenser had set out was buried with him, in what was to become a national pantheon at Poets' Corner.[14] Or perhaps the funeral had—or was orchestrated by Essex and Camden to express—a different meaning. In the shadow of the court that had failed to support a man who had played such a part in glorifying it, perhaps the proces-sion of poets to Spenser's grave represented a poetic tradition impervi-ous to the caprices of royal taste, a tradition connecting Spenser diachronically with Chaucer, synchronically with those of his colleagues who left their pens and verses in his tomb.

It is a noteworthy historical coincidence that at the very time the Londoner Spenser lay dying outside the city to the west in the precincts of the court in Westminster, Shakespeare and the Lord Chamberlain's Men were staking out a space for themselves on the south bank of the Thames. On 28 December 1598, after a physical confrontation with their landlord, they took possession of their old playhouse, the Theatre, and began to dismantle it. Over the next few weeks—during which time Spenser died and was buried—the timbers of the old building were carried across the river to the site where the Globe was to be built. As will be noted, there seems to be good evidence (from the sonnets, *A Lover's Complaint,* and *All's Well That Ends Well*) that Shakespeare was reading Spenser—and in particular the *Complaints*—around the turn of the century. Among the first plays performed at the Globe were *Julius Caesar* and *As You Like It,* and it may be possible to sense an echo of Spenser's death, and the response to it, in the way these plays present the vulnerability of poets and their verses, whether comically in the endemic mangling and misquotation of the Forest of Arden, or tragically in the horrific end of Cinna the Poet.

Many of the writers with whom Shakespeare might have competed at the beginning of the 1590s were no longer active at the end of the century. Greene and Marlowe, of course, were dead by the time the theaters reopened after the plague of 1594. Nashe, whose extraordinarily diverse writing career testifies in part to the instability of the literary market-place, and to its unreliability as a sole or main source of income, had become by 1598 embroiled in the reactions to his satirical play *The Isle of Dogs* (1597). He spent time in prison for his activities, and at other times his works were banned and burned. In some respects, however, Nashe embodies almost as much as Sidney and Spenser do, although in very different ways, a distinctively 1590s idea of authorship. In his case, it is neither a laureate nor a heroic idea but something triumphantly less orthodox—innovative, youthful, playful, disrespectful, carnivalesque, intimate. In vivid contrast to the comparative stability and steady prosperity of Shakespeare's career, Nashe's abiding financial and political difficulties were inseparable from his self-construction as an author, which itself established a model that was to be much imitated over the centuries. Lorna Hutson has observed how Nashe's works "shape themselves by exaggerating the features of those discourses which would exclude them," and she claims that they "transform drab contemporary restrictions surrounding the authorship and reception of printed texts into the exhilarating new resources of creative and interpretative freedom."[15] Nashe's career, like Spenser's and Jonson's, shows that, despite censorship and small print runs, it was slowly becoming possible for an artistically ambitious writer to imagine an existence outside the system of court patronage.

The Court

Elizabeth's court and its associations with literature have been much studied in recent years, and there is space here only for the briefest remarks about the court in the 1590s. In some ways, it continued in the cultural practices of earlier generations, with a great deal of its literature (plays, poems, masques, entertainments) being primarily part of the private, enclosed manuscript culture traditional to a monarch's household.[16] Elizabeth's reluctance to engage in direct patronage is well known (she gave royal pensions to only two poets, Thomas Churchyard and Edmund Spenser, and it is by no means clear that either award was delivered).

Elizabeth's cult was based on a hybrid form of Petrarchism, in which political discourse was eroticized. Ministers and advisers were required to "woo" the Queen to show "favour" to their policies (Norbrook, 117). It has been plausibly argued that Petrarchan poetry was popular among courtiers because it was a way they could express the conditions of their lives allegorically, through the fiction of a doomed love relationship.[17] Court culture was oblique, indirect, often downright deceitful. It prized open-endedness, ambiguity, and riddles.[18]

It took time for Elizabeth to train her courtiers, some of whom were, or regarded themselves to be, potential suitors. It was perhaps not until the 1570s that the court fully developed into a culture of institutionalized obliquity. It became an environment in which George Puttenham in *The Arte of English Poesie* (1579) could say of a courtier that "in any matter of importance his words and meaning very seldom meet," and could define Allegoria as "the courtly figure . . . when we speak one thing, and thinke another, and . . . our words and our meanings meet not."[19] A fine instance of courtly training occurs in Lyly's play *Endimion* (1591), in which young Endimion has to be taught the limits set on his love for the moon. Only when he comes to terms with the fact that he may never possess her is he able to resume his life. And she rewards him with a kiss, with which the young man has now learned to be happily satisfied.[20]

One of the problems Elizabeth faced in the 1590s was that she was outliving the men she had trained. One by one, her trusted councilors and courtiers died, leaving behind a younger generation that had been educated to expect greater responsibilities than the gerontocratic power structure was likely to yield them. At least Leicester, Sir Christopher Hatton, and Sir Henry Lee had grown old with the literary fiction of the queen as Petrarchan mistress. For younger courtiers, the culture of the court must have seemed to be characterized by a huge, at times grotesque and bizarre, gulf between words and actuality.[21]

This is the context in which Arthur Marotti has placed the sonnet-writing vogue. For him, the sonnet became a vehicle for the expression of discontent, criticism, and analysis that would otherwise need to be kept silent.[22] Allegory, therefore, often in obscure and apparently innocent manifestations, became the dominant court mode. In *The Arte of Rhetorique* (1553) Thomas Wilson had remarked that "the miseries of the courtier's life" could be "described" by the use of "similitudes, examples, comparisons from one thing to another, apte translacions, and heaping of allegories."[23] The contrast between Elizabeth's relations with the earl of Leicester (who died in 1588) and her tempestuous dealings with his stepson, the earl of Essex, in the 1590s shows how much harder it was for her to operate as the focus of the culture of Petrarchan politics as she became older. It also shows an impatience on the part of the younger generation with the cultural and literary forms of their parents. Shakespeare's critiques of Petrarchism, even when he is most Petrarchan—as in Sonnet 130 or in *Venus and Adonis*—need to be seen in this political context, as will be noted later.

London

As a literary marketplace, London was increasing in importance throughout the period.[24] One of the most interesting features of the literature published in London during the 1590s is that publishers and writers seem increasingly to have been more confident about producing fiction. The print marketplace had, until very recently, been generally hostile to modern vernacular verse and to fiction. The same urban forces that were opposed to the prodigality and folly of the theaters were opposed to the dangerous frivolity of fiction and the potential licentiousness of verse. Works of instruction, of fact, of moral improvement and spiritual uplift were all preferable to such vanity.

Yet London was a difficult city to control, a place where restrictions and distinctions had a way of collapsing under the sheer pressure of space and the struggle to live everyday lives.[25] Authority, whether governmental, parental, or patriarchal, rightly perceived itself as threatened by the unprecedented accumulation of people in such a confined space. The very presence of large numbers of literate citizens, many of them with disposable incomes, together with the increased sophistication of city writers in learning (with some notable exceptions) how to evade the censors in print, helped create a marketplace that publishers and writers could exploit. Households in London were larger than those in other parts of the country because immigrants from rural areas would move in with their relatives, but, of course, they were pressed for living space.

Emrys Jones has written about the conditions of city life at the time, which he contrasts with the modern tendency to express social separation by physical and spatial separation:

> The pre-industrial city is characterised by great social mixing for two reasons. Firstly streets of substantial houses often had lanes and alleyways of squalor immediately behind them. . . . The parish was more like a microcosm of the city as a whole than a social quarter. Secondly, social mix prevailed even within the prosperous houses, which often consisted of a shop or workshop on the ground floor, proprietor on the first, journeyman on the second and servants in the attic.[26]

It was to the city of London that Essex appealed in vain for assistance when he rose against the queen—or at least her advisers—in February 1601. One of the reasons he might have expected a more favorable response is that he had sought to identify himself with the city's governing myth, the story of Troy. The notion that London was New Troy, and that the Britons were descendants of the Trojans, had extremely powerful implications for the legitimacy and imperial ambitions of the Tudor and Stuart monarchs. It placed them, inevitably, in competition with Spain for the imperial mandate. From about 1595—at the time Essex was presenting himself as a general who could fight the Spanish anywhere in the world—there was an unprecedented spate of works concerning the story of Troy; although evocations of Troy were plentiful earlier, as in Britomart's lament (*FQ,* III.v.55–60) and Lucrece's contemplation of the image of the fall of the city (*Lucrece,* 1366ff.). Chapman's translation of Homer, dedicated in 1598 to Essex as a new Achilles, is the most prominent example, but there are many others.

The myth of Troy, with its implications for the succession of empires that followed it, was a source of pride to the city. So too was the legend that the Tower of London had been created by Julius Caesar. Such stories could be used to inspire notions of nationhood and national identity. But while Homer, Virgil, Lydgate, Caxton, and Chaucer were newly visible in the marketplace, the younger generation, in tune with a very different form of classicism, found in Ovid and, to a lesser degree, in Horace, authors who spoke to their situations. In Ovid's case, this was especially true now that his texts could be read outside the moralizing tradition of medieval commentary. Alongside the official, the civic, and the imperial, a vogue existed for the erotic and the satirical. Likewise, along the margins of sober Protestant civic culture, there was space for the grotesque and carnivalesque.[27] And just as Petrarchism was a way for courtiers to talk indirectly about their own circumstances, so classical literature and history served those who lived and worked in the city.

It is some time now since Richard Helgerson identified the ubiquity of the story of the prodigal son (whether as a direct model or as a structural pattern) in Elizabethan prose fiction.[28] One of the great virtues of the story—and perhaps the most accessible exemplar might be Nashe's *The Unfortunate Traveller* (1593)—is that it permits the writer to wander, to take the reader on a journey into uncharted, dangerous, even subversive territory, because the structural principle of a chastened protagonist is encoded in the genre. Rape, murder, religious satire, disrespect to the king, all of these can be defended (with an impeccable scriptural backing) on the grounds that our hero comes back and resolves not to travel again. In cultural terms, the story speaks to the generational divide, to the energy of a younger generation frustrated by the plodding and literalistic old order and finding a way around some of its restrictions. This is the context Shakespeare's Tarquin uses to justify his attack on Lucrece, when he dismisses "frozen conscience" by declaring, "My part is Youth, and beats these from the stage" (278).

Shakespeare's two long narrative poems are innovative and unusual works, but their subject matter, style, and generic diversity make them very characteristic products of the 1590s. At the time, the vogue for the sonnet was matched by the vogue for the so-called epyllion, or minor epic. This form is even harder to define than the sonnet sequence (or collection); and is equally aggregative, accumulative, and competitive.[29] Writers performed with a definite sense of what others had done or might do with similar or cognate material. When Shakespeare quotes Marlowe's *Hero and Leander* in *Venus and Adonis,* just as much as when he quotes Sidney's *Astrophil and Stella* in the sonnets, he is operating within the decorums of 1590s writing in signaling debts, modifying contexts, indicating twists and turns of genre. The English epyllion was inaugurated by Thomas Lodge, in his *Scillaes Metamorphosis: Enterlaced with the unfortunate love of Glaucus* (1589). Other examples include, in addition to the works of Shakespeare and Marlowe, Thomas Heywood's *Oenone and Paris* (1594), Michael Drayton's *Endymion and Phebe* (1595), Thomas Edwards's *Cephalus and Procris* (1595), John Marston's *The Metamorphosis of Pygmalion's Image* (1598), John Weever's *Faunus and Melliflora* (1600), and Francis Beaumont's *Salmacis and Hermaphroditus* (1602). Many of these were published in volumes characterized by diversity, accompanied by translations from Ovid, sometimes with satirical texts added. These are, for the most part, the products of very young writers, most of them recent university graduates. In their transgressiveness, their hybridity, their stress on sex and change, they embody the energetic rebelliousness of their generation, which was one of the first in English culture to consider itself a "new" generation, regarding its experiences as qualitatively different from what had gone before. Tarquin's line cited earlier epitomizes the typical pose of these poets. If Petrarch was the poet of the court, Ovid was the poet of the city and the university. While the poet of the most distant mythological past, he was also the poet of urban sexual intrigue. Where Petrarchism offered stasis, frustration, despair, devotion, and subjection (Elizabeth's motto was *semper eadem*—"always the same"), Ovidianism seethed with change, driven by the fantastic possibility of endlessly satisfied desires.[30]

The importance of this generational and cultural tension is considerable. It can be argued that from it springs the distinctive 1590s literary attitude that is based on the questioning of just about everything. It might be said that Elizabeth was the ideal ruler for this generation, in that her own persona was based on ambiguity and paradox, not just of utterance but in other spheres as well. Elizabeth adopted both male and female role models, and frequently represented herself in a way that was androgynous or that at least questioned conventional gender boundaries. And so she effectively licensed the interrogation and reversal to which gender roles are subjected in 1590s literature.

The prevailing attitude of the time called into question many roles and relationships, both in the city and in the court. The nature of authorship—what it means to be an author, what the purpose of authorship might be, what its value and status should be—inevitably lead to consideration of how authorship relates to authority, and how that may be defined. As the early modern state perfected its techniques of control and surveillance, there was a competing imperative for individuals to construct themselves, to fashion a self.[31]

The innovative treatment of genre in the 1590s may also be related to social phenomena. The cultivation of what might be thought of as marginal forms—verse letters, satires, minor epics, essays, epithalamions, epigrams, romances, and sonnets—can be seen as a conscious repudiation of self-consciously lofty literature. Forms that had traditionally been regarded as marginal are suddenly drawn to the center, with powerful implications not just for literary hierarchies but for other systems of value and status as well. We might recall that Essex, in addition to orchestrating Spenser's funeral, also arranged for a performance of

Shakespeare's *Richard II* at the Globe on the day before his failed uprising. It has already been noted that the patronage system was under some threat, as publishers and writers from time to time were able to secure a degree of independence. A consideration of marginal ideas and attitudes inevitably leads to the London playhouses, which were located in the recreational areas just outside the city walls, next to taverns, madhouses, brothels, sporting venues, and so forth. Their marginal position gave them a license to speak and perform.[32] Some authors were able to cross class and political divisions, but in general it was much easier for actors to do so, since they enjoyed remarkable license in access, dress, and behavior.

Richard Helgerson has commented on the writing of this period as that in which "self and nation are caught in a mutually self-constituting process"; and he focuses on the writing of "culturally uprooted young men," of whom Shakespeare was one. In his analysis these men not only "wrote England," but they also "opened a discursive space for dozens of uprooted generations to come."[33] The confidence of these writers, that they were at least the equal of the Greeks and Romans, not just as writers but as people and as a nation, encouraged innovation, experiment, and an unruffled attitude to literary and social authority. This is the generation of which Shakespeare was a significant member and the context for Francis Meres's remarks in *Palladis Tamia* (1598):

> As the soul of Euphorbus was thought to live in Pythagoras: so the sweet witty soul of Ovid lives in mellifluous and honey-tongued Shakespeare. . . . As Epius Stolo said, that the Muses would speak with Plautus tongue if they would speak Latin, so I say that the Muses would speak with Shakespeare's fine filed phrase, if they would speak English. (Riverside, 1970 [modernized])

As far as can be discerned from the records, which show him occasionally late with his property taxes and fined in Stratford for hoarding malt at a time of scarcity, William Shakespeare led a life perhaps less eventful than those of some other writers of the time. He was not beheaded as Ralegh was, or disgraced like Bacon. He did not suffer the internal exile that Donne and Sidney underwent or the failure to pursue the career he sought. He did not endure the poverty that Chapman and Spenser did. Unlike Jonson and Nashe, he spent, as far as we know, no time in prison.

Instead, he secured wealth and status, ending the decade with a coat
of arms and substantial property holdings. He had also achieved prominence in several distinct spheres, as a writer of scripts, as a published
poet, as a published playwright, and as a writer in the manuscript tradition. His mastery of many genres, and his ability to triumph in a variety
of forms, venues, and traditions, astonishing as they are, are achievements perhaps best appreciated when set against the accomplishments
of his extraordinary contemporaries.

Chapter Two

Venus and Adonis

Venus and Adonis (1593) was William Shakespeare's first acknowledged publication. Even so, the author's name, which had not acquired the marketing value it would subsequently possess, does not appear on the title page.[1] It is, however, addressed to the 18-year-old Henry Wriothesley, third earl of Southampton. The dedication, in keeping with convention, contains a frank appeal for patronage. Some critics have argued that Shakespeare's tone is slightly less servile than the norm for such requests. Nevertheless, there can be little doubt that the dedication eloquently embodies the social gulf separating the two men in the culture of Elizabethan England:

> Right Honourable, I know not how I shall offend in dedicating my unpolished lines to your Lordship, nor how the world will censure me for choosing so strong a prop to support so weak a burden. Only if your Honour seem but pleased, I account myself highly praised, and vow to take advantage of all idle hours, till I have honoured you with some graver labour. But if the first heir of my invention prove deformed, I shall be sorry it had so noble a godfather, and never after ear so barren a land, for fear it yield me still so bad a harvest. I leave it to your honourable survey, and your Honour to your heart's content, which I wish may always answer your own wish, and the world's hopeful expectation.
>
> Your Honour's in all duty,
> William Shakespeare
> (Riverside, 1799 [modernized])

Much about this passage is highly conventional, almost formulaic. The author represents himself to the prospective supporter as a novice poet. The phrase "first heir of my invention" has suggested to some critics that it is the first piece he has written— some in the past took it precisely in that sense and supposed the poem had been written in the 1580s. Rather he seeks to classify it as his first proper publication, his first really substantial work as an author. The implicit distinction, of course, is based on the performance and publication of dramatic scripts, activities deemed inescapably ephemeral and socially inferior. In addition, the neophyte author presents his work with a semblance of nonchalant self-deprecation, which, as gentlemanly ease or *sprezzatura,* was a valued characteristic of courtly culture at the time. He offers his poem as a nobleman's recreation to read, as it had been his to write "in all idle hours." Only if the dedicatee "seem but pleased" does he undertake to follow up with something "graver"—that is, less "unpolished," more mature and significant. The fact that the poet's "idle hours" are a consequence of the closure of the theaters brought on by the plague in 1592 and1593 is glossed over. The image of the text as offspring is standard Elizabethan usage (Sidney presented *Arcadia* as "this child I am loathe to father"), and is specifically extended into the discourse of patron-client relations with the request that the nobleman take on the role of godfather.

It was quite common for such dedications to be essentially speculative. And it is generally held that Shakespeare's tone argues no special intimacy. Indeed, the final sentence falls short of asking Southampton even to read the poem (which is left merely to his "honourable survey"). Yet the poet concludes by offering his work as a potential source of reinforcement for the young lord's "heart's content" whenever there is a conflict between Southampton's "own wish" and "the world's hopeful expectation." Shakespeare's formulation deftly situates his poem— and its author—on the side of youth, prodigality, recreation, and freedom, as opposed to duty, responsibility, convention, and expectation.[2]

It is possible that the implications of this passage are more specific. At the time the poem was written, for example, Southampton was one of many prominent young aristocrats who had been brought up as wards of the queen's chief minister, William Cecil, Lord Burleigh. Southampton had been placed in this position after the death of his father in 1581. At Cecil House, together with other wards, he received an education devised to train courtiers. After that he spent four years at St. John's College in Cambridge (a college with which Burleigh was powerfully connected), proceeding as M.A. in 1589, when he was 15 years old. From 1590 on, Southampton was strongly urged by Burleigh to consider marriage to the minister's granddaughter, the Lady Elizabeth Vere. Such a match (one of many that grew out of the lucrative wardships) would have been socially and financially advantageous to Burleigh, and would have established a series of family ties across one of the deeper fault lines in Elizabethan court politics. Southampton refused, and was obliged in 1592 to pay a fine of some 5,000 pounds to his guardian for failing to agree to the marriage. It is perhaps tempting to express this dispute, in the terms of Shakespeare's dedication, as a conflict between the young man's "own wish" and the desires of his powerful guardian, represented as "the world's hopeful expectation."

Indeed, Southampton's family history reminds us that such terms are more than attractive or conventional ways of describing freedom or independence of thought. Whereas Southampton's grandfather had served as lord chancellor during the reign of Henry VIII, the young man's father, a Catholic, had been involved in the intrigues in favor of Mary, Queen of Scots, and had been fortunate to escape the collapse of the conspiracy with his life. In 1601 Southampton was to become a central actor in the failed rebellion by the earl of Essex, escaping execution only because his mother interceded personally with Queen Elizabeth on his behalf. Traditionally, Shakespeare's editors have minimized both his connections with Southampton and Southampton's connection with rebellion. Thus Evans (187) reports blandly that Southampton "was later imprisoned at the time of the Essex rebellion," while Roe concludes (14) that with the reopening of the theaters in 1594, Shakespeare and Southampton "were going their separate ways."

Support for the notion of a conflict between Southampton's "own wish" and the "world's hopeful expectation" may be derived from the fact that in 1591 a short Latin poem called *Narcissus* was dedicated to Southampton. The author was one of Burleigh's secretaries, John Clapham; and there can be little doubt that the poem—a retelling of Ovid's myth of Narcissus, Echo and, Venus—was designed to persuade Southampton to marry as his guardian wished and to warn him against the dangers of excessive self-love. There are some parallels between Clapham's poem and *Venus and Adonis,* and an even more evident thematic connection between it and the first 17 of Shakespeare's sonnets printed in the 1609 edition.[3]

We also learn from the title page that the volume was "Imprinted by Richard Field, and are to be sold at the signe of the white greyhound in Paules Church-yard." The printer Richard Field was a man of considerable professional accomplishment. He served as warden of the Stationers Company in 1605 and as master in 1619 and 1622. He was also a Stratford neighbor, born three years before Shakespeare in 1561. The boys' fathers knew each other well from their activities in leather-working. Henry Field had been a tanner, living in Back Bridge Street, less than five minutes' walk from the Shakespeare house in Henley Street. When Henry Field died in 1592, John Shakespeare—who, among other things, was a manufacturer and retailer of leather goods—was one of those who appraised his estate.[4]

On his arrival in London, Richard Field had been apprenticed to Thomas Vautrollier, whose printing shop was in Blackfriars. When Vautrollier died in 1587, his widow, Jacqueline, married Richard, only recently out of his apprenticeship, an arrangement that was fairly common at the time. Vautrollier's firm had specialized in printing high-quality work, including Richard Mulcaster's *Elementarie* (1582) and Thomas North's translation of Plutarch's *Lives of the Noble Grecians and Romans* (1579). In 1591 they had printed Sir John Harington's translation of Ariosto's *Orlando Furioso,* and in 1598 they would produce the handsome folio edition of Sidney's *Arcadia* and other collected works. Starting in 1589, Field began to issue a distinguished list of books under his own imprint, including George Puttenham's *The Arte of English Poesie* (1589), the 1596 edition of Spenser's *The Faerie Queene,* as well as revised editions of the same poet's *Daphnaida* and *Fowre Hymnes* (1596). In the complex system of interlocking family and political ties, Field's association with the leading stationer, William Ponsonby, connects him with the Sidney-Herbert family—with whom Ponsonby worked closely in the construction of the Sidney canon and, indeed, in shaping the idea of authorship in the 1590s.[5]

There may be a more specific connection with Ovid and with the vogue for Ovidian writing in Shakespeare's choice of a printing house. In 1594 Field would bring out a third edition of one of Thomas Vautrollier's successful collections of Ovid's verse (earlier published in two editions in 1583), including the *Heroides,* the *Ars Amatoria,* and the *Amores.*

It follows from these preliminary observations that, long before the reader arrives at the first lines of *Venus and Adonis,* the dedication and the choice of printer have established, among other things, the author's declared ambition to associate himself with unambiguously high art. And the quotation from Ovid's *Amores* (I.xv.35-36) displayed on the title page is explicit on this point:

> *Vilia miretur vulgus: mihi flavus Apollo*
> *Pocula Castalia plena ministret acqua.*

("Let worthless stuff excite the admiration of the crowd: as for me, let golden Apollo ply me with full cups from the Castalian spring" [i.e., the

spring of the Muses].) Marlowe's contemporary version was more impe-
rious:

> Let base conceited wits admire vile things;
> Fair Phoebus lead me to the Muses' springs.[6]

Such scorn, such lofty repudiation of the mundane and vulgar, was
probably calculated to appeal to the teenaged Southampton, as well as
to the taste of the younger, classically educated generation, tired of
moralistic post-Reformation literature.

All available evidence suggests that this attitude also appealed to a
sizable part of the reading public in the plague year of 1593. During a
time of appalling suffering, in the midst of horror, disease, and death,
Shakespeare was offering access to a golden world, showing the delights
of applying learning to the pursuit of pleasure rather than drawing obvious morals from classical authors facing catastrophe. At least on the surface, what he was offering was literature as sport, as recreation, rather
than as a vehicle for stern moral instruction.[7]

With *Venus and Adonis* Shakespeare sought direct aristocratic patronage in a conventional and wholly traditional manner, but he also entered
the marketplace as a professional author. He seems to have enjoyed a
degree of success in the first of these objectives, as will be noted in the
next chapter. In the second, his triumph must have outstripped all
expectation. The poem went though 15 editions before 1640, and even
at that date it was clearly still regarded as a sufficiently profitable literary property for John Benson to be unable to include it (or, indeed,
Lucrece) in his edition of 1640.

The Poem

Venus and Adonis was entered in the Stationers' Register on 18 April
1593. It is a fine and elegantly printed book, with a text to which a
great deal of care had been given. It is not known how closely Shakespeare was involved in the publication after the manuscript had been
handed over.

The poem consists of 1194 lines in 199 six-line stanzas rhymed
ababcc. The verse form itself was a token of social and literary ambition
on Shakespeare's part, and would instantly have been recognized as
such. Its aristocratic cachet derived from its popularity at court, being

favored by several courtier poets, including Sir Walter Ralegh, Sir Arthur Gorges, the earl of Essex, the earl of Oxford, Sir Edward Dyer, Sir Thomas Heneage, and Ferdinando Stanley, Lord Strange.

Some of this courtier verse was circulating in manuscript and might have been available for Shakespeare to read. Some had been published in anthologies like *Brittons Bowre of Delights* (1591) and *The Paradyse of Daynty Devises* (1576). Seven poems in Sidney's *Arcadia* use the form, and Shakespeare would have been able to read at least four of them by 1593. Spenser used it in the January and December eclogues of *The Shepheardes Calender* (1579) and in *Astrophel* (1595). In 1589 it had been used by Thomas Lodge in his Ovidian poem entitled *Scilla's Metamorphosis, Interlaced with the Unfortunate Love of Glaucus,* whose title page claims it is "very fit for young courtiers to peruse and young dames to remember."

Much of the poem's narrative material is drawn from Ovid's *Metamorphoses*, translated by Arthur Golding (*The XV Bookes of P.Ovidius Naso, entytuled Metamorphosis, translated oute of Latin into English meeter, by Arthur Golding Gentleman*), published in 1567 and frequently quarried by Shakespeare. The story of Venus and Adonis itself is told in Book 10, lines 519–59 and 705–39; and Shakespeare adds to it elements of the stories of Salmacis and Hermaphroditus (4.285–388) and of Echo and Narcissus (3.340–500). Ovid's short account tells how Venus was driven by her love for the celebrated hunter Adonis to disguise herself as Diana so that she could also hunt. She counsels Adonis to keep away from savage beasts such as lions and boars, citing as an example the tale of Atalanta and Hippomenes, whose impiety in love caused them to be transformed into lions. Nevertheless, Adonis proceeds to hunt a boar and is fatally wounded. In mourning, Venus sprinkles nectar on his blood and the anemone springs from it as a memorial.[8]

Shakespeare's narrator throws us immediately into the action of the poem, which starts at daybreak, as "Rose-cheek'd Adonis" (3), who loved hunting but "love . . . laugh'd to scorn," is accosted by the "sick-thoughted" (lovesick) goddess Venus, who instantly embarks on a protestation of love "like a bold-fac'd suitor" (1–6). Promising unimaginable delights, she urges the young man to dismount and join her on the grass, but before he can reply the goddess's desire gives her the strength "courageously to pluck him from his horse" (30).

The narrator (31–94) then describes her physical blandishments and verbal entreaties, to all of which the young man seems impervious; he "turns his lips another way" (90). Venus responds to this coldness with a lengthy speech (95–174, 186–216, 229–40), in the course of which she pauses for breath a couple of times, and Adonis objects "Fie, no more of love!" (185). Once her resources appear to be exhausted, he breaks free of her embrace, ignores a final plea for pity, and seeks to rejoin his horse (257–58).

The horse's attention is distracted by a small Spanish mare in season, and in a celebrated passage (259–324) the narrator describes the "courtship" of the animals, whereby the female initially hails the male, who then bursts free of his restraints to pursue her. In the narrator's anthropomorphic account, the mare affects coldness, "puts on outward strangeness" (310), in order to inflame the horse; and the two beasts run off together into the forest, leaving Adonis disconsolate and silent at the loss of his mount.

Venus takes occasion of this loss to return to her attempts at persuasion, and to suggest that Adonis follow the example of his horse and "learn to love" (407). When every argument is met with flat refusal, and Venus suspects some final hostile remark, she pretends to faint (462). Her strategy is successful: Adonis now touches and kisses her in an attempt to revive her. But when she speaks to him again, asking for more kisses, his response, though gentler, is still the same—he is too young and inexperienced for her: "Before I know myself, seek not to know me" (525). She agrees to let him go, but begs for just one kiss in farewell. When he kisses her, she tries energetically to prolong the contact (547–82) before asking for a promise that they meet the following day. When Adonis announces that he plans to hunt the boar, she embarks on a lengthy speech designed to dissuade him (589–768), in the course of which she warns against the danger of dying without an heir. His response, in his most forceful speech (769–810), is based on a distinction between love—which he praises—and lust (typified by her "wanton talk" [809])—which he scorns.

Suddenly left alone, Venus spends a wretched night (811–52), during which her cries of "Woe, woe" echo through the woods. At sunrise, she begins a search of the countryside, and at first can find no trace of Adonis or his pack of hounds. In time she hears the dogs surrounding an animal at bay, and races to the source of the noise, coming face to face with a fearsome boar with its "frothy mouth bepainted all with red, / Like milk and blood being mingled all together" (901–2).

She is thrown into despair and addresses an angry speech to personified Death (931–54), before subsiding in grief (955–72). From a distance, she hears the sound of a hunter's horn, immediately persuading herself (975–96) that Adonis is not the boar's victim, apologizing to Death, withdrawing her earlier complaints ("No, no . . . sweet Death, I did but jest" [997]), and racing joyfully toward the sound (1009–26).

What she finds, even as a "merry horn" (1025) sounds in the distance, is the body of Adonis, who lies in a pool of blood gushing from a wound in his flank; and for a time she is unable to see, think, or speak (1031–68). When her speech is restored, she delivers a lengthy lament over the boy's body, in which she imagines the boar's fatal attack to have been an attempt to express a love for Adonis almost as intense as her own (1069–1120), at the end of which she falls in the blood, staining her face with it.

After gazing for a moment on Adonis's eyes, she puts a curse on love, crying that it shall forever be waited on by sorrow and become a truly terrible thing, characterized by madness, deceit, restlessness, inequality, and death (1133–64). As she speaks, the young man's body vanishes from view, and out of his blood a red and white flower grows. Venus plucks the flower, which she addresses as Adonis's offspring, and places it in her bosom before, "weary of the world" (1189), she flies off through the air to find privacy and consolation in her temple at Paphos on the island of Cyprus.

The Tradition

Many of Ovid's fables in the *Metamorphoses* invoke events in a mythic past as a means of "explaining" familiar situations or phenomena (how the cycle of the seasons came about, why the nightingale sings, and so forth). *Venus and Adonis* unquestionably participates in this tradition, as a "just so" story whose application is made clear at the end. The final speech by Venus "explains" that the inseparability of love and sorrow has its origin in her reaction to the death of Adonis:

> Since thou art dead, lo here I prophesy,
> Sorrow on love hereafter shall attend;
> . . . .
> . . . all love's pleasure shall not match his woe.
> (1135–40)

> Sith in his prime, Death doth my love destroy,
> They that love best, their loves shall not enjoy.
> (1163–64)

The Ovidian fictional tradition possesses an immediately accessible contemporary edge. At the heart of the poem, for example, Venus's praise of the lips of her beloved seems to collapse historical distance and connect the fabulous world of Ovid very specifically to plague-ravaged London in 1592–1593:

> O, never let their crimson livery wear!
> And as they last, their verdour still endure,
> To drive infection from the dangerous year!
> That the star-gazers, having writ on death,
> May say, the plague is banish'd by thy breath.
>   (506–10)

At the conclusion of the poem, with Venus's departure, the reader is in effect returned to the present day of the poem's publication. In other words, the poem's conclusion defines its readers' world (England in 1593) as one ruled over by a frustrated and self-isolating queen-goddess, who has immured herself in her own temple, while humanity is doomed to live under her valedictory curse, in which love is a source of pain and confusion. It is both a sinister variation on the plot of Lyly's *Endimion* and an anticipation of the bleak conclusion of the Faunus/Diana episode in the "Mutabilitie Cantos" of Spenser's *Faerie Queene*.

Further applications may derive from the fact that the speaker of Ovid's story is not the poet-narrator himself but Orpheus, as he wails to the trees after the death of his beloved Eurydice. In retelling the story, therefore, Shakespeare ambitiously associates himself with the prototype of ancient poets, and with the primal origins of poetry itself.

Further reflection on Ovid's Orpheus, however, may suggest, as Jonathan Bate has argued, that the implications of Shakespeare's retelling may be more complex and transgressive. Orpheus's reaction to Eurydice's death is to repudiate the love of women and—taking the example of the gods themselves as his precedent—to praise the love of boys, to which end he tells the tales of Ganymede and Cyparissus. And he goes on to tell of sexual desire crossing conventional boundaries, such as Myrrha's love for her father, and Pygmalion's intense physical desire for his statue.[9] In the end, Orpheus's songs are overcome by the savage clamor of the Thracian women he had scorned, and, defenseless, he is torn to pieces by the women (*Met,* 11.1–65).

Beginning with its title, *Venus and Adonis* invites its readers to experience pairs and conjunctions, to engage with a series of venerable and

commonplace oppositions and contrasts—male/female, love/lust, youth/
age, precept/experience, art/nature, and comedy/tragedy. Yet the cumulative effect of the poem is not to reinforce or validate such dichotomies.
Rather it is, in a fashion typical of the 1590s and of its own genre, to
hold these distinctions up to question, and to generate, especially
through the treatment of sexual desire, a radical and disturbing sense of
the potential fluidity and instability of things conventionally regarded as
static. One such distinction is between the past and the present, the
ancient and the contemporary.

   The ancient sources of the poem have already been noted. In addition, *Venus and Adonis* connects itself at crucial points in the narrative to
celebrated contemporary works. Space considerations will limit the
demonstration of this feature to a few selective illustrations. The first
stanza introduces the hero as "Rose-cheek'd Adonis" (3), quoting a passage from Marlowe's *Hero and Leander:*

>   The men of wealthy Sestos, every year,
>   For his sake whom their goddess held so dear,
>   Rose-cheeked Adonis, kept a solemn feast.[10]

In the same way, the poem's apparently ancient and conventional
opening lines, "Even as the sun with purple-color'd face / Had ta'en his
last leave of the weeping morn" (1–2), contains another allusion to Marlowe, this time to the end of *Hero and Leander,* where Hero's shame gen-
erates a blush that fools the world into thinking dawn is about to
break—and the new day that bursts into life is one on which Leander is
doomed to die:

>   Thus near the bed she blushing stood upright,
>   And from her countenance behold ye might
>   A kind of twilight break, which through the hair,
>   As from an orient cloud, glimpse here and there.
>   And round about the chamber this false morn
>   Brought forth the day before the day was born.
>   So Hero's ruddy cheek Hero betrayed.
>   (2.317–23)

   The echoes of Marlowe's poem heighten the sense of contrast
between the sun god, with his face ruddy from sexual exertions, and the

flushed cheeks of the youthful and naive Adonis. But they also omi-
nously presage a catastrophe: the weeping Aurora prefigures Venus at
the end of the poem.[11]

Shakespeare's Predecessors

The first three books of *The Faerie Queene* were published in 1590.[12] In
them and especially in Book III, Spenser had incorporated narrative and
stylistic elements of the epyllion within his epic romance.[13] Thus, for
example, his story of Marinell (III.iv.12ff) adds to the 1590s catalogue of
reluctant males who are pursued by females. Of more specific relevance
to Shakespeare's poem is Spenser's use of the story of Adonis, which is
featured in several places in Spenser's poem. The chief instance is the
episode of the Garden of Adonis (III.vi.29–49); but the story had
already been told in a tapestry at Castle Joyous (III.i.34–38) and evidently features on one of the tapestries in the House of Busyrane (III.xi),
because they are bordered with a depiction of a "long bloudy river"
(III.xi.46) traditionally associated with the death of Adonis. The concluding image of Book III in the 1590 text shows the reunited lovers
Amoret and Scudamor embracing. The narrator describes them melting
into each other and comments:

> Had ye them seene, ye would have surely thought,
> That they had beene that faire *Hermaphrodite,*
> Which that rich *Romane* of white marble wrought,
> And in his costly Bath causd to bee site:
> So seemd those two, as growne together quite.
> ([1590] III.xii.46)

The image may lie behind Shakespeare's account of the kiss between
Venus and Adonis:

> Her arms do lend his neck a sweet embrace;
> Incorporate then they seem, face grows to face.
> (539–40)

> He with her plenty press'd, she faint with dearth,
> Their lips together glued, fall to the earth.
> (545–46)

Spenser places the "stately mount" of Venus, the mons veneris, "Right in the middest," at the numerical center of Book III of *The Faerie Queene* (III.vi.43). Similarly, Chaucer had placed the physical conjunction of the lovers in *Troilus and Criseyde* at the numerical center of his romance, thereby imitating the poem's structure—"Fro wo to wele, and after out of joie" (1.4).[14] He did so in language that explicitly drew attention to its position:

> And for thow me, that koude leest disserve
> Of hem that noumbred ben unto thi grace,
> Hast holpen, ther I likly was to sterve,
> *And me bistowed in so heigh a place*
> That thilke boundes may no blisse pace,
> I kan namore; but laude and reverence
> Be to thy bounte and thyn excellence!
> (III.1268–74, italics mine)

It will be recalled that this central stanza in Chaucer's epic is addressed by Troilus to Venus in celebration of his sexual union with Criseyde. It is literally the highest point of their fortunes, and the beginning of the tragedy that will consume both of the lovers: the passage has at its core the self-referential line "And me bistowed in so heigh a place."

Shakespeare provides an aptly modified version of this model at the numerical center of *Venus and Adonis*. At the mention of the boar, Venus collapses, dragging Adonis with her—"He on her belly falls, she on her back" (594)—and the narrator comments on the irony of her situation, giving special, ominous significance to the line at the poem's midpoint (italicized below):

> Now is she in the very lists of love,
> Her champion mounted for the hot encounter;
> *All is imaginary she doth prove,*
> He will not manage her, although he mount her,
> > That worse than Tantalus' is her annoy,
> > To clip Elysium and to lack her joy.
> > (595–600)[15]

If Chaucer's *Troilus* was acknowledged at the time as the greatest English love story, it was soon rivaled by a text introduced to the reading public by Thomas Nashe as a "tragicomedy of love performed by starlight," namely Sidney's *Astrophil and Stella* (1591). Sidney's sequence tells of Astrophil's love for Stella, but also of his certainty that he will never possess her. The last three lines of the final sonnet read:

> So strangely (alas) thy works on me prevail,
> That in my woes for thee, thou art my joy:
> And in my joys for thee, my only annoy.
> (108.12–14)

Shakespeare alludes to this passage in a number of his works. In *Venus and Adonis* he signals some connection with Sidney's work, whether of kinship or indebtedness, by providing Venus with the joy/annoy rhyme on two separate occasions. One, at the very heart of the poem (599–600), has been mentioned earlier. The other instance is even closer to the spirit and style of Astrophil's expressions of his predicament:

> "O, where am I?" quoth she, "in earth or heaven,
> Or in the ocean drench'd, or in the fire?
> What hour is this? or morn or weary even?
> Do I delight to die, or life desire?
> But now I liv'd, and life was death's annoy,
> But now I died, and death was lively joy."
> (493–98)

Shakespeare's Contributions

Clearly *Venus and Adonis* is a work of its age. In it a young writer of the "middling sort" courts literary respectability and patronage from both the nobility and the burgeoning reading public. Like so many texts of the 1590s, it features an innocent hero, whose characterization anticipates elements of *Candide* and *Tom Jones*. Adonis encounters a world in which the precepts he has acquired from his education are tested in the school of experience. His knowledge of love, inevitably, is not first-hand ("I have heard it is a life in death, / That laughs and weeps, and all but with a breath" [413–14]). There is a staidly academic quality to his repudiation of Venus's "treatise" (774), her "idle over-handled theme" (771). Indeed, the poem is in many respects a dense and revealing epitome of English literary practices in the 1590s; and though space considerations preclude a full demonstration of this assertion, some of its more significant features may be readily noted.

Echoing Ovid, John Lyly observed that "in love there is much variety." Likewise Spenser commented:

> Wonder it is to see, in diuerse mindes,
> How diuersely loue doth his pageants play,
> And shows his powre in variable kindes.
>
> (*FQ*, III.v.1)

A consequence of this view—and it becomes a commonplace—is that in Elizabethan treatments of love, narrative and thematic diversity and hybridity are to be expected. Indeed, Spenser's suggestive phrase "variable kindes" hints also at new mixtures and hybrids of genres; the mingling of forms represents the unstoppable coupling urge of erotic energy. In such a context, where variety and mixture are anticipated by the reader, even the most ostensibly conventional features of the poem are nuanced and modified.

As has been suggested, Shakespeare's literary and social aspirations seem to be declared at every turn. In his Petrarchism, for example, he adopts a mode that had become a staple of courtly discourse. Elizabethan politicians considered themselves and their personal and political conditions in Petrarchan terms. The inescapable and enduring frustrations of the courtier's life were habitually characterized via the analogy of the frustrated, confused, but devoted Petrarchan lover.

Petrarchism typically includes and incorporates anti-Petrarchism.[16] And on closer inspection, Shakespeare's poem inverts the procedures of Elizabethan courtly discourse, where lines like "the love-sick queen began to sweat" (175) are understandably rare.[17] Power relations expressed through the gendered language of Elizabeth's eroticized politics are reversed: "Her eyes petitioners to his eyes suing, / . . . Her eyes wooed still, his eyes disdain'd the wooing" (356–58). It is Venus who is given a version of the conventional carpe diem arguments ("Make use of time, . . . Fair flowers that are not gath'red in their prime, / Rot, and consume themselves in little time" [129–32]); and she even provides a blazon of her own charms: "Thou canst not see one wrinkle in my brow, / Mine eyes are grey, and bright, and quick in turning" (139–40).

The poem's use of the habitual tropes of Petrarchism—typically in the voice of the narrator—is so crude as to be almost comic at times, at least initially. Thus of Venus we read that "She bathes in water, yet her fire must burn" (94), and Adonis had earlier been described as "red for shame, but frosty in desire" (36). The most obvious Petrarchan convention is the ubiquitously reiterated white/red figure. It starts with Venus praising Adonis as "More white and red than doves or roses are" (10). His oscillating between "crimson shame and anger ashy-pale" pleases Venus: "Being red, she loves him best, and being white, / Her best is better'd with a more delight" (77–8). The narrator describes Venus and the "fighting conflict of her hue, / How white and red each other did destroy" (345–46), and later uses similar terms to indicate her reaction to the news that Adonis plans to hunt the boar:

> . . . a blushing pale,
> Like lawn being spread upon the blushing rose,
> Usurps her cheek.
>
> (589–91)

These colors are in due course fatally transferred to the dreaded boar, "Whose frothy mouth bepainted all with red, / Like milk and blood being mingled all together" (901–2), and then finally to the flower that springs up from Adonis's blood:

> A purple flow'r sprung up, check'red with white,
> Resembling well his pale cheeks and the blood
> Which in round drops upon their whiteness stood.
>
> (1168–70)

No less Petrarchan are the representations of divided, antithetical inner states, as when Venus describes the impact of Adonis's speech on her:

> Thy mermaid's voice hath dome me double wrong:
> I had my load before, now press'd with bearing:

> Melodious discord, heavenly tune harsh sounding,
> Ears' deep sweet music, and heart's deep sore wounding.
>   (429–32)

Moments before, Adonis had begun his speech by telling what he knew of love, and had connected himself with the same set of conventions—"I have heard it is a life in death, / That laughs and weeps, and all but with a breath" (413–14). But as far as Venus is concerned, his ability to list such rhetorical conventions merely confirms his sterility. She had earlier dismissed him as a

> . . . liveless picture, cold and senseless stone,
> Well-painted idol, image dull and dead,
> Statue contenting but the eye alone,
> Thing like a man, but of no woman bred!
>   (211–14)

Her words, of course, ironically recall that in Ovid's story of Pygmalion and his love for the statue he made (*Met*, 10.260ff), it was Venus who had responded to the sculptor's prayers and brought the statue to life. Her speech also raises the issue, as Sidney did in his *Defence* and in *Arcadia* of how art and nature are, or may be, related. (Shakespeare also brings up the point in *The Winter's Tale,* 4.4.79-97). And shortly afterward Shakespeare slyly follows Venus's description of her own charms with an account of a young stallion:

> Look when a painter would surpass the life
> In limning out a well-proportion'd steed,
> His art with nature's workmanship at strife,
> As if the dead the living should succeed;
>   So did this horse excel a common one,
>   In shape, in courage, color, pace, and bone.
>   (289–94)

No less sly is Shakespeare's return to this theme. At the very moment when he asks his readers to imagine Venus's frantic attempts to arouse Adonis "in the very lists of love" (595), he explicitly connects the distinction between Adonis's appearance and his failure to perform sexually with the illusory quality of fictions, especially pictures.[18] Venus is compared to a bird tricked by a trompe l'oeil painting:

> Even so poor birds, deceiv'd with painted grapes,
> Do surfeit by the eye and pine the maw,
> Even so she languisheth in her mishaps,
> As those poor birds that helpless berries saw.
>
> (601–4)

Visual and verbal structures receive similar scrutiny in the poem. Sidney's Astrophil asks, "What may words say, or what may words not say?" (*AS*, 35). These questions are recalled by the fact that *Venus and Adonis*, so preoccupied with eloquence, so dazzling in its rhetorical display, is also much concerned with inexpressibility, with the limitations of language and utterance, as well as with the fatal inaccessibility of meaning to interrogation.

Although such inexpressibility was often acknowledged, it nonetheless becomes increasingly commonplace in the 1590s for erotic discourse—whether in lyrics, sonnets, prose fiction, or other fictional forms—to seek to render the inner workings of the mind, as well as explore the psychology of perception ("Oft the eye mistakes, the brain being troubled" [1051]). A characteristic device is to shift between dramatic and narrative modes in such a way that each informs the other, giving the illusion of depth. Thus, after Venus's dramatic outburst at Adonis (211–16), the narrator describes her outer appearance so as to convey a sense of her inner turmoil. He tells us not that she is silent, but that "impatience chokes her pleading tongue / And swelling passion doth provoke a pause" (217–18). When she is again silent shortly afterward, he asks rhetorically, "Now which way shall she turn? what shall she say?" (253). These passages are an attempt to represent the workings of Venus's mind, an attempt that becomes more ambitious and complex as the poem proceeds. Her solitary night watch is a vivid example (811–65), leading to a remarkable switch of point of view. As we are led towards Adonis's body, we follow the twists and turns of her emotions as she tries to interpret the sights and sounds she encounters. This leads to a fully developed soliloquy, erupting from an inner dialogue, in which Venus "exclaims on death" (931–54). In the narrator's words,

> Variable passions throng her constant woe,
> As striving who should best become her grief;
> All entertain'd, each passion labors so,
> That every present sorrow seemeth chief,
> > But none is best; then join they all together,
> > Like many clouds consulting for foul weather.
> > (967–72)

Having argued herself into believing Adonis is dead, she embarks on an assertion of the opposite, a switch signaled by the narrator—"Now she unweaves the web that she hath wrought, / Adonis lives, and Death is not to blame" (991–92).

Shakespeare's Narrator

Passages such as this draw attention to the vital, but elusive, role that Shakespeare's narrator plays in *Venus and Adonis*, most particularly in relation to the complex issue of the poem's tone, a subject that has proven a problem to generations of critics and commentators. While there is a good deal of comedy in the poem, its story deals with frustration, anger, brutal death, loss, and bitter recrimination.

Shakespeare's most significant native model was Chaucer's narrator in *Troilus and Criseyde*. While Chaucer's performance had been brilliantly imitated in the first version of Sidney's *Arcadia,* it is unclear how much of that work Shakespeare could have seen before writing the poem. John Harington's re-creation of Ariosto's narrator in his translation of the *Orlando Furioso* was certainly available to him, as was the narrator of the first three books of *The Faerie Queene* (1590). The closest modern precedent, of course, was the urbane yet occasionally compassionate narrator of Marlowe's *Hero and Leander.*

Venus and Adonis contains numerous instances of the narrator's often sardonic urbanity. As Venus rants in grief—"Hard-favor'd tyrant, ugly, meagre, lean, / Hateful divorce of love"—the narrator deflates her with, "thus chides she Death" (931–32). And throughout the poem his most common function is to highlight absurdities, excesses, and paradoxes inherent in the situations he describes. While the narrator frequently comments on language and rhetoric, he also functions in many places as a point of view, or as a means of directing the reader's visual imagination. A crude index of the importance and prominence of visual effects in the poem is the proliferation of directions to the reader to see or imagine, such as "Lo here the gentle lark, weary of rest" (853). A simple instance is the narrator's reiterated injunction to the reader to "look": "Look how a bird lies tangled in a net" (67); "Look when a painter would surpass the life" (289); "Look what a horse should have he did not lack" (299); "Look how a bright star shooteth from the sky" (815); and "Look how the world's poor people are amaz'd" (925). Adonis uses the same device in drawing Venus's attention to nightfall—"Look the world's comforter with weary gait / His day's hot task hath ended in the west"—(529–30); and the narrator, perhaps for comic effect, imagines the phrase as part of Venus's silent contemplation of Adonis: "Look how he can, she cannot choose but love" (79).

There is a world-weary, melancholy tone to some of the narrator's utterances ("All in vain, good queen, it will not be" [606–7]), as when he mournfully and self-referentially observes of lovers that "Their copious stories, oftentimes begun, / End without audience, and are never done" (845–46). There are other comments that are a good deal less brittle, more compassionate in their observations of human weakness or self-delusion. A striking instance is the narrator's account of Venus's discovery of the body, which concludes with the semiproverbial "For oft the eye mistakes, the brain being troubled" (1051–68), a remark that invites the reader to understand Venus's emotions and perceptions in unequivocally human terms.

Venus and Adonis is a densely and continuously allusive poem. It addresses artistic preoccupations characteristic of the 1590s, such as the relationship of poetry to painting, social concerns such as the phenomenon of "masterless women," and (for men) the alarming and unknowable forces unleashed by female desire, an issue that—for a host of reasons—fascinated Elizabeth's subjects. Its language is elusive, slippery, and stocked with puns and multiple meanings. The ubiquity of polarities and paradoxes manifests itself in the poem's abundant punning and wordplay; just two of the hundreds of examples are that the lark is "weary of rest" (853), and there is a kind of thought that "kills thee quickly" (a pun on *quick,* meaning alive [990]). An implication of these characteristics is that the poem constructs a view of authority (whether social, political, literary, historical, or cultural) that was implicitly oppositional, potentially rebellious, and specifically youthful. In its day Shakespeare's poem was appreciated in part as an erotic fantasy with a veneer of learning and the snob appeal of association with a celebrated aristocrat. But also, like other successful works of the 1590s, *Venus and Adonis* flirted with taboos, and seemed to glory in the inversion of established categories and values, typified by the Queen of Love herself in her semiblasphemous words to the object of her desire:

> Be prodigal: the lamp that burns by night
> Dries up his oil to lend the world his light.
> (755–56)

Later Criticism

Venus and Adonis appeared at least nine times during Shakespeare's lifetime (1593, 1594, 1595, 1596, 1599 [twice], 1602 [three times]), an additional six times in the following 20 years (1617, 1620, 1627, 1630 [twice], 1636), and again in 1675. It was included in the major editions of the eighteenth century, and its place in the canon has never seriously been challenged. Yet it has occupied a marginal position in Shakespeare's works, and historically has attracted most attention when related to the plays. Developments in the latter part of the twentieth century—notably the revived interest in rhetoric and the reading of *Venus and Adonis* in terms of gender—may have the effect of modifying the comparative neglect of the poem; although it seems inconceivable it will ever again be, as it was for a time during his life, the major plank on which Shakespeare's reputation was built.[19]

There is hardly a tradition of criticism of *Venus and Adonis* before Coleridge. Early comments are collected, together with information about editions, in Rollins's New Variorum edition.[20] Some editorial comments appeared in print, however. Capell, in his introduction to his 10-volume Shakespeare in 1768, observed of the poems that they are "plain marks of his [Shakespeare's] acquaintance with some of the *Latin* classicks at least."[21]

In 1780, Edmond Malone amused himself with the poem:

> To exhibit a young man insensible to the caresses of a transcendent beauty is to describe a being too rarely seen to be acknowledged as a natural character . . . .The deity, from her language, should seem to have been educated in the school of Messalina; the youth, from his backwardness, might be suspected of having felt the discipline of a Turkish seraglio.

In finding the poem wanting and adding little to Shakespeare's reputation, he nonetheless cites respectfully the esteem in which it had been held in Shakespeare's day and suggests the poem is worth studying for that reason at least. He also anticipates some of the directions of more recent criticism when he identifies Shakespeare's variations from classical models, and when he notes that the poem does not give unequivocal moral guidance to its reader: "It is not . . . clear," he says, "whether Shakespeare meant . . . to recommend continence as a virtue, or to try his hand with Aretine on a licentious canvas" (Vickers, 6.1774–1801 [1981], 284). Ten years later he added to his comments two significant remarks. One asked that "if we except Spenser, what poet of Shakespeare's age produced poems of equal, or nearly equal, excellence to those before us?" The second asserted, "It appears to me in the highest degree improbable that Shakespeare had any *moral view* in writing this poem" (Vickers, 6.549–50).

Coleridge's observations on the poems are presented as part of an overall view of the way Shakespeare's imagination worked. In his appreciation of *Venus and Adonis,* he cites with admiration a number of descriptive passages, seeing in them the operation of a poetic imagination. For example, discussing the moment when Adonis breaks free of Venus's embrace (811–16), he writes, "How many images and feelings are here brought together without effort and without discord, in the beauty of Adonis, the rapidity of his flight, the yearning, yet hopelessness of the enamoured gazer, while a shadowy ideal character is thrown over the whole!" (*Literary Remains,* 2.55–56). In his lectures he connected the poem specifically with Shakespeare's youth and identified the country images with the poet's life in Warwickshire.[22] Keats manifested a similar enthusiasm in a letter of 22 November 1817.[23]

In the *Biographia Literaria* (1817 [cited in Rollins, *Poems*]) Coleridge addresses, as Malone had, the question of the poem's tone and moral direction, concluding, "though the very subject cannot but detract from the pleasure of a delicate mind, yet never was poem less dangerous on a moral account" (2.16). At times his praise is lofty: "His 'Venus and Adonis' seem at once the characters themselves, and the whole representation of those characters by the most consummate actors. You seem to be told nothing, but to see and hear everything" (2.15). But the place of the poem in the Shakespearean canon is clear: "In Shakespeare's *poems,* the creative power and the intellectual energy wrestle as in a war embrace. Each in its excess of strength seems to threaten the extinction of the other. At length in the DRAMA they were reconciled" (2.19). Coleridge's approach—highlighting moments of beauty, especially those related to natural description and seeing the poems in relation to the plays, understood as the natural medium of Shakespeare's imagination—has proven extremely influential and underlies many academic studies up to the present.

Since the Restoration, it seems that the frank sexuality of Shakespeare's Venus appealed to literary and academic critics a good deal less than it had to Elizabethan and Jacobean readers. Cringing male embarrassment since the time of Coleridge has conceded grudging praise to the description of the horse and the snail and a few other natural details. In some quarters there was even a little praise for Adonis's defense of his chastity, but the orthodox view for many years was that overall the poem was a failure, the tone comically grotesque. The most eloquent articulation of these views is to be found in C. S. Lewis's judgment:

> Shakespeare's Venus is a very ill-conceived temptress. She is made so much larger than her victim that she can throw his horse's reins over one arm and tuck him under the other, and knows her own art so badly that she threatens, almost in her first words, to "smother" him with kisses. Certain horrible interviews with voluminous female relatives in one's early childhood inevitably recur to the mind. . . . Words and images which . . . ought to have been avoided keep on coming in and almost determine the dominant mood of the reader—"satiety," "sweating," "leaden appetite," "gorge," "stuff'd," "glutton," "gluttonlike," Venus's "face doth reek and smoke, her blood doth boil," and the wretched "boy" (that word too was dangerous) only gets away "hot faint and weary from her hard embracing." And this flushed, panting, perspiring, suffocating, loquacious creature is supposed to be the goddess of love herself, the golden Aphrodite. It will not do. If the poem is not meant to arouse disgust it was very foolishly written.[24]

Lewis's opinion was shared by many of his contemporaries and followers. Received wisdom in the academic world, until very recently, was that there was something unappealing, tasteless, and extreme about the poem. Reading the editions by J. C. Maxwell and F. T. Prince is to be made aware of the editors' struggles with what they regard as intractable, tedious, frankly unworthy material.[25] Both editors make no real attempt to disguise their reluctance, bordering on distaste, in confronting the poem. Prince praises Coleridge for reading the poem to illuminate Shakespeare's dramatic writing. He goes on: "Nothing else was likely then, or is likely even now, to win an attentive reading of these poems. For one thing, their eroticism is hardly more acceptable than it was in Coleridge's day; few English or American readers nowadays will respond to such happily wanton fancies as *Venus and Adonis*" (Prince, xxv).

To Robert Ellrodt, "the situation could have been handled in a Cervantic manner, but the contrast between the actions of the characters and the prevailing prettiness of the descriptive style creates in the reader an unresolved conflict of impressions . . . the highly artificial style keeps us at a distance . . . through the poem the artist seems at once hesitant about tone and too confident in the power of rhetoric."[26]

Venus and Adonis has received a more careful attention in the last 20 years, which began, as Lewis predicted it would, with a renewed interest in rhetoric. Richard Lanham, in *The Motives of Eloquence,* established a dynamic competition between rhetoric and plot.[27] In his words, "The faddish sexual role-reversal in the poem creates its comedy largely by disenfranchising its Petrarchan rhetoric" (85), and he sees the two characters as essentially "disputants" (87). Attention to rhetoric led naturally to interest in the decorum and genre of the poem, as well as to a critical reexamination of the sources and the traditions on which it drew, including two especially influential studies by William Keach and Clark Hulse.[28]

There has been a lively tradition of allegorical readings and commentaries on the poem, some drawing on Christian, others on pre-Christian (typically Platonic) value systems. In such terms, the poem has been decoded as a struggle between love and lust, reason and passion; and either (or both) of the characters has been imagined as making a journey up a Platonic ladder (see the many references in the introduction and commentary to Roe's edition).[29]

By far the most important studies have been Heather Dubrow's rereading of Petrarchan traditions and Jonathan Bate's account of Shakespeare's relation to Ovid.[30] Each has opened up valuable areas of inquiry and has shed much new light on the poem. There have been comparatively few studies of the poem in relation to Queen Elizabeth (which is surprising in view of her use of the persona of Venus-Virgo), although it has begun to receive attention in terms of gender roles, especially in their historical contexts and in terms of historicized readings of desire.[31]

As befits Shakespeare's most successful publication, this chapter ends with a record of the poem's appearance in a commercial setting. In a recent article, Katherine Duncan-Jones has brilliantly demonstrated its immediate impact on some Elizabethan readers and has been able to trace very early responses to it.[32] Remarkably, a record of an individual sale has survived (Kay 1992, 156). On 12 June 1593, Richard Stonley, an elderly civil servant who worked in the Exchequer, was walking among the bookstalls in St. Paul's Churchyard. He bought two books for a shilling and entered the details of the transaction into his pocket-book (now Folger Shakespeare Library MS V.a.460) with the care that might be expected from a man of his profession. One of the books he picked up from John Harrison's stall beneath the sign of the White Greyhound was John Eliot's *Suruay, or topographical description of France: with a new mappe.* The other was *Venus and Adonis.* The entry in the diary runs: "for the Suruey of Fraunce wth the Venus & Adhonay p^r Shakspere" (f.9). As Samuel Schoenbaum comments, "A figure of some consequence in his own day, but later forgotten, Stonley has the minor distinction of being the first recorded purchaser of Shakespeare's first publication" (1977, 176).

Chapter Three

Lucrece

In dedicating *Venus and Adonis* to the earl of Southampton, as noted in the previous chapter, Shakespeare had undertaken that if the young lord "seem but pleased" with his first offering, he would follow it with "some graver labour." Clearly, the elevated tone and classical subject of *Lucrece* recall the terms of that public promise. In addition, the tone in which this second poem is dedicated to Southampton invites its readers to suppose that the dedicatee had indeed seemed "pleased" with the earlier poem and had encouraged the poet in his endeavors:

> The love I dedicate to your Lordship is without end: whereof this Pamphlet without beginning is but a superfluous moiety. The warrant I have of your honourable disposition, not the worth of my untutored lines, makes it assured of acceptance. What I have done is yours; what I have to do is yours; being part in all I have, devoted yours. Were my worth greater, my duty would show greater; meantime, as it is, it is bound to your Lordship, to whom I wish long life still lengthened with all happiness.
>
> Your Lordship's in all duty,
> William Shakespeare[1]

Where the earlier dedication was speculative and void of any real indication of connections between poet and prospective patron, this passage is markedly more intimate and confident. Shakespeare's claim to have had a "warrant . . . of your Honourable disposition," together with his declaration that he is a "devoted' follower of Southampton to whom he is "bound," approximates much more closely the rhetorical norm of established patron-client literary relations than had been the case with *Venus and Adonis*. And it is worth noting the author's use of patronage in marketing the volume. In this manifestly public and published expression of a patron-client relationship, a professional writer places himself under the protection of a nobleman, while at the same time he invites his wider audience to share in the literary recreations of the nobility. Members of the book-buying public are urged to have their taste validated by the aristocratic cachet the dedication provides. Where *Venus and Adonis* had explicitly scorned the vulgar, *Lucrece* subtly courts a broader readership, or seeks to retain the readership won by the earlier poem.[2]

Like *Venus and Adonis,* it was printed by Richard Field, but the publisher was now John Harrison, to whom Field also transferred the earlier poem. The volume was carefully printed and poses only a few problems for editors. Of the 11 known surviving copies, 2 (1 at Oxford, 1 at Yale) differ from the rest in a few places. It was quite normal in an Elizabethan printing house for corrections to be made during the printing process and for the uncorrected pages to be offered for sale. The Oxford and Yale copies contain some pages that appear to represent an uncorrected state of the poem. Minor alterations may be found on lines 24, 31, 50, 125–26, 1182, 1335, 1350, and 1832. The scholarly consensus is that someone other than Shakespeare, probably a member of the printing team, made the alterations.[3]

There were to be no fewer than seven more editions of *Lucrece* before 1640 (1598, 1600[2], 1607, 1616, 1624, 1634), as well as another after the Restoration in 1675. It was with the sixth quarto in 1616—the last published in Shakespeare's lifetime—that the title *The Rape of Lucrece* was used, although the phrase had been used as a running title as early as the first edition. The poem was cited as an example of fashionable literature in the Cambridge Parnassus plays (Riverside, 1962) and is referred to in *Willobie his Avisa* (1594), whose prefatory verses contain the lines:

> Yet Tarquin plucked his glistering grape,
> And Shake-speare paints poor Lucrece' rape.

This is the earliest printed naming of Shakespeare as a poet. [4]

The Poem

What kind of poem is this "Pamphlet without beginning"? At the simplest level it might seem to be little more than a retelling of a celebrated and much interpreted tale from Roman history. Rome at the time of the story was ruled by kings. Lucrece was the virtuous wife of a Roman nobleman, Collatine. Tarquin, the king's son, rapes her and leaves her to be discovered by her family. Overcome by the shame the event has brought on her clan, she commits suicide. Her death inspires the Roman patricians to rebel against their kings, drive them out of Rome, and, with enthusiastic popular support, found the republic that would last for centuries.

Shakespeare took his story from Ovid (*Fasti,* 2.721–852), from Livy (*Historia,* I.57–60), from Chaucer (*The Legend of Good Women,* 1680–885), and from William Painter's version of Livy's narrative in his *Palace of Pleasure* (1566). A more contemporary model was Samuel Daniel's *The Complaint of Rosamund,* published at the end of his sonnet sequence *Delia* (1592). In this work, the ghost of Rosamund, the neglected mistress of Henry II, laments her state, in a more sophisticated version of the tradition of ghostly testimonies established in the *Mirror for Magistrates.*[5]

Lucrece is much more than a mere retelling or another recycling of an ancient story. To begin with, as in *Venus and Adonis,* it represents a massive expansion of its source material.[6] Ovid's 73 lines are swollen to 1855. But the nature of the text's engagement with its many predecessors—not all of which are as clearly signaled as Ovid, Livy, and Chaucer—is a much more profound and complex issue, as some commentators have recognized. Jonathan Bate, for example, correctly draws attention to the copiousness of the retelling. Copiousness (from the Latin *copia*—plenty or plenitude) is understood rhetorically, in the tradition of Erasmus's hugely influential *De Copia,* in terms of permitting the separate components of the material to be articulated as fully, variously, and often—and as eloquently—as possible.[7] Copiousness may also be understood hermeneutically in the context of reading and interpretation, in that it refers to the way a word, a phrase, a proverb, an image, a story may have its potential for meaning—as broadly understood—unlocked, or at least offered to the discerning reader to unlock.[8]

In Livy and Ovid the Lucrece story begins, as Shakespeare's Argument does, with Roman noblemen boasting about the virtue of their wives and then testing that virtue for a wager. All versions indicate that it was the wager that inflamed Tarquin's lust.

In contrast, the Argument of Shakespeare's *Lucrece*—whose authorship is unclear and which differs in emphasis and some points of substance from the poem—unequivocally presents the story in the context of Roman political history. The Argument provides a context for the Roman army's siege of Ardea:

Lucius Tarquinius (for his excessive pride surnamed Superbus), after he had caused his own father-in-law Servius Tullius to be cruelly murd'red, and contrary to the Roman laws and customs, not requiring or staying for the peoples' suffrages, had possessed himself of the kingdom, went, accompanied with his sons and other noblemen of Rome, to besiege Ardea; during which siege, the principal men of the army meeting one evening at the tent of Sextus Tarquinius, the King's son, in their discourses after supper every one commended the virtues of his own wife; among whom Collatinus extolled the incomparable chastity of his wife Lucretia. In that pleasant humor they all posted to Rome, and intending by their secret and sudden arrival to make trial of that which every one had before avouched, only Collatinus finds his wife (though it were late in the night) spinning amongst her maids; the other ladies were all found dancing and revelling, or in several disports; whereupon the noblemen yielded Collatinus the victory, and his wife the fame. At that time Sextus Tarquinius being inflamed with Lucrece' beauty, yet smothering his passions for the present, departed with the rest back to the camp; from whence he shortly after privily withdrew himself, and was (according to his estate) royally entertained and lodged by Lucrece at Collatium. The same night he treacherously stealeth into her chamber, violently ravish'd her, and early in the morning speedeth away. Lucrece, in this lamentable plight, hastily dispatcheth messengers, one to Rome for her father, another to the camp for Collatine. They came, the one accompanied with Junius Brutus, the other by Publius Valerius, and finding Lucrece attired in mourning habit, demanded the cause of her sorrow. She, first taking an oath of them for her revenge, revealed the actor, and whole manner of his dealing, and withal suddenly stabbed herself. Which done, with one consent they all vowed to root out the whole hated family of the Tarquins; and bearing the dead body to Rome, Brutus acquainted the people with the doer and the manner of the vile deed; with a bitter invective against the tyranny of the king, wherewith the people were so moved, that with one consent and general acclamation the Tarquins were all exiled, and the state government changed from kings to consuls.

Because the style here is somewhat different from Shakespeare's normal range of prose styles, there have been suggestions that he did not write it. Whoever did write it was closely influenced by the style and language of the major sources: Baldwin showed that behind the Argument lie, among other texts, an annotated edition of Ovid's *Fasti* and a text of Livy's *Historia*.[9]

From the outset, then, the Tarquins are presented as a murderous, tyrannical, usurping crew whose government sets itself against the will of the people. The opening phrase locates the poem in the midst of the vigorous sixteenth-century debate about the proper response to a tyrannical government and establishes that controversy as a significant component in the poem's context. The Argument goes on to stress the historical and political significance of Tarquin's act. His rape of Lucrece was to be understood as the final outrage that stirred the Romans to "root out the whole hated family of the Tarquins," after which "the state government changed from kings to consuls." The focus of the Argument, in other words, is on the rape as a political act whose political consequences, namely the establishment of the Roman Republic, were abiding.

Interest in republican ideas was widespread in early modern Europe, and many intellectuals in England were as curious about the phenomenon as their Continental counterparts. At first sight, the poem that follows the Argument may appear less politically risqué, less explicit in connecting the rape with a hated form of government that a united population might overthrow. Those commentators who, for a variety of cultural and political reasons, have sought to keep Shakespeare out of politics are prone to deny a connection between the Argument and the poem. It is important to remember that it was always necessary to treat republican ideas obliquely in Elizabethan England. The normal strategies adopted by authors for doing so included fables and allegories, or locating stories in a remote and foreign past, or presenting the work as a translation or an exercise in historical accuracy (as Ben Jonson would—to little effect, as he was nevertheless imprisoned for it—in *Sejanus* {1605}).

Lucrece's Argument, no matter who wrote it and positioned it, undeniably occupies a prominent and powerful position in the volume. It adds an ominous political and historical weight to the narrative's conclusion, where the display of Lucrece's body in the streets of Rome "with speedy diligence" inspires the population to give its enthusiastic "consent / To Tarquin's everlasting banishment"(1851–55).

The poem's final adjective slyly recalls the dedication's elusive reference to the piece as a "Pamphlet without beginning." In that single phrase Shakespeare may be doing more than merely referring to his narrative's opening in medias res. He could be hinting that the choice of subject was his own, not that of a politically motivated patron. There may be a preemptively defensive suggestion that the choice of the story had no immediate contemporary occasion, no prompting or "beginning" or occasion, in the politics of 1593 and 1594. Or perhaps he was cautiously laying the groundwork for a defense of the poem by apparently sealing it off from the Argument.[10] There is some evidence that at least one contemporary reader saw the poem being directed to a more discerning and curious readership than its predecessor. In the much discussed manuscript note written in his copy of the 1598 edition of Speght's edition of Chaucer's *Works* (fol. 394v), Gabriel Harvey remarked on the popular success of *Venus and Adonis* with younger readers, but added that Shakespeare's "Lucrece, & his tragedie of Hamlet, Prince of Denmark, haue it in them, to please the wiser sort" (Riverside, 1965).[11]

Lucrece consists of 1855 lines, disposed in 265 stanzas. The stanza (as in Daniel's *Complaint of Rosamund*) is the seven-line rhyme royal (*ababbcc*) immortalized in Chaucer's *Troilus and Criseyde*. It was a stanzaic form held to be especially appropriate for tragedy (as in Thomas Sackville's Induction to the *Mirror for Magistrates*), for complaint (as in Spenser's *The Ruines of Time* [1591]), and for philosophical reflection, as in Spenser's *Fowre Hymnes* (1596). Shakespeare would also use it in *A Lover's Complaint*. Of particular significance to the subject and concerns of *Lucrece* is the fact that Sir Philip Sidney associated the form both with female lament (as in Gynecia's lament in *The Old Arcadia*, 22), beginning "With two strange fires of equal heat possessed"), and with antiquity and political allegory, as in the pastoral allegory set on the Danube ("As I my little flock on Ister bank" [*The Old Arcadia*, 66]) that relates ancient Arcadia to central European politics and to Sidney's relationship with his mentor Hubert Languet.[12]

The 1616 quarto helpfully, though with some inaccuracies, prefaced the poem with a numbered list of major events, keyed in most cases to marginal numbers in the body of the poem.[13] And indeed the main events of the poem may be readily summarized.

The narrative bursts into action in medias res. Instead of opening with the siege of Ardea or the wager of the Roman nobles and their return home to test their wives, it begins with the arresting image of the "Lust-breathed" (3) Tarquin speeding "all in post" (1) to Lucrece. His motivation is the "lightless fire" of desire for "Lucrece the chaste" (4,7). The narrator then furnishes very briefly the history of this desire, which in this telling is stirred up by a conversation among the soldiers in their tent during the siege. He castigates Collatine for his heedless pride in bragging of his wife's chastity and faithfulness—"why is Collatine the publisher / Of that rich jewel he should keep unknown / From thievish ears?" (33–35). The precise details of the origins of Tarquin's desire are left obscure. The narrator affects uncertainty in several places, but the result is starkly stated:

His honor, his affairs, his friends, his state,
Neglected all, with swift intent he goes
To quench the coal which in his liver glows.
                                        (45–47)

Upon his arrival at Collatium, Tarquin is courteously and hospitably received by Lucrece, and the narrator provides a view of the "Roman dame" (51) as interpreted by Tarquin's "traitor eye" (73), where every sign of beauty or virtue serves merely to inflame his lust. This dual perspective continues into a conversation between the two (84–124), where the straightforward, almost naive language and behavior of "modest Lucrece" (123) are in marked contrast to the "subtle shining secrecies" (101) deployed by Tarquin to win and maintain her confidence.

As the evening ends, Tarquin is shown to a bedchamber where the narrator gives us a view of the prince's interior perturbations as he lies "revolving" (127), the likely consequences of the act he is determined to carry out. He is clear about what is at stake, and that the crime he will commit will result in "Pawning his honor to obtain his lust" (156). In the darkest hour of the night he prepares to move, sharpening his dagger in readiness. At this point the narrator gives him a lengthy speech of self-examination that occupies almost 100 lines (190–280), after which, "By reprobate desire thus madly led, / The Roman lord marcheth to Lucrece' bed" (301–2). On the way he has first to overcome various physical obstacles—which serve merely to arouse him more—before he discovers his hostess's glove, which he interprets as a token of his success (316–22). Eventually he strides forward to the bed and pulls back the curtains.

In language that echoes *The Faerie Queene,* the appearance of Lucrece is likened to that of the sun emerging from behind a cloud (372–78). Then follows a blazon of Lucrece's physical attributes, rehearsed with specific reference to Tarquin's powerful response to them, which leads to the moment when he gathers up all his resolution and places a hand on her breast (435–41). In a series of vivid similes, the narrator describes Lucrece's terror at the intrusion (441–69) and reports, but does not quote, the "vehement prayers" (475) of her speech of protestation. Tarquin's response is to declare that only the most pressing imperatives of desire have, quite against the rules of law and duty (497), brought him to this place and that "nothing can affection's course control" (500). He reinforces this declaration with physical threat, embodied in his sword, before offering to keep Lucrece's consent a secret from her family. Tarquin claims, as she watches like "the picture of pure piety" (542), that by yielding to him without a struggle, she has the the power to protect the good name of her clan.

Lucrece's response (575–644) is essentially an appeal to Tarquin's better nature and to his sense of honor and shame. Holding up her hands, Lucrece explains that she is petitioning for "exil'd majesty's repeal" (640) for Tarquin to return to himself. As Lucrece continues to plead for Tarquin to consider the consequences of what he is about to do, the prince cuts her off—"No more . . . by heaven, I will not hear thee" (667)—and threatens to take her, after the rape, to be discovered naked and abused in the bed of a slave (668–72). The narrator then briefly and obliquely tells of the rape, which takes place in darkness and silence (677–84). We are then given our final view of Tarquin, now self-divided and disgusted as he recognizes that "his soul's fair temple is defac'd" (719) and that his action will cause him to be remembered in infamy through the centuries. Carrying this "burthen of a guilty mind" (735), he slinks away, another Cain, "like a thievish dog" (736), leaving behind his victim "like a wearied lamb" to bear "the load of lust he left behind" (737, 734).

Lucrece now becomes the focus of the poem, and the following 800 lines are taken up with the way she passes the remainder of the night. The first section is structured around a series of speeches directed against the personified Night (762–812), Opportunity (876–924), and Time (925–96). Night, characterized as "vaporous and foggy" (771) and explicitly associated with Tarquin's crime, is offered the chance of expiating its guilt by going to war with the sun in order to keep Lucrece's shame and grief at being "martyr'd with disgrace" (802), hidden from the light of day (773–84). The address to Opportunity, which includes a number of parallels to the speech on "commodity" in *King John* (2.1.574–98), is a catalogue of examples in which virtue is destroyed or subverted in an instant because the opportunity for sin presented itself or in which, because of opportunity's willful neglect, evils remain unpunished and wrongs unrighted—

> When wilt thou sort an hour great strifes to end?
> (898)

> The poor, lame, blind, halt, creep, cry out for thee,
> But they ne'er meet with Opportunity.
> (902–3)

This leads to a characteristically Shakespearean attack on "injurious shifting Time" (930), in which the ferocious and destructive qualities of Time are enumerated, Time is declared to be the enemy of beauty and virtue and the master of Opportunity, as well as a force that can promote reconciliation and repentance and that can"wrong the wronger till he render right" (943). At the end of this lengthy section, however, Lucrece dismisses her speeches as "idle words . . . unprofitable sounds" (1016–17) and comes to the conclusion that her only honorable course of action is to take her own life, since, as she puts it, "The remedy indeed to do me good / Is to let forth my foul defiled blood" (1029-30).

At this point she rises from her bed and starts to look for "some desp'rate instrument of death" (1038) and, as she does so, develops her chief argument in favor of suicide. She realizes that her death will be a means to "clear this spot" (1053) of dishonor from her family, whose stock has been polluted (1063), and also to secure Tarquin's condemnation by ensuring that her story is told:

> My tongue shall utter all, mine eyes like sluices,
> As from a mountain spring that feeds a dale,
> Shall gush pure streams to purge my impure tale.
> (1076–78)

As she moves around the room, the first birdsong of the dawn is heard, then the first light breaks, with each of these tokens prompting additional speeches, as "deep drenched in a sea of care," she "Holds disputation with each thing she views, / And to herself all sorrow doth compare" (1100–1102). In particular, the nightingale's song is the occasion of comparisons between the rape of Philomel by Tereus and Lucrece's story, after which she rehearses the provisions of her will and the terms of the report she will make to her husband.

The shorter second section begins with the entrance of a maid, who will set in motion the summons to Lucrece's family. In an instant of wordless recognition, the maid, struck by Lucrece's distress, begins to weep in sympathy (1217–69). Composing herself, Lucrece establishes that Tarquin has left the house long ago, urges the maid to stop crying, and then asks that writing materials be brought and a messenger be provided (1270–94). Lucrece, after several faltering starts, writes the letter (1295–316) and has it sent to Collatine. An index of Lucrece's sense of her own defilement is that she interprets the bashful and awkward silence of the runner as a sign that he "blushed to see her shame" (1344); as the narrator puts it, "The more she saw the blood his cheeks replenish, / The more she thought he spied in her some blemish" (1357–58).

In the third section, Lucrece finds herself drawn to contemplate an image (either a painting or a tapestry) of the fall of Troy. It is an episode rich in literary associations, recalling such passages as the incident in the *Aeneid* where Aeneas sees images of the fall of Troy (1.453–93) and Spenser's account of Britomart's emotional response to a similar tapestry in the House of Busyrane (*FQ*, III.ix.38–39). The picture is first described as any viewer might see it—the narrator tells the reader that "There might you see" (1380) the major incidents and personalities of the fall, as well as hints and tokens of further scenes that the spectator is invited to imagine (1421–28). Lucrece approaches the picture with a particular purpose: "To find a face where all distress is stell'd" (1444).[14] Soon she pauses before the image of Hecuba (1447–63), after which her eye is drawn to every representation of sorrow, and she finds herself weeping at each of their stories in turn—"She throws her eyes about the painting round, / And who she finds forlorn, she doth lament" (1499–500). Eventually she sees a mild, innocuous figure which represents the deceitful Sinon (1501–26). Her initial reaction is that it is implausible for evil to lurk in such an unexceptional figure, but in the act of articulating the thought, the memory of Tarquin comes back to her (1524–40) and becomes a parallel story—"As Priam him did cherish, / So did I Tarquin; so my Troy did perish" (1545-46). Thereupon she attacks the image of Sinon with her nails (1561–68) before returning to her private sorrows.

It is in this condition that her husband finds her and asks the reason for her distress (1590–603). She prepares herself and then addresses both Collatine and his "consorted lords" (1609), telling the story of her rape succinctly, though holding back her attacker's name and concluding with the assertion: "Though my gross blood be stain'd with this abuse, / Immaculate and spotless is my mind" (1655–56). As Collatine, "the hopeless merchant of this loss" (1660), adopts the traditional melancholy posture of crossed arms and downcast eyes and silently conveys pent-up grief and anger (1661–73), Lucrece stirs up the assembly to thoughts of revenge, of the duty of knights to repair wrongs done to ladies (1681–94).

Although her audience rejects the notion that she is guilty or that she has been stained by the attack, Lucrece refuses to listen to them and draws up her strength to name Tarquin. The effort of the act deprives her of almost all power of speech. After struggling with herself, she summons the strength to blame Tarquin for what she is about to do—then stabs herself (1722–24) with his knife. Along with their followers, Collatine and old Lucretius are "Stone-still, astonish'd with this deadly deed" (1730), as Lucrece lies dead in a pool of blood. As the amazement abates, first Lucretius (1751–71), then Collatine (1772–90), claim primacy in grief. They begin to compete with each other for ownership of the dead woman and of the sorrow (" 'My daughter!' and 'My wife!' with clamors fill'd / The dispers'd air" (1804–5). Meanwhile Brutus, a man regarded as a fool by the Romans, plucks the dagger out of Lucrece's body and drops the guise of folly by which he has preserved his life during the rule of tyranny. He improvises a ritual of kneeling by the body of Lucrece and swearing—by the gods, by the city, and by Lucrece's blood on the knife that slew her—to bind the Roman nobility together to rise up against the Tarquins and seek revenge for "the death of this true wife" (1841). As a result, the body is carried into the city, where it inspires the people to support Brutus and banish the Tarquins (1841–55).

Shakespeare's Meanings

Even from such a brief summary, it should be clear that the poem combines, in the usual manner of the epyllion, the narrative and the dramatic, and that set-piece rhetorical display is one of its important features. Even the most casual reading of the poem will suggest that, notwithstanding what has been noted about some of the political implications of his subject, Shakespeare was writing for a readership who evidently relished the numerous sententiae, such as "The old bees die, the young possess their hive" (1769); "Poor women's faces are their own faults' books" (1253); "It easeth some, though none it ever cured, / To think their dolour others have endured" (1581–82)"

In fact, several sententious passages are indicated typographically in the first quarto (although no modern edition preserves this feature). It may be instructive to consider them as an illustration of the passages below that someone in 1594—whether the author or the printer—highlighted as being especially worthy of note.

> For unstain'd thoughts do seldom dream on evil;
> Birds never lim'd no secret bushes fear. (87–88)

Such shadows are the weak brain's forgeries. (460)
A little harm done to a great good end. (528)
The poisonous simple sometime is compacted. (530)
Tears harden lust, though marble [wear] with raining. (560)
How he in peace is wounded, not in war.
Alas, how many bear such shameful blows. (831–32)
But no perfection is so absolute. (853)
The sweets we wish for turn to loathed sours
Even in the moment that we call them ours. (867–68)
A woeful hostess brooks not merry guests. (1125)
Distress likes dumps when time is kept with tears. (1127)
For fleet-wing'd duty with thought's feathers flies. (1216)
For sparing justice feeds iniquity. (1687)

One longer passage is highlighted:

> For mirth doth search the bottom of annoy,
> Sad souls are slain in merry company,
> Grief best is pleas'd with grief's society;
>   True sorrow then is feelingly suffic'd
>   When with like semblance it is sympathiz'd.
>
> 'Tis double death to drown in ken of shore,
> He ten times pines that pines beholding food,
> To see the salve does make the wound ache more,
> Great grief grieves most at that would do it good;
> Deep woes roll forward like a gentle flood.
>   (1109–18)

It is unclear why these particular passages, and not similar ones, were marked; although it is evident that they confirm the Elizabethan reader's well-attested relish for antithetical formulations and proverb-like utterances. In addition, however, it might be argued that some of the marked passages, especially when lifted from their context and gathered in this way, relate to two of the poem's concerns—the representation of the inner life as conflicted, contradictory, and turbulent, and the tendency of absolute power to foster abuses that, if not addressed, may fuel rebellious resentment (as in 831–32, 853, and 1687).

Not only the "wiser sort" identified by Gabriel Harvey, but also, presumably, their more frivolous counterparts, would have appreciated the poem's ubiquitous verbal dexterity and rhetorical display. Wordplay is often of a highly self-advertising kind: "To shun the blot, she would not blot the letter" (1322) and "Ere she with blood had stain'd her stain'd excuse" (1316).

Such self-conscious rhetorical display is also found at some of the most critical points in the narrative, as in the following passage immediately following the rape. The stark antitheses, whose power is increased by their formality, establish a vivid contrast between predator and prey, between guilt and innocence:

> She bears the load of lust he left behind,
> And he the burthen of a guilty mind.
>
> He like a thievish dog creeps sadly thence,
> She like a wearied lamb lies panting there;
> He scowls and hates himself for his offense,
> She desperate with her nails her flesh doth tear;
> He faintly flies, sweating with guilty fear;
>   She stays, exclaiming on the direful night,
>   He runs, and chides his vanish'd, loath'd delight.
>
> He thence departs a heavy convertite,
> She there remains a hopeless castaway,
> He in his speed looks for the morning light,
> She prays she never may behold the day.
>   (734–46)

There are places where the narrator provides something close to a commentary, explicitly drawing attention to the various rhetorical set pieces. Thus, the narrator announces Lucrece's attack upon sleep as a time when defenses are down—"Here she exclaims against repose and rest" (757). In the same way, after her apostrophes to "comfort-killing Night, image of Hell" (764–805)—a passage that recalls Prince Arthur's complaint in *The Faerie Queene* (*FQ,* III.iv.55–60)—to Opportunity (874–924), and to Time (925–1022), Lucrece comments on her own performance:

> In vain I rail at Opportunity,
> At Time, at Tarquin, and uncheerful Night,
> In vain I cavil with mine infamy,
> In vain I spurn at my confirm'd despite:
> This helpless smoke of words doth me no right.
>   (1023–27)

The narrator, in a much less obvious way than his precursor in *Venus and Adonis,* directs the reader's perceptions, as when the reader is instructed to "Imagine her as one in dead of night" (450). He also sums up several episodes, announces others, and signals transitions in the story by several devices, most obviously by the frequent use of "thus":

> Teaching them thus to use it in the fight. (62)
> And to the flame thus speaks advisedly. (180)
> And justly thus controls his thoughts unjust. (189)
> Thus graceless holds he disputation. (246)
> By reprobate desire thus madly led. (300)
> Thus treason works ere traitors be espied. (361)
> Thus he replies. (477)
> Frantic with grief thus breathes she forth her spite. (762)
> Thus cavils she with every thing she sees. (1093)
> At last she thus begins. (1303)
> "It cannot be" she in that sense forsook,
> And turn'd it thus. (1538–39)
> Thus ebbs and flows the current of her sorrow. (1569)
> At last he takes her by the bloodless hand,
> And thus begins. (1598)
> Why art thou thus attir'd in discontent? (1601)
> And his untimely frenzy thus awaketh. (1675)

This is the state of mind—"To see sad sights moves more than hear them told" (1324)—in which Lucrece begins her contemplation of the image of the Trojan War, a representation of "Certain sorrow, writ uncertainly." (1311).[15] Tarquin's blazon of Lucrece (386–410) is the act of a spectator "Rolling his greedy eyeballs in his head" (368), whose wonder arouses lust:

> With more than admiration he admired
> Her azure veins, her alabaster skin,
> Her coral lips, her snow-white dimpled chin.
> (418–20)

Lucrece's colors, her "heraldry," are figured as red and white (52–63)— "This heraldry in Lucrece' face was seen, / Argued by beauty's red and virtue's white" (64–65). An opposite figure to Lucrece is the Trojan traitor Sinon, whose image appears in the painting of the Trojan War. As the embodiment of ambiguity and duplicity, his face has cheeks that are

> . . . neither red nor pale, but mingled so
> That blushing red no guilty instance gave,
> Nor ashy pale the fear that false hearts have
> (1510–12).

To Tarquin's eye, Lucrece's face is the battlefield for a "silent war of lilies and of roses" (71). Under his influence, the meaning of the colors changes to the white of terror and the red of shame. Lucrece and her maid gaze with ashen faces on each other (1219–53); then she blushes with shame when the blushing groom comes to her (1342–58). Collatine bathes his pale face in Lucrece's blood (1774–75).

Related Poetry

The context of Shakespeare's rhetorical performance in *Lucrece,* as much as in his plays, is crucial throughout. And an inescapable, vital context for *Lucrece* is the memory of *Venus and Adonis.* Emrys Jones long ago demonstrated conclusively that Shakespeare borrowed at least as much and as frequently from himself—especially scenic structures—as from anyone else.[16] Undoubtedly, one of the most important sources for *Lucrece* is *Venus and Adonis.* Of course, there are many differences in subject, style, tone, and narrative strategies between the two poems. Nevertheless, they might in some respects be seen as twinned, almost as mirror images of each other. The concluding pageants of the bodies of Adonis and Lucrece, with their circling streams of blood, recall the fact that each story shows rampant, errant, uncontrolled royal desire leading to the death of unwilling subjects. In each case the royal aggressor does not deliver the fatal blow and is far away when the death occurs. One poem ends with Venus in self-imposed retreat, the other with Tarquin in exile. It has been argued that the two protagonists and the two victims may have more in common than at first appears.[17]

In the same way, the contrasts between the poems may be mutually illuminating. For example, the ominous, gloomy, menacing interior journey of the predatory Tarquin appears more sinister when compared with the open-air directness of Venus.

Unlike *Venus and Adonis, Lucrece* is not set in a mythical past, close enough to be nostalgic about it, but in a fallen, violent world. This is particularly apparent in the rhetorical and ultimately (645–72) physical competition of their debate, which contrasts Tarquin's speeches (477–539) with Lucrece's eloquent appeals (575–645) to his better nature. Tyranny, lust, and greed translate the metaphors of Petrarchism into the actuality of rape. This is signaled by the rhetorical figure known as *gradatio* or climax: "What could he see but mightily he noted? / What did he note but strongly he desired?" (414–15). For added emphasis, the figure of *gradatio* is repeated a few lines later: "His drumming heart cheers up his burning eye, / His eye commends the leading to his hand, / His hand as proud of such a dignity" (435–37).

The poem also can be placed among significant contemporary literary contexts. Shakespeare connects his work with the most important and most ambitious contemporary poem, as if he were announcing himself as Ovid to Spenser's Virgil. Thus, just as Lucrece takes on the persona of Spenser's great heroine of married chastity, Britomart, when she confronts the image of the fall of Troy, Tarquin contains elements of several figures from *The Faerie Queene*. There are obvious echoes of the Ovidian seducer and rapist (and also, it should be added, historian of both Troy and Rome) Paridell. When Tarquin pulls back the curtain and has an epiphany of Lucrece (371–78), Shakespeare recalls the moment where Paridell is "smitten . . . with great amazement" as Britomart removes her helmet (*FQ,* III.ix.21–24).[18]

Tarquin also restages, in parodic form, elements of two of Spenser's heroes, one female, one male. Tarquin's journey to the bedroom is evocative of Britomart's journey to the House of Busyrane (*FQ,* III.xi–xii). It

also recalls the opening incident in *The Faerie Queene,* where the Red
Cross Knight enters Error's den in the Wandering Wood: in the darkness he is able to see the monster only because "his glistring armor made
/ A litle glooming light, much like a shade" (*FQ,* I.i.14-15).[19] Tarquin
has a "lightless fire" (4), then a torch whose flame is sparked from the
fatal dagger (176–92). And just as the Red Cross Knight s eventually
enwreathed by Error's tail and is described as being "in great perplexi-
tie," Lucrece is "perplex'd in greater pain" (733)—literally "wrapped
around," also metaphorically "troubled" or "confused"—after Tarquin
leaves her.

The Poem and the 1590s

Such a typically 1590s self-consciousness is found in many places in the
poem. Tarquin, for example, is at one level an exemplary tyrant from a
familiar part of ancient history. Yet his inner debate is highly contemporary. It features the conventional 1590s conflict between willful, youthful prodigality and sententious experience; and he displays an awareness
of his situation, as when he comments, "My part is youth, and beats
these from the stage" (278). The arguments in his "disputation / 'Tween
frozen conscience and hot burning will" (246–47) are those of the
rebellions youth of the morality tradition (as found both in interludes
such as *Youth* and *Lusty Juventus* and in Shakespeare's own construction
of Hal in the two parts of *Henry IV*). But they are also manifestly those
of the Petrarchan sonnet-lover—"nothing can affection's course control"
and then "Yet strive I to embrace mine infamy" (500–504). In language
that anticipates the sonnets, male lust is depicted as "this ambitious foul
infirmity," which "In having much, torments us with defect / Of that we
have," causing men to "Make something nothing by augmenting it"
(150–54) and leading to disgust rather than satisfaction.

The combination of ancient and contemporary strengthens the political elements in the poem. It demonstrates tyranny in its most intimate
form, the private outrage that is inescapably public: hence the rape is
figured in terms both domestic (as a burglary) and public (as a hunt, a
war, a siege). It also reveals the essential violence of many conventional
erotic metaphors. That context adds urgency to Tarquin's otherwise
conventional conflation of military and erotic metaphors, with his
"drumming heart" beating as he attacks the citadel of Lucrece's body
and honor (428–70). Shakespeare also draws on the powerful Elizabethan myth of the island nation as woman.[20]

The poem abounds with images of hunting and predation. Tarquin is regularly depicted as a hunter—"Into the chamber wickedly he stalks" (365)—and as a bird of prey: "The dove sleeps fast that this night-owl will catch" (360). His sword is compared to "a falcon tow'ring in the skies," while Lucrece is like a "fowl" who hears the falcon's bells "with trembling fear" (506–11). Her innocence is expressed by the aphoristic "Birds never lim'd no secret bushes fear" (88). Elsewhere Tarquin is like a "grim lion" fawning over his prey (421).[21] Just before the rape Lucrece is described as

> Wrapped and confounded in a thousand fears,
> Like to a new-killed bird she trembling lies.
>
> (456–57)

When Tarquin pauses, Lucrece is "the picture of pure piety / Like a white hind under the gripe's sharp claws" (542–43) and later a "weak mouse" grabbed by a "vulture" (555–56). In her attempt to fend him off, Lucrece appeals to his sense of sportsmanship: "He is no woodman that doth bend his bow / To strike the poor unseasonable doe" (580-81). During the rape itself—"The wolf hath seiz'd his prey, the poor lamb cries" (677)—there is a return to images of predation, when Tarquin is compared to a "full-fed hound or gorged hawk" (694). The poem concludes with Lucrece as "this pale swan in her wat'ry nest" (1611).

The poem oscillates between narrative and dramatic, visual and verbal, simplicity and complexity. Both Lucrece and Tarquin, for example, are summed up with unambiguous epithets: Tarquin is "this lustful lord" (169), and Lucrece is "Lucrece the chaste" (7)—an echo of Marlowe's "Hero the fair" (Hero and Leander, 5)—and "Harmless Lucretia" (511).

There is also a considerable amount of information about the inner workings of their minds, especially Tarquin's. The poem begins with much uncertainty about his motivation (8, 36, 39, 43). He is likened to insomniacs with "troubled minds" (126), and then

> As one of which doth Tarquin lie revolving
> The sundry dangers of his will's obtaining,
> Yet ever to obtain his will resolving,
> Though weak-built hopes persuade him abstaining.
>
> (127–30)

In the manner of David in Wyatt's *Penitential Psalms,* Tarquin, we are told, "in his inward mind doth much debate" (185) "And justly thus controls his thoughts unjust" (189). Yet despite its apparent access to the minds of the protagonists, the poem is just as remarkable for what it does not show or tell, which speaks both to its treatment of gender relations and to its handling of political material. In the painting of Troy, the presence of Achilles is left for the viewer to conjure up:

> . . . for Achilles' image stood his spear,
> Grip'd in an armed hand, himself behind
> Was left unseen, save to the eye of mind:
> A hand, a foot, a face, a leg, a head
> Stood for the whole to be imagined.
> (1424–28)

The rape itself is also unseen, passed over in two stanzas (673–86), whose focus is on darkness, the covering of Lucrece's eyes, and Tarquin's muffling her cries. Lucrece's first speech is not quoted but reported: "she with vehement prayers urgeth still / Under what color he commits this ill" (475-76); later on, "With untun'd tongue she hoarsely calls her maid" (1215). Then Lucrece and Collatine gaze at each other (1591–95), and Collatine's voice is "damn'd up by woe" when he hears her story (1661). When Lucrece writes her letter to Collatine, she "dares not . . . make discovery" (1314) of what has happened to her. Instead

> Here folds she up the tenure of her woe,
> Her certain sorrow, writ uncertainly.
> (1310–11)

The articulation of her final monosyllabic words is depicted as an heroic struggle:

> Here with a sigh as if her heart would break,
> She throws forth Tarquin's name: "He, he," she says,
> But more than "he" her poor tongue could not speak,
> Till after many accents and delays,
> Untimely breathings, sick and short assays,

> She utters this, "He, he, fair lords, 'tis he,
> That guides this hand to give this wound to me."
>   (1716–22)

Whereupon Collatine is reduced to silence:

> The deep vexation of his inward soul
> Hath serv'd a dumb arrest upon his tongue.
>   (1779–80)

In his discussion of speaking pictures in *The Defence of Poesie,* Sidney referred to the pictorial image of "the constant though lamenting look of Lucretia, when she punished in herself another's fault."[22] More obviously accessible to Shakespeare at this time was the account of the death of Amavia "In whose white alabaster brest did sticke / A cruell knife," described as "Pitifull spectacle, as euer eye did view" (*FQ,* II.1.39–40), a passage that seems to lie behind lines 1723–50. This is the state of mind—"To see sad sights moves more than hear them told" (1324)—in which Lucrece begins her contemplation of the image of the Trojan War.

After the rape, the poem raises important issues of reputation, reading, and interpretation. Interpretation is shown to be a complex business in a wilderness of parallels and comparisons, where the story of Troy, combining rape and siege, also raises the idea of empire—and of the role of Brutus—that connects Troy to Rome and, inescapably, to Britain. Lucrece imagines herself becoming, like Criseyde, a watchword for faithlessness—"The orator to deck his oratory / Will couple my reproach to Tarquin's shame" (815–16). She proclaims herself a speaking picture:

> . . . the illiterate that know not how
>   To cipher what is writ in learned books,
>   Will cote my loathsome trespass in my looks. (810–12)

The Tradition

It is with the issues of memory and reputation that the poem seems to invoke most powerfully the previous tellings of the Lucrece story and the ethical "disputations" to which it had given rise over the centuries.

Several scholars have traced the history of the story of Lucrece from ancient times to the Renaissance and have demonstrated Shakespeare's connection with aspects of the tradition.[23] Lucrece's suicide had been much debated in Roman and Christian thought. In Shakespeare's treatments of the ancient world, speakers (like Brutus and Cassius over the body of Caesar, or Pandarus, Troilus, and Cressida contemplating their reputations, or Cleopatra imagining herself being acted by a boy-player) are often given moments when they predict a future in which they have become exemplary, when the most urgent crises in their lives have become topics for school debate and philosophical and ethical argument. In Lucrece's case, she looks to a time when "The nurse to quell her child will tell my story" and "The orator to deck his oratory" will connect her blame to the shame of Tarquin (813–15). She continues:

> "Let my good name, that senseless reputation,
> For Collatine's dear love be kept unspotted:
> If that be made a theme for disputation,
> The branches of another root are rotted."
>
> (820–23)

Suicide was already established as a "theme for disputation" when St. Augustine took it up in *The City of God,* a work designed, among other things, to demonstrate the inadequacies of classical civilization and the superiority of Christianity. Augustine's argument is simple.[24] The Romans were wrong to think of Lucrece as an ideal, a heroine, and a martyr; and she should not have killed herself. The sin of suicide ensures the loss and damnation of her soul, whereas in the rape itself, as was a commonplace in Augustine's day, "there were two persons involved, and only one committed adultery." So, Augustine asks, if she were innocent, why should she have killed herself? By what authority is an innocent life to be taken without trial? Is not such a person in effect a murderer? If, however, she regarded herself, rightly or wrongly, as guilty of adultery, of taking pleasure in the act, other issues are raised. In either case, she ought not to be held up as an ideal (29–30).

Augustine contextualizes his account in important ways (28). He was writing at a time when Christian women were being raped prior to execution in the arena; and his analysis is a means of explaining to the Romans that their acts of torture and rape could only affect the bodies, not the souls, of the women. Where a sense of shame would have driven a Roman female to seek redemption through suicide, Augustine explains that these Christian women believed their souls were unaffected by their suffering. Therefore they refused to commit suicide in order to safeguard their eternal happiness in heaven. He also grants the context of Lucrece's act, describing her as a "noble example" in the light of the values of her own culture of shame:

> She was ashamed of another's foul deed committed on her, even though not with her, and as a Roman woman, excessively eager for honour, she was afraid that she should be thought, if she lived, to have willingly endured what, when she lived, she had violently suffered.... She blushed at the thought of being regarded as an accomplice in the act if she were to bear with patience what another had inflicted on her with violence. Such has not been the behaviour of Christian women. (30)

Scholars have recognized that, like Augustine, Shakespeare provides pagan and Christian frameworks for crucial points in the action. Lucrece dies crying for revenge in the high Roman fashion, because "life is sham'd" (1155), but had earlier asked, in a distinctly Christian phrase, " 'To kill myself,' quoth she, 'alack what were it / But with my body my poor soul's pollution?' " (1156–57). She goes on to use Christian formulations when she raises theological questions about sin and guilt to which future Christianity will propose answers that she was born too early to hear (1478–84).[25] Both pagan and Christian values inform parts of her self-examination:

> My body or my soul, which was the dearer,
> When the one pure, the other made divine?
> Whose love of either to myself was nearer,
> When both were kept for heaven and Collatine?
> (1163–66)

The dense, paradoxical language describing the suicide maintains the sense of the distinction between the body and the soul:

> Even here she sheathed in her harmless breast
> A harmful knife, that thence her soul unsheathed;
> That blow did bail it from the deep unrest
> Of that polluted prison where it breathed.

Her contrite sighs unto the clouds bequeathed
　Her winged sprite, and through her wounds doth fly
　Live's lasting date from cancell'd destiny.
                                          (1723–29)

Lucrece's story was told often in the Middle Ages, as in the *Roman de la Rose* and John Gower's *Confessio Amantis* (7.4754–5130). In one of the stories collected in Chaucer's *Legend of Good Women* (Riverside *Chaucer,* 618–20), the Lucrece narrative ("*Legenda Lucrecie Rome, Martiris*") appears to be based on Ovid, although the narrator does mention Livy (1684). Chaucer's narrative is brisk and the exchanges brief and direct. He encapsulates her predicament, with the sword of the rapist she knows is the king's son at her throat, in language that anticipates Shakespeare:

　　What shal she seyn? Hire wit is al ago.
　　Ryght as a wolf that fynt a lomb alone,
　　To whom shal she compleyne or make mone?
                                          (1797–99)

The narrator describes how, under pressure of the immediate circumstances and because of Lucrece's ingrained belief in the Roman value system, with its horror of shame, she faints. Thus the rape happens when she is so unconscious that someone could have struck off her arm or head before she could regain her senses (thereby deflecting Augustine's insinuation that she took pleasure from the rape):

　　These Romeyns wyves lovede so here name
　　At thilke tyme, and dredde so the shame,
　　That, what for fer of sclaunder and drede of death,
　　She loste bothe at ones wit and breth,
　　And in a swogh she lay, and wex so ded
　　Men myghte smyten of hire arm or hed;
　　She feleth no thyng, neyther foul ne fayr.
                                          (1812–18)

Chaucer's narrator had begun, somewhat disingenuously, by claiming that Augustine had expressed "gret compassioun" (1690) for Lucrece.

Toward the end he remarks on the Roman elevation of Lucrece into a kind of saint, with a festival day, before locating the poem in its political context and pointing out that after Lucrece's death there were no more kings in Rome ("Ne never was ther kyng in Rome toun Syn thilke day" [1870–71]). Then he ends by relating politics to gender relations, directing his readers to look truly and hard at how men behave—"as of men, loke ye what tirannye they doon alday" (1883–84).

There are also some obvious parallels between Shakespeare's *Lucrece* and the broadly sympathetic treatment accorded by the narrator to Criseyde in *Troilus and Criseyde*. In this text, Chaucer repudiated some of the central elements of the Criseyde story as it had come down to him. In particular, he took issue with a tradition that blamed Criseyde for her faithlessness and rejoiced in her punishment and misfortune. Chaucer presents Criseyde not as a whore, an embodiment of female inconstancy and heartlessness, but as a victim.

The imagery describing the moment of her sexual union with Troilus is strikingly violent and changes the dynamic of the relationship. While Pandarus is reading romances, and while the conventional rhetoric of love pours out of Troilus, the narrator signals a new, much more brutal actuality. In language that anticipates *Lucrece* and parallels the description of the futility of Lucrece's utterances in the *Legend,* Criseyde is suddenly presented as an innocent lark, trapped by the talons of a bird of prey. The narrator asks, "What myghte or may the sely larke seye, / Whan that the sperhauk hath it in his foot?" (*TC,* III.1191–92, Riverside *Chaucer,* 529).

Lucrece utters a complaint (1464–91) in the character of Hecuba, whose silent image in the painting provokes her to comment on the artist: "He did her wrong, / To give her so much grief, and not a tongue" (1462–63). As she "feelingly . . . weeps Troy's painted woes," she echoes Britomart's planctus or complaint: "O lamentable fall of famous towne" (*FQ,* III.ix.38–39). But when she is moved to scratch the image of Sinon, who recalls Tarquin, she acknowledges the futility of her response: "his wounds will not be sore" (1568).

Lucrece's references to Philomel at 1079 and 1127 are more than formulaic, in that they argue for an irrepressible voice eternally proclaiming rape and injustice. They recall both Ovid and the ominous comparison of Criseyde to the nightingale while she is in bed with Troilus (*TC,* III.1233–39). In this context, Lucrece's meditation on suicide (1044–211) is rendered morally complex for a Christian readership. The web of allusion seems designed to show, and also to arouse compassion for, a woman trapped by the values of a patriarchal society ("What is the quality of my offence, being constrained with dreadful circumstance?" [1702]).

Her death arouses amazement (1730) and gives rise to yet another debate. It expresses the patriarchal values of the world Lucrece had lived in, as it consists of a rhetorical competition between her father and husband over who owns her and who has more right to mourn (1795–806). Yet while our attention is inescapably taken up with this verbal display, the action, precipitated by Brutus, is centered on the fatal dagger, which, brought into her house by Tarquin as the instrument of violence that lit his way to the rape, now becomes an instrument less of personal vengeance than of popular resistance and political transformation. And of course the historically validated interpretation of her suicide for Shakespeare's readers—descendants of Brutus in New Troy—is provided by Brutus, who "pluck'd the knife from Lucrece' side" (1807). It is through the dagger, more than through words, that Lucrece is connected to historical processes still under way for Shakespeare's readers.

When Brutus steps forward, casting off his lifelong reputation for folly, he improvises a ritual—kissing the knife (1843)—that transforms grief and outrage at Lucrece's death into a determination to "publish Tarquin's foul offense" and change the political system (1814–55). Brutus emerges from the shadows in a characteristic 1590s oscillation between foreground and background, center and margin. Like the silence at the rape, like the omission of material from the argument at the beginning of the poem, this incident reminds us that *Lucrece,* notwithstanding its powerful speeches and harrowing images, is no less remarkable for its silences and its shadows, for what is "left unseen, save to the eye of mind" (1424).

Traditions of Interpretation

The story of the responses to Lucrece over the centuries is initially very similar to that of *Venus and Adonis.* One difference is that, perhaps because of the more obviously declamatory nature of some of the speeches and because of similarities between the dramatic scenes and various moments in the plays, there has always been a tendency to read *Lucrece* as a version of, or as a preparation for, the plays.[26]

The poem certainly has much in common with some of the early plays, especially *Titus Andronicus.* There are at least four references to the

story of Lucrece in *Titus* (2.1.108, 3.1.298, 4.1.64, 4.1.95), and there
are many other connections between the two works. Passages that have
been noted to resemble each other in the two texts include:

Lucrece	*Titus*
552–53	2.3.51
577	5.3.171
579–80	2.3.25–26
592–94	3.1.37–42
664–65	4.3.45
1136	3.2.16–17
1520–61	5.3.79–86[27]

The traditional view of *Lucrece* in academic literary criticism—which
has showed slightly more enthusiasm for it than for *Venus and Adonis*—is
that the poem is little more than a bookish, pedantic dry run for Shakespeare's tragedies—in William Empson's phrase, "the Bard doing five-
finger exercises at the piano" (cited in Roe, 27).[28] There are a variety of
similar comments, such as F. T. Prince's identification of "excesses in
rhetoric" in the treatment of an "uninteresting" story, resulting in a
"failure" that "reveals itself ever more disastrously as the poem proceeds" (Prince, xxxv). It is hard not to find hints of misogyny in remarks
like Prince's "After her violation, Lucrece loses our sympathy exactly in
proportion as she gives tongue" (xxxvi) or in Roe's grudging concession
that, compared to Thomas Kyd's *The Spanish Tragedy,* Lucrece's speeches
are "not at all excessive" (27). Writing of both of Shakespeare's narrative
poems, Robert Ellrodt comments that

> one may complain of prolixity and one would like to think the poet
> mocked the Elizabethan partiality to copia when he compared the
> "tedious" lament of Venus to "copious stories" that "End without audi-
> ence, and are never done." (ll.841–46) Vain wish, since wordiness grew
> worse in *Lucrece*! (Ellrodt 1986, 45–46)

It was often held that the poem was an uneasy hybrid of narrative
and dramatic, and that it had been more successfully treated by Ovid
and Chaucer. Another common complaint was the poem's apparent
two-part structure, one half concentrating on Tarquin, the other on
Lucrece. To quote Prince again:

Until the crime is committed, Tarquin is the focus of our attention, and convinces us that he is a tragically complex character. After the deed, Lucrece becomes the tragic heroine, but we are never wholly convinced that she deserves the part, and the more we ponder the more clearly we can see why she does not. Not only is she a less interesting character than Tarquin: she is forced to express herself in a way which dissipates the real pathos of her situation. (xxxvi)

Conclusion

As noted, the connections between Lucrece and the moral and ethical issues it raised have been much discussed. There have been several studies of the history of the Lucrece story.[29] Some commentators have argued that Shakespeare engaged with this material in a subtle way, perhaps injecting critiques of orthodox views.[30] Richard Levin, however, has offered a skeptical riposte to such arguments.[31]

In a way that will perhaps by this stage of the present study seem to be a familiar reaction to the hybrid, unclassifiable literature of the 1590s, many commentators have wrestled with the genre of Lucrece. They have noted that the poem combines political fable and tragedy within a highly contemporary milieu of self-conscious antiquity. Following J. W. Lever, Maurice Evans defines the poem as a "moral narrative on a tragic theme" (Evans, 32), whose first half is the tragedy of Tarquin—in the sense used in both Chaucer and Boethius of an exemplary fall from greatness—and whose second is the planctus—on Daniel's model—of Lucrece. In a significant development, the poem's connection specifically to Samuel Daniel's *Complaint of Rosamund* and more generally to the genre of female poems of lament or complaint has now been conclusively established as a major element in its context.[32]

The tradition of rhetorical readings has continued from the days of the New Criticism to the present and has at times offered ways of finding unity in a text that other readers have found divided, hybrid, or incoherent. More recently, rhetoric has been used to explore the poem's treatment of the inherent theatricality of life—"Lucrece teaches that history happens on a stage to begin with . . . In history so construed . . . speeches offer not less verisimilitude but more."[33] A more problematic view of language, together with an account of verbal and visual rhetorics, is found in Katharine Eisaman Maus's influential study in 1986.[34] Language is approached in a psychoanalytical/deconstructive way in Joel Fineman's "Shakespeare's Will," which is related to his study of Shakespeare's construction of a "new" subjectivity in the sonnets.[35] Heather Dubrow in *Captive Victors* identifies the union of opposites, or *syneciosis,* as the poem's central trope and a way of understanding the complex relations between the various opposed forces, characters, languages, and settings the poem displays (80–142).

Perhaps the most significant recent developments since the reawakened interest in rhetoric have been the feminist discovery of the poem and a dawning awareness of its political engagement. There has been for many years a trickle of studies that have read the poem historically— seeing it as closer in spirit to Livy than to Ovid. Until fairly recently, the historical readings tended to locate the poem in the "advice-to-a-prince" genre and read it as specifically directed towards Southampton.[36] As noted earlier, historical readings have been taken in a more political direction in such studies as Annabel Patterson's *Reading Between the Lines* (1993).

Much of the most interesting work on the poem in recent years has grown out of feminism. Whereas, in the passages cited earlier, Prince (and other editors) did not refer to the rape as a rape, but rather by some circumlocution, Coppelia Kahn has argued for the centrality of the rape to the poem and that it exposes the violent operation of a patriarchy in which women were chattels and rape a property crime.[37] In an analogous study, Nancy Vickers has explored the latent savagery inherent in the descriptions and catalogues of female beauty in much the same way that both of Shakespeare's epyllia reveal the potentially bloodthirsty and destructive implications of Petrarchism.[38]

As Dubrow points out in her judicious summary of modern criticism (Riverside, 50–52), feminist readings tend to connect the opening wager, where men lay bets about their wives' chastity, with the incongruous tussle near the end of the poem between Collatine and Lucretius for ownership of Lucrece's body and for primacy in grief. (There is an instructive cross-generic parallel with *The Taming of the Shrew.*) Political readings, by contrast, focus on the "Argument" and on the emerging figure of Brutus, whose sudden transformation from marginal and scorned figure to history maker is a version of—perhaps a transformation of—the figure of Sinon.

Lucrece, like so many of Shakespeare's historical tragedies, renders problematic the categories of history and myth, of public and private, and exemplifies the bewildering nature of historical parallels. The self-conscious rhetorical display and the examination of representation is daringly politicized, explicitly, if inconclusively, connecting the aesthetic and the erotic with politics both sexual and state. Lucrece was Shake-speare's most profound meditation to date on history, particularly on the relations between public role and private morality, and on the conjunc-tion of forces—personal, political, and social—that creates turning points in human history. In it, he not only articulated, albeit indirectly, the concerns of his young patron, who was already closely associated with the doomed earl of Essex, but he also gave voice to some of the most urgent concerns of his generation.

Chapter Four

Miscellaneous Poems

This chapter discusses *The Passionate Pilgrim* (1599) and *The Phoenix and Turtle* (1601), as well as a miscellaneous group of poems, mainly occasional writings, that have been attributed to Shakespeare at various times. In doing so, the chapter addresses, although in a somewhat different set of contexts, the issues of authorship and reputation that are considered in other chapters and also touches on the question of the Shakespeare canon.

The Passionate Pilgrim

The inconsistent treatment of *The Passionate Pilgrim* by Shakespeare's editors may at times confuse students and other readers. For example, whereas the 1997 *Riverside Shakespeare* prints the entire collection, as its predecessors have done, David Bevington, in the preface to the 1997 edition of *The Complete Works of Shakespeare,* comments

> This edition does not include, however, *The Passionate Pilgrim,* a little volume of 1599 attributed to Shakespeare by its unscrupulous publisher but containing no new poems that are convincingly his.[1]

The complex story of the publication of *The Passionate Pilgrim* sheds some light on Shakespeare's reputation and on his conception of himself as an author. It may even provide some valuable clues as to the chronology of some of his works and to possible connections between them. In addition, study of this "little volume" and its "unscrupulous publisher" may provide insight into important aspects of the literary profession in which Shakespeare worked, in particular the shifting power relationships between writers and publishers. It may also prompt, at least by implication, reflections about volumes—big and little—and about publishers—scrupulous or otherwise—in the Shakespeare industry four hundred years after a much maligned London publisher sought to participate in it.

In late 1598 or early 1599 the printer William Jaggard brought out an anthology of 20 miscellaneous poems. Time has not served the flimsy volume well. The title page of the first edition is lost; the volume, discovered in 1920, survives in an incomplete form in the Folger Shakespeare Library. A second edition, *The Passionate Pilgrime. By W. Shakespeare,* appeared in 1599. This edition was to be sold by William Leake, who was also selling the 1599 fifth and sixth quarto editions of Shakespeare's perennial best-seller *Venus and Adonis* at the sign of the Greyhound in St. Paul's Churchyard. Presumably, Jaggard was hoping that the volume would benefit from the new (post-1598) visibility of Shakespeare's name in the literary marketplace and from physical proximity to the commercially successful *Venus and Adonis.*

In 1612—three years after Thorpe's publication of *Shake-speare's Sonnets*—Jaggard brought out a third edition, *The Passionate Pilgrime. Or Certaine Amorous Sonnets, betweene Venus and Adonis, newly corrected and augmented. By W. Shakespere.* The Bodleian copy of this edition features a canceled title page, which omits "By W. Shakespere." The omission probably indicates that there had been a disagreement between Jaggard and Shakespeare.

It was not the only controversy Jaggard had to face as a result of this publication. The major change that had occurred to the volume since the 1599 edition was the inclusion of a group of nine poems by Thomas Heywood, which Jaggard had already published in 1609 in a volume called *Troia Britannica.* Heywood vigorously protested the 1612 edition, in which, he claimed, some of his own poems had been printed without acknowledgment, alleging that they had been incompetently printed by Jaggard in the earlier book. Furthermore, he argued, the title page, by implying that the poems had actually been written by Shakespeare, left Heywood vulnerable to charges of dishonesty. In his *Apologie for Actors* (1612), Heywood complains to his friend Nicholas Okes:

I must necessarily insert a manifest injury done me in this worke [*Troia Britannica*], by taking the two Epistles of *Paris to Helen,* and *Helen to Paris,* and printing them in a lesse volume [*The Passionate Pilgrim*], under the name of another [*Shakespeare*] which may put the world in opinion I might steale them from him: and he to do himselfe right, hath since published them in his owne name, but as I must acknowledge his lines not worthy the patronage, under whom he hath publisht them, so the Author I know much offended with M. *Jaggard* (that altogether unknowne to him) presumed to make so bold with his name. (Chambers, II.218)

It should be noted that Shakespeare had been, as far as we know, silent since the first publication of Jaggard's volume, and there is no corroboration of Heywood's story other than the removal of Shakepeare's name from the 1612 title page. What is more, Jaggard and his son Isaac would be part of the consortium that published the Shakespeare First Folio in 1623; so if there were a breach with Shakespeare it cannot have been especially serious or long lasting. It would be a mistake to assume that Shakespeare was inclined to side with exploited writers against opportunistic businessmen.

An important context of the first publication of *The Passionate Pilgrim* in 1599 is the fact that Shakespeare's name had recently appeared for the first time on the title page of new editions of *Richard III* and *Richard II* in 1598. The second Quarto of *Henry IV, Part I,* like *The Passionate Pilgrim* published in 1599, was advertised as having been "Newly corrected by W. Shakespeare." In addition, and perhaps of greatest significance for Jaggard's volume, a quarto text of *Love's Labour's Lost* had been published in 1598, with a title page declaring to its potential readers that it had been presented before the Queen herself and that it had been "Newly corrected and augmented by W. Shakespere."

Jaggard was one of an emerging class of powerful and entrepreneurial publishers. *The Passionate Pilgrim* as a commercial venture may have been very successful—that is certainly one possible implication of the extreme scarcity of the volume—but just as significantly, it testifies eloquently to the rapidity with which Shakespeare's name had acquired commercial value.

In Jaggard's numbered collection, at least 5 of the 20 poems are demonstrably Shakespearean. Poem 1 is a text of Sonnet 138 ("When my love swears that she is made of truth"), containing a sufficient number of readings different from the 1609 edition of the sonnets to suggest to some editors that it comes from a different source and probably represents an earlier, unrevised version. Poem 2 is a text of Sonnet 144 ("Two loves I have, of comfort and despair"); 3 of Longaville's sonnet to Maria in *Love's Labour's Lost,* 4.3.58–71 ("Did not the heavenly rhetoric of thine eye"); 5 of Berowne's "If love make me forsworn" from *Love's Labour's Lost,* (4.2.105–18); and 16 of Dumaine's song "On a day (alack the day)" from *Love's Labour's Lost* (4.3.99–118). Jaggard seems to have worked either from the 1598 printed text of the play or from a lost, but accurate, earlier edition. Poems 8 and 20 are by Richard Barnfield (whose *Poems* had been published in 1598 by Jaggard's brother); and 19 is a somewhat mangled version of the much anthologized exchange, attributed to Marlowe and "Ralegh" of "The Passionate Shepherd." (For texts of all the poems in the volume, see the Riverside, 1883–88, and Roe, 238–62.)

As already noted, the remarkable longevity of *Venus and Adonis* in the marketplace seems to have been an important commercial factor in Jaggard's decision to compile his volume. And Poems 4, 6, 9, and 11 are explicitly related to the story of Shakespeare's poem and to its mythological sources, although some commentators argue that the unknown poet or poets exhibit more influence of Ovid's *Ars Amatoria* (Roe, 241). At least four other poems—10 ("Sweet rose, fair flower, untimely pluck'd"), 12 ("Crabbed age and youth cannot live together"), 13 ("Beauty is but a vain and doubtful good"), and 14 ("Good night, good rest, ah, neither be my share")—may also refer, albeit obliquely, to the same story. Because Poem 11 also appears in Bartholomew Griffin's *Fidessa* of 1596, commentators have tended to assume that Griffin wrote it and wrote the other three "Venus and Adonis" poems. Neither assumption may be correct.

There has been much speculation since Malone's time that Shakespeare was the author of some of these unattributed pieces. Perhaps these were some of Shakespeare's "sugred Sonnets" circulated "among his priuate friends"—or at least versions of them that were in circulation; they certainly harmonize with Meres's praise of Shakespeare in *Palladis Tamia* as an Ovidian writer; and might offer insight into Jaggard's sense of the Ovidian taste of his market. As we will see later, evidence has survived that indicates Shakespeare may have revised his sonnets, possibly revisiting them after gaps of several years over a lengthy period.

The inclusion of a good text of Sonnet 144, the speaker's summing up of the erotic triangle of the sonnets, reinforces the view that the essential elements of the sequence were in place at an early stage of composition (see chapter 5). Furthermore, all the sonnets in the volume, including both the genuinely Shakespearean texts and the others, reinforce the view that the central emotional dynamic of the sonnets, with their speaker's relationships with an androgynous and narcissistic young man and a physically passionate Queen of Love, in some sense grew out of *Venus and Adonis* (see Kerrigan, 443–44).

Investigation of Jaggard's volume has yielded, and will continue to yield, further insight into such matters as the relationship of manuscript to print culture in the 1590s, the changing nature of the literary profession, and the evolving status of the author. It may also, as with *The Phoenix and Turtle,* lead to increased knowledge of the chronology and circumstances of Shakespeare's literary career and afford some glimpses of him at work revising his texts.

The Phoenix and Turtle

The Phoenix and Turtle is Shakespeare's contribution to *Loves Martyr: or, Rosalins Complaint, Allegorically shadowing the Truth of Love, in the constant Fate of the Phoenix and Turtle* (1601), a volume of poems associated with Sir John Salusbury and compiled by Robert Chester. Appended to this work are "Some new compositions, of severall modern writers whose names are subscribed to their several workes, upon the first subject: viz., the Phoenix and Turtle." These modern writers are "Ignoto" (possibly John Donne), Shakespeare, John Marston, George Chapman, and Ben Jonson. Shakespeare's poem appears without a title.

Chester's *Love's Martyr* is an allegorical poem (treating the myth of the phoenix's rebirth from its own ashes) whose occasion and meaning remain obscure. Chester was a member of the household of Sir John Salusbury of Lleweni in Denbigh, North Wales.[2] Salusbury was distantly related to Queen Elizabeth. In 1586, he married Ursula, the illegitimate daughter of the fourth earl of Derby; and in 1601, the year Chester's poem was published, he was knighted by the queen. In 1586, just three months before the wedding, Sir John's brother Thomas was executed for treason. One possible reading of Chester's poem and its publication, then, is that it was composed as private consolation at the time of the execution and the marriage in 1586, and then published—with a dazzling group of authors lending their luster to the occasion—at the time of Salusbury's knighthood and the family's rehabilitation in 1601. It is relatively easy to see why the younger poets—each of whom was in need of patronage—might have been drawn to write for Chester's volume in praise of the Salusburys and the queen.

Given the importance of the phoenix in Queen Elizabeth's cult, connections with her have been proposed: many scholars have claimed to find an allegory of her relationship with the earl of Essex, executed in 1601.[3] Most commentators support the connection between Chester's poem and the circumstances of Salusbury's wedding in 1586 and suggest that Shakespeare's piece was written at the same time as the other "modern" poems, some time before 1601.[4] Nevertheless, such a connection by no means rules out the possibility that the poem was written, or perhaps revised, in the context of the Essex rebellion and the queen's conduct during and after it. Marie Axton's subtle suggestion—that the relationship at the core of the poem involves the queen and her subjects—indicates that a profitable area of study would be the continued exploration of the connections between the poem and the cult of Elizabeth.[5]

In a radical assault upon received wisdom, E. A. J. Honigmann goes further and argues, as part of his "early-start" view of Shakespeare's writing career, that his poem is much earlier than 1601 and that it should be seen as contemporary with the Salusbury nuptials.[6] He makes this argument as part of his attempt to revive and justify the speculation that William Shakespeare was the same person as a William Shakeshafte, who was a retainer of a gentry household at Hoghton Tower in Lancashire in the 1580s—at a time when the historical record for William Shakespeare is essentially blank.

The Hoghtons of Hoghton Tower were connected with the Stanley earls of Derby. Ursula, who married Salusbury, was the sister of Ferdinando Stanley, also known as Lord Strange, who was later, and briefly, earl of Derby. Lord Strange had a company of players, including at various times Richard Burbage, Edward Alleyn, and, as Honigmann argues, William Shakespeare. Among other pieces of evidence, the presence of compliments to ancestors of the Stanley family in Shakespeare's early history plays may not be accidental.[7]

From what we know about Shakespeare's early life, Honigmann's theory must remain speculation, but he may have opened up a vein of research that will prove fruitful. Even if Shakespeare's "early start" is not accepted, Honigmann's fuller demonstration of his connection with the Stanley family plausibly connects Shakespeare to the Chester volume. It might also be noted that in 1601 Shakespeare's own relation to the patronage system was clouded in ambiguity. His patron Southampton was sentenced to death in February 1601 in the aftermath of the Essex rebellion and, although reprieved, was to remain in prison for several years. Also in 1601, Shakespeare's father died (buried on 8 September), and shortly afterwards his right to bear the coat of arms that had been granted in 1596 was challenged (albeit unsuccessfully) by the York Herald.[8]

My following remarks, pending the discovery of further evidence to support Honigmann's claim, assume a later date for *The Phoenix and Turtle*. Shakespeare's poem owes something to the Eighth Song ("In a grove most rich of shade") in Sidney's *Astrophil and Stella* and seems to be related in setting and subject to Matthew Roydon's *Elegie* on Sidney, published in *The Phoenix Nest* (1593). In themselves these possible connections do not necessarily contradict Honigmann, since Sidney had died in 1586, and Roydon's poem was clearly written quite soon afterwards.[9]

Shakespeare's poem is brief, a mere 67 short lines disposed in 17 stanzas. The formal components of the piece are immediately apparent. The first of two marked sections consists of 13 four-line stanzas rhymed *abba*. It is followed by the Threnos, consisting of 5 three-line stanzas. The first section is further divided into two parts, namely an invocation of 5 stanzas followed by the explicit announcement "Here the anthem doth commence" (21). There are some obvious symmetries about this arrangement—5 stanzas of Prologue, 8 of Anthem, 5 of Threnos. Furthermore, the numerical center of the poem is occupied by a stanza expressive of stasis, a still point in defiance of time:

> So between them love did shine,
> That the Turtle saw his right
> Flaming in the Phoenix' sight;
> Either was the other's mine.
>
> (33–36)

Such features may (or may not) indicate the presence of architectural or numerological structural principles in the poem, just as the line total may (or may not) relate to Queen Elizabeth's age (she turned 68 in September of 1601). The poem also seems to imply some form of ceremonial actuality beyond the imagined procession, with its reference to the "tragic scene" (52), to "this urn" (65), which is "Here" (55).

Shakespeare's poem connects with the end of Chester's piece—which he had evidently read attentively—where from the funeral pyre of the phoenix and turtle rises up a new phoenix in whose heart lives "a perpetual love / Sprong from the bosom of the turtle dove." In other words, before Shakespeare's poem begins, we are to imagine the funeral pyre and the placement of the ashes in the urn.

The beginning invocation, in the tradition of poems (such as Skelton's *Philip Sparrow* and the rhyme "Who Killed Cock Robin?") purporting to be funeral masses for dead birds, summons to the burial service the "bird of loudest lay," the swan, the crow, and the presiding eagle, and banishes the screech owl, as well as "Every fowl of tyrant wing." At the head of the procession is the "death-divining swan" in the office of the priest, accompanied by the proverbially long-lived crow, whose breath engenders its offspring. There is a perhaps a suggestion of comprehensiveness in this anthology of birds, with the four elements implied by the crow (the earth), the swan (water), the eagle (the air), and the phoenix (fire)

(Roe, 51). Such compendiousness is a common elegiac *topos*, which was held to be both panegyric and implicitly consolatory. The "bird of loudest lay" ought, of course, to be the phoenix, having risen again; but since we learn that the Phoenix and Turtle left "no posterity" (59), some scholars have argued that it cannot be and is in fact the nightingale, or the crane, or cockerel. Others, with equal confidence, have argued that it must be the phoenix.[10]

The congregation sings its anthem on the lovers' unity in diversity:

> So they loved as love in twain
> Had the essence but in one,
> Two distincts, division none:
> Number there in love was slain.
> (25–28)

Shakespeare uses the languages of academic logic and philosophy paradoxically in the service of metaphor and ambiguity—"How true a twain / Seemeth this concordant one!" (45–46). The implication that love can be so powerful as to overwhelm logic and reason is a Shakespearean commonplace, although hardly unique to him. For example, one of the lovers in John Donne's *Songs and Sonnets* speaks thus to his mistress of the riddle of the phoenix—"We two being one, are it" ("The Canonization").

Much of the interpretive difficulty, as well as much of the richness and strange beauty of the poem, is generated by Shakespeare's attempt to express the mysteries associated with the idea of union. As with many Renaissance writers, he approaches this challenge through the medium of paradox—whereby he conveys through words a meaning that highlights the limitations of words to convey meaning. Commenting on such lines as

> Hearts remote, yet not asunder;
> Distance, and no space was seen
> 'Twixt this Turtle and his queen:
> But in them it were a wonder.
> (29–32)

and

> Single nature's double name
> Neither two nor one was called.
>   (39–40)

Maurice Evans writes, "This love is something which at once preserves and destroys incompatibility, which simultaneously negates and maintains distinction" (Evans, 55). Many commentators have remarked upon the abstract language—love, constancy, essence, reason, property, and so on. Such terminology, as well as the use of paradox in these stanzas, has given rise to many Neoplatonic readings of the poem.

Shakespeare is vague about the identity of the speakers of the first two sections. The opening set of instructions, with its imperative tone—"Let the bird of loudest lay . . . Let the priest in surplice white"—is followed by an announcement from another unidentified speaker—"Here the anthem doth commence," after which a third speaker, with a more philosophical tone of abstraction and paradox, takes over.

The union of the Phoenix and Turtle is celebrated and defined as a moment in which Reason is "in itself confounded." Reason's response is twofold. First it proclaims, rounding off the anthem with the rhymes that had begun it,

> "How true a twain
> Seemeth this concordant one!
> Love hath reason, Reason none,
> If what parts, can so remain."
>   (45–48)

Reason is then allocated the role of "chorus" to the "tragic scene" of the dead lovers and responds with the final Threnos, in which an attempt is made to interpret the miraculous events that have gone before. The passage perhaps recalls Hymen's injunction at the end of *As You Like It* to "Feed yourself with questioning; / That reason wonder may diminish" (5.4.138–39). At this point in the poem, 52 lines have elapsed, which may be expressive of the completion of an annual cycle as a consoling metaphor for death and continuity.

The core of Reason's second speech, in a style markedly different from its exclamation in the immediate aftermath of the Anthem, is the understanding that the unique union of the Phoenix and Turtle—the

logic-defying conjunction of "two distincts," beauty and truth—has left
the world. In other words, the Phoenix and Turtle are dead and gone:

> Beauty, Truth, and Rarity,
> Grace in all simplicity,
> Here enclosed in cinders lie.
> (53-55)

The self-consuming uniqueness leading to the final, issueless incinera-
tion of the Phoenix and Turtle is summed up in the vaguely Neoplatonic
phrase "married chastity," which implies a rarefied turning away from
carnality. There is an analogous, though less renunciatory, passage in
Spenser's *Prothalamion* (1596), where the poet imagines a blessing being
pronounced over the two betrothed couples—

> And let your bed with pleasures chast abound,
> That fruitfull issue may to you afford,
> Which may your foes confound,
> And make your joyes redound. . . .
> (103–6: *Shorter Poems*, ed. Oram, 766)

—a wish that yokes married chastity and abundance. In fact the
Chesters' married chastity was closer to the Spenserian than to the
Shakespearean model celebrated in the poem. They were far from child-
less and indeed by 1601 had ten children, one of whom was 14 years
old. This fecundity was a point John Marston was quick to make in his
own poem that followed on the heels of Shakespeare's:

> O twas a moving *Epicedium*!
> Can Fire? can Time? can blackest Fate consume
> So rare creation? No, tis thwart to sense,
> Corruption quakes to touch such excellence,
> Nature exclaimes for Justice, Justice fate,
> Ought unto Nought can never remigrate.
> Then looke; for see what glorious issue (brighter
> Then clearest fire, and beyond faith farre whiter
> Than Dians tier) now springs from yonder flame?
> (Cited by Roe, 46)

Shakespeare's strange and haunting poem was published, as we have seen, in 1601. There was a reissue in 1611. And there seems little reason to doubt the accuracy of the attribution to Shakespeare, unusual though the poem is. None of the other authors whose work was included raised any objection. Since Malone, and despite a period in the nineteenth century when some doubts were raised, its place in the canon is now established. F. T. Prince (xlii) calls it "a priceless addition to Shakespeare's lyrics," and it has inspired some remarkable critical responses over the last 60 or 70 years.

There has been little agreement, however, among commentators about the tone of the conclusion:

> Truth may seem, but cannot be,
> Beauty brag, but 'tis not she,
> Truth and Beauty buried be
> To this urn let those repair
> That are either true or fair;
> For these dead birds sigh a prayer.
> (62–67)

Some critics have argued that the Phoenix and Turtle have bequeathed to mortals an image of ideal love to which they can aspire.[11] Others view the conclusion as tragic, as a recognition of the gulf separating mortal comprehension (which sees only "dead birds") from the essential nature of the creatures and their union. Still others try to hold both views: Roe, for example, claims that the poem "views its Platonism from the perspective of a tragic denouement and regards its subject as a melancholy one. And yet its tone is buoyant" (54).

The academic criticism of the poem is of recent origin, really beginning in the mid-twentieth century, when its inclusion in Helen Gardner's *The Metaphysical Poets* (1957) stimulated interest. Since then it has continued to enjoy rarefied acclaim.[12] The separate tradition of biographical/historical reading has continued and remains vigorous. But there was for many years—outside and inside the academy—a vogue for treating the poem as almost abstract "pure poetry" ("the magic of sound and cadence," in the words of Robert Ellrodt, "making comment unnecessary"). Here are some of the other comments the poem has nonetheless elicited:

[The poem] floats high above the plane of intellectual apprehension . . . There is surely no more astonishing description of the highest attainable by human love . . . an immediate intuition into the nature of things. It is inevitable that such poetry should be obscure, mystical, and strictly unintelligible . . . it necessarily hovers between the condition of being the highest poetry of all and not being poetry at all.[13]

. . . in celebration of a mystical love-union beyond sex, as we understand it, and all biological categories . . . .[14]

. . . the beauty of the poem consists in a marriage between intense emotion and almost unintelligible fantasy. It is inexhaustible because it is inexplicable; and it is inexplicable because it is deliberately unreasonable, beyond and contrary to both reason and nature. (Prince, xliv)

As an anonymous work it would command our highest admiration. The oracular, which of all styles is the most contemptible when it fails, is here completely successful; the illusion that we have been in another world and heard the voices of gods is achieved.[15]

The Phoenix and Turtle has inspired many such remarks. Taking the scholarship as a whole, it is clear that the poem has generated less unease or embarrassment than the longer narrative poems. Critics repelled by Venus or made impatient by Lucrece seem to be reduced to wordless awe by *The Phoenix and Turtle*. The comparative rarity of comment on the piece by female scholars and critics is also notable.[16]

Miscellaneous and Occasional Poems

Over the centuries attempts have regularly been made to augment the canon of Shakespeare's poems. The Wells and Taylor Oxford *Works* in particular made cases for several poems that had some traditional association with Shakespeare's name. No attribution is contemporary, although some have circumstantial and traditional claims to authenticity.

It would be surprising, however, if Shakespeare had not written occasional verses. Extempore versifying was a prized social skill, and the legends that grew up around Shakespeare's life inevitably included demonstrations of spontaneous verbal brilliance. In 1681 John Aubrey famously recorded in his notes that

. . . his father was a Butcher, & I have been told heretofore by some of his neighbours, that when he was a boy he exercised his father's Trade, but when he kill'd a Calfe, he would do it in a high style, & make a Speech. (Chambers, II.252–53)

Many of the short poems attributed to Shakespeare are consistent with the construction of an image of the vigorous, spontaneous, witty Bard. Since their appearance in editions is spasmodic, since they are brief, since some or all of them may well be authentic, and since even if they are not they testify to the way in which Shakespeare was seen by his near contemporaries, I will give texts and brief contexts in the pages that follow.

It is possible that Shakespeare's last professional work was an occasional commission. He was paid forty-four shillings in March 1613 for providing the words, while his colleague and friend Richard Burbage received the same amount for making the painted emblematic image for the impresa that Francis Manners, earl of Rutland, wore at the king's Accession Day tilt on 24 March in that year. We do not know if Shakespeare had performed such work for hire before, but he had composed an enigmatic collection of imprese (mottoes worn on shields) for the tournament scene in *Pericles* just a few years earlier.

This particular tilt seems to have featured an especially obscure and riddling set of shield devices—which perhaps explains why an ambitious nobleman would have hired Shakespeare to match his wits against other writers. In the words of a contemporary observer, the courtier and diplomat Sir Henry Wotton, writing some time later, "some were so dark [obscure], that their meaning is not yet understood, unless perchance that were their meaning, not to be understood" (Chambers, II.153). Wotton went on to judge that the best devices had been worn by the Herbert brothers—later, of course, to be the dedicatees of the Shakespeare First Folio.

In 1594 the widower Alexander Aspinall, master of the grammar school at Stratford-upon-Avon from 1582 to 1624 (too late to have taught Shakespeare, who was 18 in 1582), married the widow Anne Shaw (one of whose sons, July [or Julyus] witnessed Shakespeare's will in 1616). In the seventeenth century Sir Francis Fane of Bulbeck (1611–1680) recorded in his commonplace book a "posy" alleged to have been given by Aspinall to Shaw to accompany a present of a pair of gloves:

> The gift is small:
> The will is all:
> Asheyander Asbenall.

These lines are attributed to "Shaxpaire upon a peaire of gloves that master sent to his mistris."[17]

In a similar Stratford milieu are two epitaphs said to be written for Shakespeare's friend John Combe. The poems survive in a wide variety of versions, not always connected with Combe and only rarely, and much later , attributed to Shakespeare. Combe was a friend and business associate of Shakespeare's and one of Stratford's wealthiest men. As legend has it, he was also a miser whose coffers had been swollen by money-lending (as had, for a time, John Shakespeare's), an activity in which the officially permissible interest rate was 10 percent, or "ten in the hundred." In the version of the tale told by Nicholas Rowe in his 1709 life of Shakespeare, Combe told the poet he planned to outlive all his contemporaries and accordingly asked for his epitaph to be made while he lived and was able to enjoy verses from the Bard of Avon. "Upon which," Rowe writes, "*Shakespeare* gave him these four Verses":

> Ten in the Hundred lies here ingrav'd,
>
> 'Tis a hundred to Ten, his Soul is not sav'd:
>
> If any Man ask, Who lies in this Tomb?
>
> Oh! ho! quoth the devil, 'tis my *John-a-Combe*.

After that, Rowe reports, "the Sharpnes of the satyr is said to have stung the Man so severely, that he never forgave it" (Schoenbaum, 242).[18] A similar account of the story had appeared in John Aubrey's *Brief Lives*.

Versions of this epitaph had also appeared in William Camden's *Remaines* (1614) and in an anthology called *The More the Merrier* (1608) before its publication—described as an epitaph for Combe of Stratford, but with no mention of Shakespeare—in Richard Braithwait's *Remains after Death* (1618). Shakespeare is first associated with these verses in 1634, in a manuscript narrative of a journey through England by a Lieutenant Hammond (British Library Lansdowne MS 213 fol.332[v] cited in Chambers, II.243).

What we know of Shakespeare's generally amicable relationship with his neighbor, and indeed with Combe's large family, suggests that the legend—or at least the tone of it—may be ill-founded. In his own will the poet left his sword to Thomas Combe, John's nephew and heir. This was a gesture rich in symbolic meaning that might, for example, have indicated that responsibility for the well-being of the poet's wife was being passed on to another. John Combe was born three years before

Shakespeare, in 1561, and died two years before him, in 1614. The two men did business together for more than a decade without any recorded suggestion of difficulty between them—no small accomplishment given Combe's propensity for suing people. Combe had also been appointed to conduct important business for Shakespeare's parents. In his will, made in January 1613, he left money to endow an annual sermon, 20 pounds for the poor of the parish, and, among numerous bequests to friends and family, 5 pounds to William Shakespeare. We may imagine that Shakespeare teased his friend as a hard-hearted skinflint with verses he might have picked up in London.

In a manuscript owned by Nicholas Burgh now in the Bodleian Library in Oxford (MS Ashmole 38, p. 180), there is a second epitaph on Combe, also attributed to Shakespeare, in which the poet responds to the generous provisions Combe had made in his will for the relief of poverty in Stratford.

> How ere he liued Judge not
> John Combe shall neuer be forgott
> While poor, hath Memorye, for hee did gather
> To make the poore his Issue; hee their father
> As record of his tilth and seede
> Did Crowne him in his Latter deede.
>
> Finis W: Shak.[19]

Burgh's manuscript contains a number of anecdotes celebrating a lost golden age of literary one-upmanship and jousts of wit between the great writers of an earlier generation. On the following page (181) he records:

m^r Ben: Johnson and m^r. W^m: Shake-speare Being Merrye att a Tauern, m^r Jonson haueing begune this for his Epitaph

> Here lies Ben Johnson that was once one

he gives ytt to m^r Shakspear to make vpp who presently wrightes

> Who while hee liu'de was a sloe things
> and now being dead is Nothinge.
>
> finis.[20]

The Oxford *Works* follows a number of manuscript miscellanies in attributing to Shakespeare a poem in praise of King James printed prominently on the frontispiece of the king's *Works* (1616) beneath the image of the king himself. The scribe of Bodleian MS Ashmole 38, however, attributes it (p. 39), perhaps with more plausibility, to the printer Robert Barker, as do other scribes (for example, in Bodleian MS Rawl. D. 1372, fol. 2ᵛ). The text of the poem is:

> Crounes haue their compasse, length of dayes their date,
> Triumphes their tomes, felicitie her fate:
> Of more than earth, can earth make none partaker,
> But knowledge makes the KING most like his maker.

Three reports from the late seventeenth century—by a Mr. Dowdall (1693), by William Hall (1694), and an anonymous note in a copy of the Third Folio—ascribed to Shakespeare the authorship of the famous epitaph placed on his grave in the chancel of Holy Trinity Church in Stratford (Chambers, II.259–61):

> GOOD FREND FOR JESUS SAKE FORBEARE,
> TO DIGG THE DUST ENCLOASED HEARE:
> BLESTE BE YE MAN YT SPARES THES STONES,
> AND CURST BE HE YT MOVES MY BONES.[21]

Of particular interest to scholars investigating the early years of Shakespeare's career, and especially his connections with the family of Ferdinando Strange, earl of Derby, are two epitaphs at Tong church in Shropshire, attributed to Shakespeare in William Dugdale's *Visitation of Shropshire,* on Sir Thomas Stanley (d.1576) and on his son Sir Edward, who was two years older than Shakespeare and died in 1632. Dugdale reports the verses were "made by William Shakespeare, the late famous tragedian." If genuine, the poems reinforce the suggestion, noted earlier, that Shakespeare had been associated with Lord Strange's Men (Lord Strange was Sir Thomas's nephew, Sir Edward's cousin). Given the dates involved, Shakespeare would have had to compose the epitaphs while the subjects were still alive, but there are plenty of contemporary instances of such a practice. The text of the epitaphs (mistranscribed in the version used by Chambers), carved on the east and west sides of the monument, is as follows:

[EAST]

Ask who lies here, but do not weep;
He is not dead, he doth but sleep.
This stony register is for his bones,
His fame is more perpetual than these stones;
And his own goodness, with himself being gone,
Shall live when earthly monument is none.

[WEST]

Not monumental stone preserves our fame,
Nor sky-aspiring pyramids our name;
The memory of him for whom this stands
Shall outlive marble and defacers' hands:
When all to Time's consumption shall be given,
Stanley, for whom this stands, shall stand in heaven. (Evans, 184)

In 1613, although he was spending most of his time in Stratford, Shakespeare invested in the complex of former monastic buildings in London called the Blackfriars. His three partners in the deal were William Johnson, the landlord of the Mermaid Tavern; John Hemming, presumably his friend and colleague from the King's Men (and subsequent compiler of the First Folio); and a man called John Jackson. Jackson was related by marriage to the brewer Elias James, who lived at the foot of Puddle Dock Hill, a stone's throw from Blackfriars. A poetical manuscript miscellany compiled mainly in the 1630s (Bodleian MS Rawl. Poet. 160) contains an epitaph on James, which is attributed to Shakespeare. The text, which has been modernized, is as follows:

> When God was pleased (the world unwilling yet),
> Elias James to Nature paid his debt,
> And here reposeth. As he liv'd, he died,
> The saying in him verified,
> "Such life, such death." Then, a known truth to tell
> He liv'd a godly life, and died as well.
>
> (fol. 41)

It has been argued that James's demonstrable connection with Shakespeare's friends and business associates adds weight to the ascription.[22]

More controversial has proved the second Shakespeare attribution in Rawl. Poet. 160 of a lyric in nine short stanzas, beginning "Shall I die?" The attribution was recorded in catalogues and scholarly works, but ignored by Shakespeareans until accepted by Gary Taylor prior to the publication of the Oxford *Works*.[23] In the sometimes bitter debate that followed, a second manuscript copy, without attribution, was identified in the Osborn Collection (b 197, dated 1638–1639) at Yale.[24] The controversy played a part in the advance publicity of the Oxford *Works* and was perceived by some as an element in that edition's claim to novelty and uniqueness. In the present state of knowledge, the matter has not been resolved, with editors taking very different views of the poem. For example, Evans includes it, but Roe and the Riverside do not. Whatever the outcome, a valuable consequence has been the stimulation of debate about the canon and research into the relation of Shakespeare to the manuscript culture of his time.[25] Each of these developments has already changed the way Shakespeare is perceived and has altered the way the works are presented to readers.

For many years the defense of the Shakespearean canon has been mounted with all the vigor of a Vatican *advocatus diaboli* scrutinizing the claims of a candidate for sainthood. For a variety of cultural, economic, and historical reasons this is no longer the case. As in the 1590s, modern publishers seem to be convinced that new editions of Shakespeare need to be justified by being advertised as, in the words of Elizabethan promotional copy, "newly corrected and augmented." Scholars have gone back to manuscripts, to anonymous plays, to plays hitherto deemed "apocryphal" (such as *Edward III,* now included in the Riverside), and to works attributed to writers sharing Shakespeare's initials. The latest instance is Donald Foster's campaign for the acceptance of a funeral elegy from 1612, written by a poet named as "W.S." on the death of a man called William Peter.[26] Foster has employed a number of research techniques, but not all of them have persuaded specialists either in Shakespeare or in the study of authorship of their validity. The debate is still being vigorously pursued at the time of writing, both in the pages of *PMLA* (see vol. 112 [May 1997], 429–34) and in a volume of *Shakespeare Studies* appearing in 1997.

Presumably the inclusion of some or all of the poems discussed in this chapter in "standard" editions of the "complete" works will invest them with an aura of authenticity their present unfamiliarity denies them.

What is certain is that as the twentieth century closes, the sudden renewal of interest in Shakespeare's activities as a poet, especially as an occasional poet, has helped to construct a view of his canon, indeed of his text, as unprecedentedly fluid and shifting. No doubt some readers will be excited and others confused by these developments, but as they are further read and studied and more fully processed, we are likely to find that William Shakespeare will be understood as a writer whose range and authorial identity are more complex and various than has been supposed.

Chapter Five
The *Sonnets* and
A Lover's Complaint

Shakespeare's sonnets were published only once in his lifetime. For nearly two centuries after their first appearance, in the period between the English Civil War and the American and French Revolutions—during the time when Shakespeare's emergence as the nation's Bard was a matter of political and cultural contention—they were regarded as unstable and questionable elements in his canon. Today they are very successful best-sellers. The current high critical interest in these poems, which are often regarded as having many points of contact with contemporary culture, is also related to a reexamination of the reputation and status of Shakespeare's writings, as well as of his cultural role and value.

Contexts of the Elizabethan Sonnet

The sonnet is a form that highlights the relationship between the artist and literary tradition in an especially self-conscious and often socially aware manner. At the height of their vogue in England, collections of sonnets developed an aggregative, cumulative quality, with each new volume defining itself in relation to its predecessors and rivals. Not only in style and structure, but also in the supposed personality or circumstances of the speaker, these sequences were self-consciously differentiated from each other. Most obviously, the sequences of well-known professional writers such as Michael Drayton and Edmund Spenser took pains to characterize their speakers in ways that related closely to the other works of each author. The form's very allusiveness, its intertextuality, calls upon much older traditions; and it is important to have some sense of them.

In England the sonnet sequence was particularly fashionable for a relatively brief period; and one of the main features of the history of the form is the movement from display to introspection, from secular to spiritual. Sonnets grew out of court writings of the 1570s and 1580s, but became popular at the beginning of the 1590s, due to the extraordinary impact of Sir Philip Sidney's remarkable *Astrophil and Stella,* which was composed in the early 1580s but reached a wide public through the "pirated" edition—with a dazzling introduction by Thomas Nashe—in 1591.

By the early years of the following century, sonnets were increasingly being written on spiritual subjects; and religious and meditative sequences began to rival, then outstrip in number, their secular and amatory counterparts. The following is a selective list of English sequences before Shakespeare (not including reprints or revised editions):

> 1560   Ann Lock, *A meditation of a Penitent Sinner*
>
> 1582   Thomas Watson, *Hekatompathia or passionate centurie of love*
>
> 1584   John Soowthern, *Pandora*
>
> 1591   Philip Sidney, *Sir P.S. his Astrophil and Stella* (unauthorized edition)
>
> 1592   Henry Constable, *Diana*
>
>   Samuel Daniel, *Delia . . . with the complaint of Rosamund*
>
> 1593   Barnabe Barnes, *Parthenophil and Parthenophe*
>
>   Giles Fletcher, *Licia*
>
>   Thomas Lodge, *Phillis*
>
>   Henry Lok, *Sundry Christian Passions*
>
>   Thomas Watson, *The teares of fancie*
>
> 1594   Michael Drayton, *Ideas Mirrour*
>
>   William Percy, *Sonnets to the fairest Coelia*
>
> 1595   E.C., *Emaricdulfe*
>
>   I.C., *Alcilia*
>
>   Barnabe Barnes, *A divine centurie of spirituall sonnets*
>
>   Richard Barnfield, *Cynthia*
>
>   Edmund Spenser, *Amoretti* and *Epithalamion*
>
> 1596   Bartholomew Griffin, *Fidessa*
>
>   Richard Lynche, *Diella*
>
>   William Smith, *Chloris*

1597   Richard Parry, *Sinetes passions uppon his fortunes*
       Robert Tofte, *Laura*
1598   Philip Sidney, *Astrophel and Stella* ("authorized" edition)
       Robert Tofte, *Alba*
1602   Nicholas Breton, *The Soules Harmony*
1604   Sir William Alexander, *Aurora*
       Richard Nugent, *Cynthia*
1605   John Davies of Hereford, *Wittes Pilgrimage*
1606   Alexander Craig, *Amorose songes, sonets and elegies*
1609   William Shakespeare, *Shake-speares sonnets*

Appearing in 1609, Shakespeare's sonnets were published late in the period. And so while they were written in the shadow of Sidney and broadly at the same time as Spenser, Daniel, and Drayton, in their published form they are contemporaries of John Donne, Henry Constable, William Alabaster (whose sonnets remained in manuscript), William Drummond, and George Wither.

There are several histories of the sonnet and the sonnet sequence in English.[1] In reading them, it is important first to bear in mind the inevitable tendency in such works to construct narratives that present Shakespeare as the culmination of the form rather than a participant in its development. Second, neither the renewed study of the nature of authorship in the period nor the recent reexamination of the relationships between print and manuscript culture has yet been taken into account by a broader historical survey. Third, the emphasis in such studies on "sequences" needs to be modified, with reference both to the role individual sonnets and groups of sonnets played in early modern culture and to the contentious question of the applicability of narrative to Petrarch-derived sonnets.

In addition, this immediate Elizabethan literary context of Shakespeare's sonnets needs to be seen in relation to literary traditions that had twinned erotic and introspective writing for several centuries. After all, in the culture of the late Middle Ages, the discourse of love was wrapped up with the discourse of self-inspection and analysis.

And the discourse of introspection was specifically religious in its origin. It was after the Fourth Lateran Council of 1215 that it became the duty of each Christian to confess his or her sins and seek absolution at least once a year. In order to prepare for the sacrament, sermons, instructional manuals, and devotional practices were provided, with the intention of training penitents to prepare for confession by honestly reviewing their conduct and spiritual condition. Even a casual inspection of poems and works of fiction written in the period after this ecclesiastical innovation suggests that writers were conscious of their readers' developing interest both in their own inner lives and in those of fictional speakers.

To note only the most obvious example, in the so-called religion of love that is often identified as a part of the code of *fin'amors* or courtly love, the practices of self-examination associated with the sacrament of confession are applied to the conduct of lovers. The title of John Gower's great work *Confessio Amantis* (*The Lover's Confession*) exemplifies this connection. Lovers were expected to examine their consciences, to question and test their motives and feelings in exactly the same way as a penitent preparing to be shriven by the priest. And readers found themselves in the position of coming to some form of judgment. At the end of *Sir Gawaine and the Green Knight,* the reader is left with two contrasting readings of the events of the poem. To Arthur and the court at Camelot, Gawaine is a hero. To Gawaine, his conduct has represented a fatal slipping from the ideals he had sought to uphold. The narrator presents these two views as the poem ends, an open-ended conclusion that seems to invite the readers' opinion. Indeed, the inscription at the end of the manuscript, "HON Y SOIT QUI MAL Y PENSE" ("evil be he who thinks evil") is perhaps more than merely the motto of the Order of the Garter. It could also be seen as an instruction to those readers beginning their deliberation of the final episode. As such it is a precursor of Thomas Thorpe's offering of Shakespeare's *Sonnets* to the "well-wishing adventurer" who will read them. In the same way, the speaker of Sir Thomas Wyatt's poem "They Fle From Me" in the 1530s describes both external events and his own feelings before declaring to his reader, "I would fain know what she hath deserved."

In the English Reformation—in the same decade when Wyatt wrote these lines—the sacrament of penance was summarily abolished. Just as the imposition of regular confession had had profound implications for secular and fictional writing, so too did its removal. I have argued elsewhere that the secularization of introspection was intimately connected with the development of vernacular literature.[2] The whole elaborate psychology of sin and repentance was cast out, and the customary language of introspection was suddenly called into question. It became necessary for men and women to seek secular alternatives. In English literary texts, the sonnet, like the soliloquy, the essay, and perhaps the commonplace book, can be seen in part as evolving in response to this new need.[3]

As far as the sonnet is concerned, the evolution involved a return to the form's Italian roots. Indeed, it is difficult to think of any other literary form that is so tied to its origins, whatever experiments and innovations occurred.

Thomas Roche has written that "All studies of the sonnet sequence must begin with Petrarch, for the genre sprang fullgrown from the mind of Petrarch, prefigured by Dante in *La vita nuova*."[4] *La Vita Nuova—New Life*—is a work that was written in the vernacular, partly as a demonstration of the power and scope of vernacular writing. It contains both poems and a prose commentary on them. The prose has two major functions. The first is narrative, furnishing the reader with a chronological account of those events in the life of the protagonist that are to be supposed the inspiration of the individual poems. The second is (as Dante himself notes in chapter 14) *aprire*, to "open up" the text by giving the reader the *divisioni* of each poem.[5] A typical example is chapter 26. Dante tells us that

> I then wrote this next sonnet, which begins *Vede perfettamente onne salute,* telling how her virtuous power affected other ladies, as appears in the divisions. (58)

Then follows the text of the sonnet, followed by the division:

> This sonnet has three parts. In the first I tell in whose company this lady seemed most admirable; in the second I tell how desirable it was to be in her company; in the third I speak of those things which she miraculously brought about in others. The second part begins *quelle che vanno;* the third: *E sua bieltate.* This last part divides into three . . . the second begins *La vista sua;* the third *Ed e ne li atti.* (59)

Such division was a familiar technique of scholastic analysis and commentary, but Dante's application of it to vernacular poems dealing with love was a radical and striking innovation. The highlighted divisions may appear to do little more than signal the components of each poem—they almost never hint at any interpretative consequence. Nevertheless, they are an implicit declaration of the seriousness and scope of the work and also a guide to anyone seeking to imitate it. With its remarkable interplay of narrative and dramatic elements, its suggestion of a story behind the poems, its explicit expectation of careful and trained reading, and its stress upon technical and formal accomplishment in the vernacular, Dante's *Vita Nuova* anticipated by three centuries many of the features of the sonnet sequence of Elizabethan and Jacobean England, and in particular the works of Sidney, Spenser, and Shakespeare.

In the medieval cult of courtly love, the religion of love had its own distinct terminology derived from such texts as *Le Roman de la Rose.* When writers in other European languages operated within this tradition, the normal practice was to import the French terms of art with minimal changes, without translating them. Thus in Chaucer's poetry, for example, words such as *courtesy, grace, pity, danger, dread*, and *gentleness* tend to be deployed in the specialized sense of *amour courtois.* In contrast, the works of Petrarch could be translated, as Chaucer himself showed in *Troilus and Criseyde,* in the first appearance in English of the tormented, frustrated Petrarchan lover. Troilus sings (in a version of Petrarch's Sonnet 88) to the god of love his questions about what love means—what is the nature of this force that has such contradictory elements? His song begins:

> If no love is, O God, what fele I so?
> And if love is, what thing and which is she?
> If love be good, from whennes comes my wo?
> If it be wikke, a wonder thynketh me,
> When every torment and adversite
> That cometh of him may to me savory thinke,
> For ay thurst I, the more that ich it drinke.
>   (*TC* I. 400–407)

It is the concepts that are imported from Petrarch, not an elaborate set of technical terms. The first four lines translate the Italian original while employing a simple English vocabulary. Troilus goes on to call love oxymoronically a "quike deth" (i.e., "living death") and a "swete harm" (I.411).

The final stanza of his song translates Petrarch's vision of the lover helpless on a stormy sea, again in readily accessible vernacular terms that were to become a shorthand for suggesting the Petrarchan tradition. He ends his lament

> Thus possed to and fro,
> All sterelees withinne a boot am I
> Amidde the see, betwixen wyndes two,
> That in contrarie stonden evere mo.
> Allas, what is this wondre malladie?
> For hote of cold, for cold of hote, I dye.
>
> (I.414–20)

This passage perhaps underlies Sidney's concept of Astrophil, as well as Shakespeare's Sonnet 116 and, I would suggest, the characterization of Othello.

Leonard Forster argued many years ago that Petrarch's influence was especially powerful because he inspired vernacular poets to find words in their native languages to match the Petrarchan concepts and situations.[6] Thus vernacular poetry was stimulated through an act of translation. This view, which is perhaps something of a simplification as far as Europe as a whole is concerned, could nevertheless be readily illustrated by looking at any one of hundreds of English versions of Petrarch. To cite one of the most famous examples, in *Rime Sparse* 134 Petrarch writes:

> Pace non trove et non ò da far guerra,
> e temo et spero, et ardo et son un ghiaccio,
> et volo sopra 'l cielo et giaccio in terra,
> et nulla stringo et tutto 'l mondo abbraccio.[7]

A literal translation would be:

> *Peace I do not find, and I have no desire to make war;*
> *and I fear and I hope, and I burn and I am made of ice;*
> *and I fly above the heavens and I lie on the earth;*
> *and I grab hold of nothing and embrace the whole world.*

Sir Thomas Wyatt's renowned version retains the concept but uses a completely English vocabulary. His Sonnet XVII begins:

> I find no peace and all my war is done.
> I fear and hope, I burn and freeze like ice,

> I fly above the wind yet can I not arise.
> And naught I have and all the world I seize on.[8]

A further important step in the assimilation of Petrarchism to England came with the publication of the volume influentially titled *Songes and Sonettes* (1557), or *Tottel's Miscellany*. In this work, the poems of Wyatt, Surrey, and some of their contemporaries were transcribed from a private manuscript culture into the world of print. Three features of the transcription are of particular interest. First, providing the names of the authors of many of the poems inaugurated the voyeuristic appeal of the published sonnet. Wyatt and Surrey, who lived prominent, public lives, were publishing poems that opened a window onto the world of the court and high politics. Second, Tottel, or an editor, "regularized" the meter and some of the language of the poems, making them both more familiar and more imitable. Third, titles were provided for many of the poems (as Benson would provide titles for Shakespeare's sonnets in his edition of 1640). So, for instance, Wyatt's sonnet quoted above was given the title "Description of the contrarious passions in a lover."[9]

Tottel's volume, while opening up the possibility of specific, historical readings of the poems by naming their authors, at the same time generalized each poem, distancing the "I" of the speaker from the named author. We should note that when individual sonnets by Shakespeare entered the world of manuscript circulation they did so in this fashion, with titles that generalized their subjects—with Sonnet 2 being given the title "Spes altera," Sonnet 106 "On his Mistress' Beauty," and Sonnet 8 "In laudem musicae et opprobrium contemporii eiusdem" (Kerrigan, 449–51).

The title given to Donne's collection *Songs and Sonnets*, as well as being his homage to Tottel, invites the reader both to connect the verses with the well-known details of the life of the celebrated author and to be prepared to generalize, to refrain from identifying the speaker of the poems too directly with Donne himself.[10] It may be that an early modern reader was prepared to move easily between the specific and the general in reading sonnets, a practice that appears to have been foreign to traditions of reading in more recent centuries.

Wyatt's sonnet was important in another respect. In 1549 his *Certain Psalmes* was published. The volume was a paraphrase, with narrative links, of the seven Penitential Psalms (Ps 6, 32, 51, 102, 130, and 143) and drew heavily on the paraphrase of the psalms by Pietro Aretino. These psalms had been treated as a separate group for many years and were used in the late Middle Ages as reading to prepare a person for the sacrament of penance, since their main subject is the individual's acknowledgment of sin and request for divine forgiveness.

With the Reformation, although penance was abolished, the Penitential Psalms were still prized by reformers, who encouraged people to read them in approved translations. Wyatt used a translation from the Hebrew by Zwingli. As the Reformation proceeded, the tradition of reading and studying the psalms was maintained among Catholics and Protestants; and there are, for instance, many fine musical settings by Catholic composers of the period. Wyatt's paraphrase goes beyond a simple translation. In addition to versions of the psalms themselves, he provides a narrative prologue and narrative links between them. The psalms themselves are spoken by David. The links establish a context in the story of David's relationship with Bathsheba and his betrayal of Uriah the Hittite (2 Samuel xi–xii).

The implications of *Certain Psalmes* are profound, if little recognized. It tells, in a combination of narrative and dramatic speech, the story of an adulterous love affair from the point of view of a lover who comes to recognize the implications of what he has done, and who finally experiences a conversion and a sense of forgiveness through acknowledgment of his sin. In the context of the hostility of the English Reformation to poetry and fiction, the subject was untouchable, since it was itself biblical and because David was (like at least one Tudor monarch) a king and a poet, as well as a murderous adulterer. One of the volume's formal innovations was its expression of a degree of psychological continuity, telling the story of David's state of mind and describing the external symptoms of that state. For example, in the narrative link after David has just finished Psalm 6 with the line, "Since I, O Lord, remain in thy protection," Wyatt's commentator tells us,

> Whoso hath seen the sick in his fever,
> After truce taken with the heat or cold
> And that the fit is passed of his fervour,
> Draw fainting sighs, let him, I say, behold
> Sorrowful David after his languor,
> That with the tears that from his eyes down rolled
> Paused in his plaint and laid adown his harp,
> Faithful record of all his sorrows sharp.
>
> (Rebholz, 200)

Later, as a prelude to Psalm 130 ("Out of the depths"), the narrator describes the inner workings of his mind, until David finds "the sprite of comfort" (212) and then prepares to sing again to the Lord:

> His own merit he findeth in default.
> And whilst he pondered these things in his heart,
> His knee, his arm, his hand sustained his chin
> When he his song again did thus begin.
>
> (213)

Wyatt's version of the psalms is part of the secularization of introspection discussed elsewhere in this chapter. The psalms are no longer limited to preparation for a sacrament, but, with a suitable narrative frame and a helpful vernacular paraphrase, made available for an individual to apply to the circumstances of his or her life. They are portable, imitative, exemplary, and connected with a private self-examination. Patricia Fumerton has written of the way sonnets, as physical objects, provided some of the same cultural function as portrait miniatures—as a means of defining private, individual space.[11]

Wyatt's volume, as much as Petrarch's example, provided a valuable model for the cultivation and articulation of such introspection. His volume also constituted a model in several important respects for writers of sonnets. Not the least is that it is a sequence, a story with a clear narrative structure, whose subject is both desire and the interior life of a speaker who is viewed both as an individual and as a representative, an instructive example. The numerous phrases Sidney's Astrophil takes from the psalms indicate that David is an important and acknowledged precursor, as he may also be of Shakespeare's speaker.

One further aspect of the sonnet heritage available to Shakespeare is worth mentioning. In addition to the form's association with privacy and intimacy, it was also held to be capable of a concentration, a density, or a compendiousness of meaning quite disproportionate to its small size. "We'll build in sonnets pretty roomes," says Donne's speaker in "The Canonization" (32), as if the sonnet could be imagined as a means of creating another world, a private space, in the teeth of the world's scorn or disdain. In this regard, as Rosalie Colie pointed out many years ago, the individual sonnet could be imagined as a (potentially) remarkably comprehensive form, a kind of writing that could imply or suggest immense meaning and value. In this respect, in its hospitality to "generic inclusionism," it was analogous to the epigram. Colie argued that the Renaissance, valuing large and small forms, prizing the miniature and the allegorical tapestry, the lute-song and the polyphonic mass, *Don Quixote* and the epigram, saw the sonnet as capable of expressing aspects of, for instance, epic, romance, and other large forms in a brief compass.[12] Shakespeare's Sonnets 29 and 30, each of which seems to imply a long narrative leading up to a moment of reflection and self-discovery, possess such a sense of scale. From a different perspective, Sonnet 107, if one accepts the persuasive arguments for its being written after Queen Elizabeth's death in March 1603 (see Kerrigan, 313–19, Dubrow [1996] and G. B. Evans, 216–17), might be seen as a dense evocation both of a historical moment and of a broader historical process:

> Not mine own fears, nor the prophetic soul
> Of the wide world, dreaming on things to come,
> Can yet the lease of my true love control,
> Suppos'd as forfeit to a confin'd doom.
> The mortal moon hath her eclipse endur'd,
> And the sad augurs mock their own presage,
> Incertainties now crown themselves assur'd,
> And peace proclaims olives of endless age.
> Now with the drops of this most balmy time
> My love looks fresh, and Death to me subscribes,
> Since spite of him I'll live in this poor rhyme,
> While he insults o'er dull and speechless tribes;
> And thou in this shalt find thy monument,
> When tyrants' crests and tombs of brass are spent.

Shake-speares Sonnets (1609)

None of Shakespeare's works has been so tirelessly ransacked for biographical "clues" as the 154 sonnets, published with *A Lover's Complaint* by Thomas Thorpe in 1609. Unlike the narrative poems, they enjoyed only limited commercial success during Shakespeare's lifetime, and no further edition appeared until Benson's in 1640.[13]

The title page, like Jaggard's of *The Passionate Pilgrim,* relied upon the drawing power of the author's name and promised

SHAKE-SPEARES
SONNETS
Neuer before Imprinted

The long narrative poems, as noted in earlier chapters, had been pre-
ceded by the poet's elegant, if enigmatic, dedications to Southampton.
In this volume, Thorpe provided an almost inscrutable text, perhaps
containing a conscious echo of the earlier dedication to *Lucrece* ("I wish
long life still lengthened with all happinesse"):

TO. THE. ONLIE. BEGETTER. OF.
THESE INSVING. SONNETS.
Mr. W. H. ALL. HAPPINESSE.
AND THAT ETERNITIE.
PROMISED.
BY.
OVR. EVER-LIVING. POET.
WISHETH.
THE. WELL-WISHING.
ADVENTVRER. IN.
SETTING. FORTH.
T.T.

This page has been much discussed. Some features are readily decoded,
others not (Arden, 60–4). Thorpe, clearly the "T.T." above, was an established and reputable publisher, responsible for Jonson's *Sejanus* (1605) and
Volpone (1607). His title page introduced a collection of 154 numbered
sonnets, 2 of which (138 and 144) had in fact appeared in print before, in
The Passionate Pilgrim (1599), followed (on Sig. K1v) by "A louers com-
plaint. BY WILLIAM SHAKE-SPEARE." Full title pages survive intact
in 11 of the 13 extant copies. All indicate that the book was printed by
George Eld (who had printed *Sejanus*): 7 were "to be solde by Iohn
Wright, dwelling at Christ Church gate," the other 4 "to be solde by
William Aspley." Presumably Thorpe was spreading the investment risk.
   The identity of "T.T.," then, is an uncomplicated matter to establish.
Another part of the passage that seems reasonably straightforward is the
phrase "OVR. EVER-LIVING. POET.," which presumably refers to

Shakespeare himself. It has been suggested that the hyperbole teeters on the edge of blasphemy, since the phrase "ever-living" was conventionally applied only to God or to people who had died. Premature celebrations of immortality were a common consequence of what might be termed panegyric inflation—the prefatory poems to Webster's *Duchess of Malfi* (1613) are a revealing contemporary instance. On a more prosaic level, the term perhaps alludes to Shakespeare's reiterated treatment of poetic immortality (as in Sonnets 15, 18, 19, 55, 60, 63, 81, and 101). It could also invoke his complex, emulatory relation to Ovid. In addition, the phrase both echoes the neoblasphemy of Sidney's Astrophil, who declares to Stella, "To you, to you all song of praise is due / Only in you my song begins and endeth" (First Song), and the widespread celebration of Sidney as a modern English writer whose works had already secured the immortality of his fame.[14] Beyond that, it seems fair to surmise that "the well-wishing adventurer" is the volume's ideal purchaser—someone who not only reads it with a "well-wishing" or sympathetic disposition informing the "adventure" of reading or discovery, but also someone who is prepared to venture money in order to do so.

The passage locates this volume firmly in the commercial world of the book trade and indicates that the role of the aristocratic patron, whose function, as was seen in the case of *Venus and Adonis,* had been to "seem but pleased," has been passed on to the reading public. In the poems, of course, it was Southampton's name as much as Shakespeare's that had been advertised. In the case of the *Sonnets,* Shakespeare's name is given an exclusive prominence that testifies to the marked increase in its market value between 1593 and 1609. Where the poems had offered their paying readers a glimpse into the rarefied world of aristocratic taste, the *Sonnets* entice their readers by the promise of exclusivity. To describe the poems as *"Shakespeare's Sonnets: Never before Imprinted"* implies they have had a prior manuscript existence and that Thorpe is now pleased to offer them to a discerning readership outside that circle of the poet's closest acquaintances. In addition, given that sonnets (most obviously those of Sidney and Spenser) were often held to contain teasing glimpses of their author's private lives, Thorpe's title page seems to anticipate curiosity on the part of potential purchasers as to what persons and incidents might lie behind the surface of these hitherto private poems.

The phrase "ONLIE. BEGETTER." has led to a good deal of speculation. In particular, it has often been argued that *begetter* means the person who provided the manuscript of the poems to the publisher. Study of the contemporary use of the word suggests such a reading is unlikely, and that the term more probably refers to the inspiration of the sequence, to its imaginative source.[15] If *only* is allowed its normal Elizabethan-Jacobean sense of "unique," "single," "incomparable," then Thorpe is holding out to someone he thinks of as the "thou" of the *Sonnets*—the poet's incomparable inspiration—the crown of poetic immortality that some of the sonnets offer.

Leaving until later the general question of the significance of biographical information for the *Sonnets,* it is worth pausing for a moment to consider whether the identity of Mr. W. H. may be resolved. Many candidates have been proposed, including Queen Elizabeth herself and Oscar Wilde's ingenious fictional creation Willie Hughes.[16] Such speculations are in the minority. Shakespeare's status within Western culture is such that those searching for the identity of Mr. W. H. have rarely questioned that he was from anything other than the highest social class. Since the poems had been dedicated to a nobleman, the argument goes, it follows that the *Sonnets* were also. Once that determination is made, the quest for Mr. W. H. becomes a matter of narrowing the field.

The two names most frequently proposed are the earl of Southampton, who, as Henry Wriothesley, was born with the correct initials, though in reverse order, in 1573, and the young earl of Pembroke, who was born William Herbert in 1580. Each of these men was connected with Shakespeare. Southampton, as noted earlier, received the dedications of *Venus and Adonis* and *Lucrece* and was one of the leading allies of the earl of Essex at the time of his failed coup in 1601, after which he was sentenced to death and spent some time in prison. (Riverside reproduces a portrait of him in the Tower of London, Plate 3.) Pembroke was to be the dedicatee of the First Folio in 1623; and he was also a figure of great importance in Shakespeare's Jacobean professional life (Arden, 53–69, 459–60), since he served as Lord Chamberlain and would have been the chief official liaison between the players of the King's Men and their royal patron and the court itself. It has even been suggested that it was at his recommendation that King James took on the direct and personal patronage of the company from the Lord Chamberlain in 1603.[17]

Arguments have been mounted in favor of each of these individuals, and they have been connected with the question of the date of the composition of the poems. Assuming the addressee of the first 17 sonnets to have been a real person, for example, a date of composition in the early to mid 1590s would be more plausibly connected with Southampton than with the much younger Herbert. There is clear documentary evidence of a literary connection between Shakespeare and Southampton, and it has been proposed that his name is glanced at in a couple of places and that his political fortunes are alluded to in at least one sonnet (107). But there is no scholarly consensus about the importance of Mr. W. H. to the sequence or about the date of composition, nor about which is the more likely candidate. There are no coded allusions to coats of arms, family seats, or genealogies to point the way. An argument that works equally well against the candidacy of each of these noblemen is that, in the highly stratified and class-conscious code of address that prevailed in early modern England, it would have seemed both shocking and ill-mannered to call an earl "Mr."

Such speculations are also inevitably tied to attempts to identify a real person behind the "dark lady" sonnets.[18] The chief candidates seem to be Mary Fitton, a lady-in-waiting to the queen and the mistress of William Herbert, and the noted poet Aemilia Lanier, who was for a time the mistress of Henry Carey, first Lord Hunsdon and, as Lord Chamberlain, the patron of Shakespeare's company. From a lower social class come other candidates, such as Jacqueline Field, French-born wife of Richard Field, and Lucy Morgan, also known as Lucy Negro, who was a prominent brothel-keeper in 1594.

There is one further document that has been thought by some to be related to the circumstances surrounding the composition of the sonnets. It is in a strange volume called *Willobie his Avisa, or the True Picture of a Modest Maid, and of a Chaste and Constant Wife,* published in 1594. The book is presented as a collection of papers found by one "Hadrian Dorrell," of whom no record has so far been found and who may well be one of the numerous fictional "friends of the author" in Elizabethan literature who take the liberty of publishing the private writings of someone close to them. Usually the relationship is extremely close, as in the case of George Gascoigne's *Adventures of Master F. J.* (1573)—which is introduced to the reader by its "editor," one "H. W."—and Spenser's *The Shepheardes Calender* (1579). Gentlemen authors often felt the need to create fictional screens of this kind to hide or to excuse their descent into the vulgar milieu of print.

In the first case, "Dorrell" purports to be presenting the poems of his friend Henry Willobie, in which a chaste woman named Avisa repudiates a series of suitors. Willobie was probably Henry Willobie, born in Wiltshire, who studied first at St. John's and then at Exeter College, Oxford, between 1591 and 1595. It is possible that Willobie knew Shakespeare and that the initials "W. S." in his book refer to him. The connection, admittedly tenuous, is through a man named Thomas Russell, whom Shakespeare would appoint in 1616 to oversee the execution of his will. In 1590 Russell had married Katherine Bampfield; a month earlier Katherine's sister Elinor had married William Willobie, the brother of Henry. What is incontestable is that, as noted previously (page 49), *Willobie his Avisa* contains an unambiguous reference to Shakespeare's *Lucrece,* which constitutes the earliest published naming of him as a poet.

The entire poem has attracted a variety of ingenious allegorical interpretations over the years. In addition, the initials H. W. and W. S. have exercised an obvious attraction for those who would wish to decode the sonnets. Some have taken the H. W., even though they are the initials of Henry Willobie, to stand for Henry Wriothesley and have found in the volume echoes of the supposed "story" of the sonnets. The crucial evidence for such a reading occurs in a prose passage just before Poem 44 in the collection. Here is the modernized passage:

> H. W. being suddenly infected with the contagion of a fantastical fit, at the first sight of A[visa], pineth awhile in secret grief. At length, not able any longer to endure the burning heat of so fervent a humour, bewrayeth the secrecy of his disease unto his familiar friend W. S., who, not long before, had tried the curtesy of the like passion, and was now newly recovered of the like infection. Yet, finding his friend let blood in the same vein, he took pleasure for a time to see him bleed, and instead of stopping the issue, he enlargeth the wound, with the sharp razor of a willing conceit, persuading him that he thought it a matter very easy to be compassed, and no doubt—with pain, diligence and some cost in time—to be obtained. Thus this miserable comforter comforting his friend with an impossibility, either for that he would now secretly laugh at his friend's folly, that had given occasion not long before unto others to laugh at his own, or because he would see whether another could play his part better than himself, and in viewing far off the course of this loving comedy, he determined to see whether it would sort to a happier end for this new actor than it did for the old player. But at length this Comedy was like to have grown to a Tragedy, by the weak and feeble estate that H. W. was brought unto, by a desperate view of an impossibility of obtaining his purpose, till Time and Necessity, being his best physicians, brought him a plaster, if not to heal, yet in part to ease his malady. In all which discourse is lively represented the unruly rage of unbridled fancy, having the reins to rove at liberty, with the diverse and sundry changes of affections and temptations, which Will, set loose from Reason, can devise . . . etc. (Riverside,1960)[19]

Thorpe's Volume

Thomas Thorpe's volume is a totality, and whatever Shakespeare's involvement in its production, readers should regard it as such, since it is the only major witness we have to the text of the sonnets. It is often difficult for a modern reader to experience even a semblance of its original form. G. B. Evans's New Cambridge edition of 1996, for example, does not include *A Lover's Complaint*—because in that series the text of that work is printed elsewhere, in Roe's edition of *The Poems*. In Kerrigan's excellent New Penguin edition, which does include *A Lover's Complaint*, Thorpe's title page and dedication appear only in the notes.

In an influential and persuasive study, Katherine Duncan-Jones draws attention to the fact that the contents of Thorpe's publication matched a number of earlier works.[20] Samuel Daniel's *Delia* in 1592 had consisted of a sonnet sequence of 50 sonnets, followed by a short ode in anacreontic verse, followed by *The Complaint of Rosamund*, a long poem of female complaint using the rhyme-royal stanza, on which Shakespeare drew for *Lucrece*. After *Astrophil and Stella*, *Delia* was perhaps the most influential of the Elizabethan sequences. As Duncan-Jones points out, its tripartite structure occurs in a number of other sequences of the 1590s, such as Thomas Lodge's *Phyllis* (1593), in which the second poem is entitled *The Tragical Complaint of Elstred;* Giles Fletcher the Elder's *Licia* (1593), accompanied by *A Lover's Maze*; Richard Barnfield's *Cynthia* (1595), which includes the tale of Cassandra; Edmund Spenser's *Amoretti* and *Epithalamion* (1595); and Richard Lynch's *Diella* (1596), which includes *The amorous poem of Don Diego and Ginevra*. Such precedents argue for the connectedness of Thorpe's publication and add significant weight to the idea that the volume was shaped authorially. They also suggest that the otherwise anomalous final sonnets may be contextualized as a bridge between the sequence and *A Lover's Complaint* on the model of these earlier volumes.

Since the pioneering editorial work of Edmond Malone and George Steevens in 1780, the 154 numbered sonnets have been conventionally divided between the "young man" sonnets (1–126) and the "dark lady" sonnets (127–52), with the final pair (153–54) now often seen as an envoi or coda to the collection. It is worth recalling that Malone's division was an invention. Its effect was to imply the existence of a narrative lying behind the poems. Consciously or not, his editorial work (which will be noted later), by creating the supposition of a sequential narrative, of a story, inaugurated the quest to discover the "mystery" of the sonnets. The sonnets are then followed by *A Lover's Complaint,* a poem of some 329 lines, disposed into 47 seven-line rhyme-royal stanzas. Drawing heavily on Spenser and Daniel, it is the complaint of a woman wronged by the duplicity of a man.

Shakespeare employs the conventional English sonnet form derived from the sonnets of Henry Howard, earl of Surrey: three quatrains capped with a couplet. There is one obvious error in 146, where Thorpe opens a hypermetric second line with the repeated last three words of line one, giving the following:

> Poore soule the center of my sinfull earth,
> My sinfull earth these rebbell powres that thee array
>   (*Sonnets* [1609], Sig. I3)

Apart from this, there are perhaps just three formally irregular sonnets: 99 has 15 lines; 126, taken to be the farewell to the young man of the preceding sonnets, has 12 pentameters rhymed in couplets (with two line spaces indicated typographically by the use of open brackets); and 145 uses octosyllabics. As has been noted, 153 and 154, which feature a distinct trochaic meter, are probably to be taken as formally distinct from the preceding sequence in accordance with the practice of other writers, following the example of Daniel.

There is some evidence concerning the date of composition of the sonnets. Two of them, 138 and 144, as we have seen, were published in William Jaggard's collection *The Passionate Pilgrim* in 1599. A year earlier, Francis Meres, in his *Palladis Tamia, Wits Treasury,* referred to the circulation of "mellifluous and hony-tongued" Shakespeare's "sugred Sonnets among his private friends." Later in the same passage he lists Shakespeare as one of "the most passionate among us to bewaile and bemoane the perplexities of love" (Riverside, 1970).

Copies of a small number of the sonnets have been found in surviving manuscript collections of verse from the first half of the seventeeth century.[21] Texts of as many as 12 sonnets have so far been discovered. All of them seem to have been transcribed in the 1620s or even later—after the publication of the *Sonnets* of 1609. Most are evidently derived from printed texts and have no independent textual authority.

Most, but not all. Variant readings found in manuscript versions of 4 of the sonnets suggest that, although they were copied after 1609, they descend from a manuscript tradition distinct from the text that lies behind Thorpe's edition. These 4—Thorpe's 2, 8, 106, and 128—may then be (together with 138, 144, and perhaps some of the other *Passionate Pilgrim* sonnets) surviving instances of the "sugred sonnets."

There are no fewer than 13 surviving manuscript copies of Sonnet 2, only 2 of which derive from printed texts. According to several scholars, the remaining 11 copies descend from another version of the poem, one that has been dated to the mid-1590s and that appears to indicate an earlier stage of the poem than the one published by Thorpe.[22] In several manuscripts, this earlier version is entitled "Spes Altera," which means "another hope," and comes from Virgil's *Aeneid,* Book 12.

Spes Altera

When forty winters shall beseige thy brow,
And trench deep furrows in that lovely field,
They youth's fair liv'ry, so accounted now,
Shall be like rotten weeds of no worth held.
Then being asked where all thy beauty lies,
Where all the lustre of thy youthful days,
To say "Within these hollow sunken eyes"
Were an ill-eaten truth and worthless praise.
O how much better were thy beauty's use
If thou couldst say "This pretty child of mine
Saves my account and makes my old excuse,"
Making his beauty by succession thine.
This were to be new born when thou art old,
And see thy blood warm when thou feels't it cold.[23]

Gary Taylor argues that the vocabulary of the sonnet is characteristic of Shakespeare's work in the period around 1596, and he proposes that Thorpe's 1609 published text indicates a hardening of the speaker's attitude towards the "fair youth." Taylor further points out that this manuscript version of the sonnet is closer to an acknowledged source of this and the following sonnet, Thomas Wilson's translation in his *Arte of Rhetorique* (1553) of a letter by Erasmus advocating marriage and procreation:

Now again, what a joye shal this be unto you, when your moste faire wife, shall make you a father, in bringyng furthe a faire childe unto you,

> where you shall have a pretie litle boye, running up and doune youre
> house, suche a one as shall expresse your looke, and your wiues look . . .
> by whom you shall seme, to be newe born. (Wilson, 127–28)

The reexamination of the manuscript tradition is a relatively recent phenomenon, and further discoveries can be anticipated as it develops. It is
now possible in some modern editions (such as Wells and Taylor, and
Kerrigan) to read earlier versions alongside the 1609 text.

Even at this preliminary stage, there are some significant implications
of this research. First, while single poems could be transcribed into
manuscript miscellanies from memory or from commonplace books, it
was much more normal for foliated paper to be used, suggesting that
clusters of poems would have been circulated (perhaps on the same
theme or in obviously connected groups , such as 33 and 34, 82 and
83).[24] Second, the fact that copies of Sonnets 2, 8, 106, and 128 can be
dated to texts circulating in the mid-1590s means that poems from the
opening section, from the "fair youth" section, and from the "dark lady"
section were in existence at that time. In other words, the apparent basis
for the idea that there is a "story" behind the *Sonnets,* or at least the
dynamics of the relationships the whole collection would treat, must
have been established at a very early stage.

There have been attempts to fix the date of composition of several of
the sonnets, especially those that refer to the passage of specific periods
of time. Of these, 107 may with some confidence be dated in 1603 and
1604, at the time of the death of Queen Elizabeth, the release of
Southampton from imprisonment, and the accession of King James,
who rapidly became the patron of Shakespeare's company, which
changed its name to the King's Men. Andrew Gurr's argument that 145
is an early poem, possibly predating Shakespeare's move to London and
containing puns on the name of his wife, Anne Hathaway, seems very
plausible.[25] Most conjecture as to the dating of the "procreation" sonnets (1–17) has been closely related to attempts to identify the person to
whom they were supposedly addressed.

Apart from that, there are numerous verbal parallels between many
of the sonnets (1–103, 127–54) and plays from the period between the
re-opening of the theaters in 1594 and about 1596—the years immediately after the narrative poems—out of which the sonnets very probably
grew. There are also stylistic parallels between 104–26 and plays of the
years 1604–1608. Occasional parallels with *Hamlet* and *As You Like It*
probably point to a period of revision at or about the turn of the century,

and Sonnets 1–60 may have been revised further in the four or five years prior to publication (Arden, 12–13).[26] Additional work is needed on this issue, and also in the area of Shakespeare's reading of Sidney, Spenser, and Montaigne.

Evidence suggesting a lengthy period of composition—let alone evidence of revision or indications that the poems were not composed in a chronological sequence—is inconvenient for (and therefore usually ignored by) commentators seeking to unlock the so-called mystery of the sonnets. An early date can be used to support Southampton as the boy, Marlowe as the rival poet, and Lucy Negro as the dark lady (before she took charge of her brothel). A later date brings William Herbert and George Chapman into the frame, with Mary Fitton and Aemilia Lanier as possible dark ladies. There may, of course, have been more than one young man, rival, and dark lady. Or Shakespeare, professional actor and lifelong writer of fiction that he was, may have created a work of fiction.

The textual scholarship on the sonnets has participated in the distinctive, controversial, and, to some, heretical reconfiguration of the kind of author Shakespeare was. Increasingly he has been presented as a writer who revised his work, sometimes, as in the passage noted above and as common sense would propose, drifting progressively further from his sources.[27] The implications of these judgments for Shakespeare studies are likely to be profound and far-reaching.

Bibliographical study of Thorpe's 1609 quarto, however, indicates that Shakespeare was not closely involved in the actual physical production of the volume. London was ravaged by a severe outbreak of the plague in that year. The book seems to have been almost entirely the responsibility of two compositors in George Eld's printing house, each with distinctive punctuation and spelling preferences. Thus, to cite just a few examples, compositor A has a fondness for italic and prefers the following forms: *shalbe, ritch, dost, flowre;* whereas compositor B prefers *shall be, rich, doost, flower.* These may be the same men who worked on the quarto of Shakespeare's *Troilus and Cressida* in Eld's shop the same year.[28]

What sort of document were these men working from? It was probably not a holograph. The volume yields no instances of characteristic Shakespearean spellings or of the misreadings often found when compositors worked from his handwriting. On about 15 occasions, the compositors seem to have misread the word *thy* in their copy as *their.* This suggests that in the handwriting of the text of the sonnets from which the compositors worked, *thy* would have been written in contracted form, as y^i or perhaps y^{ie}, and that the compositors misread this for the contracted form of *their*, as in y^r or y^{er}. Not only is this pattern of mis-reading found nowhere else in the printed editions of Shakespeare, but also all available evidence suggests that Shakespeare's handwriting did not feature this contraction. One conclusion must be that the manu-script copy of the sonnets from which Thorpe worked was made by a scribe—perhaps under Shakespeare's direction, perhaps not. Another is that Shakespeare was much less closely involved in the detailed work of producing the text than he had been in *Venus and Adonis,* another work produced in a time of plague.[29]

The Sonnets: A Sequence?

No Elizabethan sonnet sequence is a novel in verse in the way George Meredith's *Modern Love* (1862) was to be. The pattern had been set by Petrarch, the title of whose sequence—*Rime Sparse* ("Scattered Rhymes")—implies an improvisatory, thoughtless, and random antho-logy rather than a highly structured work. Of course, the implication is not borne out by the careful and significant patterning and organization of the *Rime,* with the reader being faced with an apparent contradiction between an insouciant, self-deprecating title and a polished literary struc-ture. An English author in the 1590s would have had, in addition to Petrarch, the elevated example of Sidney to define, as part of the charac-teristic pose of the sonneteer, a tendency to hint at some actuality behind the fiction and invite speculation as to the events that inspired the verse. It might be suggested that the roots of the remarkable history of the interpretation of Shakespeare's sonnets stretch back to the conscious ambiguity and playfulness that almost define the genre. Nevertheless, it will be useful at this stage briefly to survey the sonnets in the order in which Thorpe printed them before considering issues of interpretation.

The conventional way of identifying the volume's components is to distinguish between the first 126 sonnets, which are generally assumed to be addressed to a young man, and the remaining sonnets, 127–54, which deal with the relations between a poet who tells us that "My name is Will" (136) and a woman whose dark hair, dark complexion, and black eyes make her the opposite of the Petrarchan ideal of female beauty. It is possible to make some further refinements on this simple division. It has already been noted, for example, that the final sonnets, 153 and 154, may well have been placed to function as a distinct formal unit, representing a bridge out of the sequence proper and into *A Lover's Complaint*.

Beyond that, the first group of sonnets represent probably the most easily identifiable and coherent section in the volume, the one on which most commentators have agreed. Traditionally, the first section was identified as Sonnets 1–17. In recent times, it has been persuasively argued that the opening sequence extends to include 18 and 19 (see Kerrigan, 196–99). Katharine Wilson draws attention to the connection between these sonnets and Erasmus's *Encomium Matrimonii,* which had been translated into English and published as an "Epistle to persuade a young gentleman to marriage" in Thomas Wilson's *The Arte of Rhetorique* in 1553 (95–140).[30] The theme of the poems is clearly procreation, and the speaker urges his youthful reader to marry and produce children as the only sure way to defeat "this bloody tyrant Time" (16) and achieve immortality. This opening movement—if that is indeed what it is—ends with a resounding flourish:

> Yet do thy worst, old Time: despite thy wrong,
> My love shall in my verse ever live young.
>
>   (19)

The difficulty involved in attempting to identify discrete structural units in the sonnets is exemplified by what follows on the heels of such apparent closure. Although the couplet might suggest the end of a section, it is immediately followed by the poet telling the young man "A woman's face with nature's own hand painted / Hast thou" (20). In other words, the placement of the poems gives the impression of a degree of narrative continuity, suggesting that the poet is moving to do what he has just undertaken.

Similar problems of definition arise in relation to the eight sonnets (78–80, 82–86) in which the poet speaks of a "rival poet" who has appeared to challenge the exclusivity of his relationship with his young patron. Elsewhere (not least in 87), the poet reveals his anxiety about his own worth and originality, characterizing his writing as "poor rude lines . . . outstripp'd by every pen" (32), as old-fashioned, "barren of new pride" (76), as invariable (108) and repetitive (105). Indeed, the idea of rivalry is introduced much earlier, where he distinguishes his own truth-inspired performance from the eloquent and learned similes of writers "stirr'd by a painted beauty" (21), a phrase that takes us back to the face painted by Nature in 20.

Likewise, what looks like another distinct group of sonnets (71–74), in which the poet relates the ideas of poetic immortality to himself and meditates on how he will be recalled after his death, has many connections with other sonnets. The most obvious of these is 32, where the young man is asked to spare a "loving thought" for the poet when he comes across old verses after the writer's death.

It is rare to find agreement among commentators and editors about the presence of other clusters of three or more sonnets, but most readers are likely to find some degree of coherence in groups such as 94–96, 106–12, 116–21, and 123–25. Close study of those poems, however, is likely to generate other webs of connection with additional sonnets or groups of sonnets.

Some pairs of sonnets are positioned in the volume in such a way as to suggest they were designed as companion pieces. Examples include 44–45, 46–47, 57–58, and 113–14. Such pairs and small groups seem to be related to the circumstances of manuscript circulation as well as, perhaps, to the way the sonnets were written. Yet throughout the book there are poems that are no less linked by theme, style, and language, but that are separated. One instance is Sonnets 36 and 39 (perhaps with their companion 62); another might be Sonnet 54, which seems very close to the "procreation" sonnets at the beginning of the volume; and a third group might be the scattered sonnets dealing with sleep (27, 43, and 61).

It would be possible to identify relations between sonnets on the basis of shared stylistic or rhetorical procedures, verbal texture, or, most obviously, theme. Thus 27–28, 43–45, and 97–99 deal with absence and separation from the beloved. A list of sonnets dealing with such major preoccupations as identity, comparison, art, or time would, of course, be much more extensive.

There are also numerous connections between individual "dark lady" sonnets and the rest of the collection. The most obvious pairing is the ostensibly anti-Petrarchan 27 and 130, but others might be adduced. The speaker sums up his predicament in 144, one of the *Passionate Pilgrim* poems:

> Two loves I have of comfort and despair,
> Which like two spirits do suggest me still:
> The better angel is a man right fair,
> The worser spirit a woman colour'd ill.

The speaker's attraction to the "worser spirit" is figured in harsh language elsewhere: referring to Cupid's "heart-inflaming brand" (154),

"Till my bad angel fire my good one out" (144), "My love is as a fever, longing still / For that which longer nurseth the disease" (147), and above all "Th' expense of spirit in a waste of shame . . . and none knows well / To shun the heaven that leads men to this hell" (129). In fact the brutal juxtaposition between lyricism and lust (129 between 128 and 130) is characteristic of this section of the collection. The consequent disjointedness expresses a form of psychological verisimilitude by the standards of Shakespeare's day, where discontinuity and repetition were held to reveal the inner state of a speaker.[31]

The identification of connections in this way still leaves questions about the sequence (if that is what it is) as a whole (if it is one.) In particular, they invite speculation as to what, if any, structural or organizational principle might be at work. In the absence of clear signals from Thorpe or Shakespeare, critics have exercised considerable ingenuity in order to identify such a principle. The most notable achievements in this field have been the learned numerological readings of Alastair Fowler and Thomas Roche.[32]

Homosexuality

Whether or not the sonnets have a narrative spine, one of the subjects they unquestionably address is homosexual love. The applicability of such material to biographical speculation about Shakespeare cannot be determined. In a famous dictum, Stephen Booth wrote that "William Shakespeare was almost certainly homosexual, bisexual, or heterosexual. The sonnets provide no evidence on the matter" (548). Furthermore, the potential anachronism of applying a modern understanding of, and attitudes toward, homosexuality to early modern culture is self-evident. We cannot know where they drew their boundaries, and the surviving evidence is frequently contradictory and confusing. Nevertheless, the issue is an important one in the collection and is perhaps best approached through some brief observations on aspects of its literary and cultural contexts.

There are several official pronouncements and legal stipulations, although what they suggest is that terms such as *sodomie* and *atheists* were broadly applied to any person outside the norms of acceptable behavior, beyond what was conceivable. Sodomy was characterized and denounced as a monstrosity of unspeakable evil and incalculable consequences, on a par with atheism and Catholicism.[33] There was a degree of biblically derived legislation expressing abhorrence and announcing savage penalties. But beyond such extremes, the culture lacked a language in which to address a homoeroticism that undoubtedly and, in some cases, defiantly existed. As John Kerrigan writes of Elizabethan England,

> Its legal codes and religious discourses could not accommodate the vice they abhorred. The age was, to that extent, neither sympathetic nor antagonistic towards inversion, but pre-homosexual. As a consequence, one finds a curious lacuna in most contemporary accounts. The popular and biblical characterisations of the condition were so extreme that few people inclined to homoeroticism felt able to imagine that their own emotions and actions were of the kind condemned. (Kerrigan, 47)[34]

But in the comparatively censorship-free zone of the ancient languages, we do know that every educated person would at least have had a small glimpse of the homoeroticism of Plato's Athens and of Virgil's shepherds, not to mention the inventively gender-inclusive coupling of the *Metamorphoses*—in other words a Mediterranean world markedly different in its sexual mores from newly Protestant England.[35] The popularity and high cultural esteem of Marlowe's verses and the occasionally honored reputation of Richard Barnfield (poems by both of whom appear with Shakespeare's in *The Passionate Pilgrim*) suggest that the populist fundamentalism underlying official prohibitions did not deter all writers, publishers, or readers.[36] The most casual acquaintance with the most laureate and commercially successful texts, such as *Arcadia, The Faerie Queene,* and Lyly's *Euphues,* not to mention the distinctly homosocial atmosphere of King James's court, will indicate the widespread presence of homoeroticism, classically inspired male friendship, and, most ubiquitous of all perhaps, the Platonic concept of androgyny.

At the core of some of the anxiety such issues aroused in a few writers was the belief—or fear—that the self was originally anatomically feminine and that the alarming possibility of a return to it could not be altogether discounted. Laura Levine argues that many antitheatrical texts "exhibit the fear that femininity is neither constructed nor a superficial condition susceptible to giving way to a 'real' masculinity, but rather the underlying or default position that masculinity is always in danger of slipping into."[37] One of the strongest and most abiding components of antitheatrical polemic was that attendance at the theater (where crossdressing was inevitably witnessed) would have the effect of making the spectators literally effeminate, of eroding their masculinity.[38] In other words, just as cross-dressing could destabilize gender and precipitate a return to the feminine, so watching such a phenomenon could trigger an identical anatomical response. In the words of Philip Stubbes in his *Anatomie of Abuses* (1583), cross-dressing produces "Hermaphroditi, that is, Monsters of both kindes, half women, half men," because "to weare the Apparel of another sex, is to . . . adulterate the veritie of his owne kinde," with the result that after the plays, "every one bringes another homeward . . . very friendly, and in their secret conclaves (covertly) they play the Sodomits, or worse. And these be the fruits of Playes and Inter-luds, for the most part" (Sig. F5v, L8v: cited in Levine, 22).

And yet the theater survived, despite the fact that this strain of antitheatrical discourse became stronger with every decade, reaching a peak with William Pyrnne in *Histrio-mastix* (1633), shortly before the theaters were eventually closed. Androgyny had been prominent in the cult of various European rulers in the 1500s, most notably François I of France. And Queen Elizabeth herself, throughout her reign and espe-cially in the 1590s, represented herself in an androgynous way, as both the father and mother of the kingdom, its bride and groom, with the body of a woman and the heart of a king.[39]

The tradition of royal panegyric is echoed in Sonnet 53. Just as Lyly builds much of *Euphues and his England* on the concept of Elizabeth's inexpressibility and Spenser's Proem to Book III of *The Faerie Queene* argues that there is no single representation that can hope to express the queen, so the speaker of 53 starts from the struggle to represent the young man, who resembles both Adonis and Helen.

> What is your substance, whereof are you made,
> That millions of strange shadows on you tend?
> Since every one hath, every one, one shade,
> And you, but one, can every shadow lend:
> Describe Adonis, and the counterfeit
> Is poorly imitated after you;
> On Helen's cheek all art of beauty set,
> And you in Grecian tires are painted new;
> Speak of the spring and foison of the year,
> The one doth shadow of your beauty show,
> The other as your bounty doth appear,
> And you in every blessed shape we know.
> In all external grace you have some part,
> But you like none, none you, for constant heart.

Here androgyny is figured as a component of the subject's copiousness or fullness of excellencies (see 99 also). And like so many of the poems praising the young man, it draws as much on the language of clientage as on that of the conventions of the Petrarchan sonnet—insofar as the discourses may be separated. The androgyny coexists with a knowing display of Platonic terminology—"substance," "shade," "shadows."

As has been noted, a humanist education could open windows onto a world very different from post-Reformation England. For instance, Plato's praise of love between men was in marked contrast to the establishment of capital punishment as the penalty for sodomy in 1533. And while in the sonnets the relationship between the speaker and the young man generally both invites and resists definition, it is clearly presented as a challenge to orthodoxy. If at times it seems to correspond to the numerous Elizabethan and Jacobean celebrations of male friendship, at others it has a raw physicality that resists such polite categorization. Thus the speaker refers to the friend as "rose," "my love," "lover," and "sweet love"; and many commentators have demonstrated the repeated use of explicitly or strongly suggestive sexual language in regard to the male friend (as in, for example, 98, 99, 106, 109, 110).

Even Sonnet 20, where sexual intimacy seems to be explicitly denied, is no less ambivalent. C. S. Lewis, in an influential comment, observed:

> The precise mode of love which the poet declares for the Man remains obscure. His language is too lover-like for that of ordinary male friendship; and though the claims of friendship are sometimes put very high in, say, *Arcadia,* I have found no real parallel to such language between friends in sixteenth-century literature. Yet, on the other hand, this does not seem to be the poetry of full-blown pederasty. Shakespeare, and indeed Shakespeare's age, did nothing by halves. If he had intended in these sonnets to be the poet of pederasty, I think he would have left us in no doubt; the lovely παιδικα, attended by a whole train of mythological perversities, would have blazed across the pages. (Lewis, 503)

Sonnet 20 undoubtedly recalls Sidney's descriptions of his prince Pyrocles (who spends most of *Arcadia* dressed as an Amazon and attracts both male and female admirers) as possessing "such a cherefull favour, as might seeme either a womans face on a boy, or an excellent boyes face on a woman" (*Arcadia* [1593], 170).[40] But the sense of the poem appears simple: it seems like a declaration that, whatever else the relationship may be, it cannot be sexual:

A woman's face with Nature's own hand painted
Hast thou, the master mistress of my passion;
A woman's gentle heart but not acquainted
With shifting change as is false women's fashion;
An eye more bright than theirs, less false in rolling,
Gilding the object whereupon it gazeth;
A man in hue all hues in his controlling,
Which steals men's eyes and women's souls amazeth.
And for a woman wert thou first created,
Till Nature as she wrought thee fell a-doting,
And by addition me of thee defeated,
By adding one thing to my purpose nothing.
But since she prick'd thee out for women's pleasure,
Mine be thy love, and thy love's use their treasure.

Yet on closer inspection such certainty must be qualified by the tendency of the vocabulary to undermine it. Whatever the logic of the argument, the speaker's mind runs to bawdy puns, not just phallic double meanings such as "prick'd" and "addition," but also "controlling," "acquainted," "nothing," and "treasure," all of which refer to the female genitalia. The final couplet seems to invoke the financial imagery that is used in many other poems—the speaker, as Kerrigan (201) notes, is asking for the capital for himself ("Mine be thy love"), leaving the interest ("thy love's use") to the women. Once the reader begins to unpick such double and multiple senses, the elusiveness of language becomes itself part of the argument, as the experience of polysemy mimics the experience of androgyny (Arden, 150–1).[41]

It is also notable that the poem employs feminine rhyme throughout, thereby inviting comparison with Sonnet 87, which (excluding lines 2 and 4) is the only other sonnet that uses the device. The poems may well be companion pieces. Certainly the beginning of 87 picks up the commercial and contractual implications of the conclusion of 20:

Farewell, thou art too dear for my possessing,
And like enough thou know'st thy estimate;
The charter of thy worth gives thee releasing;
My bonds in thee are all determinate.

Although 87 seems almost willfully to avoid the double meaning that is
generally present in the collection, it begins with the double sense of the
word "dear" and possibly another in "bonds"; and it further draws attention to itself by employing feminine rhyme, which is associated with romance (as used by John Harington in his translation of the *Orlando Furioso*
[1591], by Sidney, and by Spenser in Books IV-VI of *The Faerie Queene*),
therefore jarring with the speaker's language of contracts and commercial
transactions. Such doubleness, as with so much about the collection, suggests that Shakespeare's exploration of sexual and gender relations participates both in the conscious playfulness and transgressiveness of many writers of the 1590s and later, at the time of publication, in the homosocial
culture of King James's court (Arden, 50). In addition, the avoidance of
narrative in the volume may well be of a piece with a thoroughgoing critique of categorization and distinction on a par, perhaps, with the generic
experiments in such plays as *Henry V* and *Troilus and Cressida*.

"My Name Is Will"
Shakespeare and His Sonnets

The sonnet, as we have seen, is an aggregative, accumulative genre, a
form that encourages and is nourished by intertextuality. It is probably
fair to claim that while the most immediate model for the 1609 sonnets
is Daniel's *Delia*—a connection signaled as early as 2, where Daniel's
"the world may viewe / Best in my face, how cares hath til'd deepe sor-
rowes" (4.7–8) probably lies behind "When forty winters shall besiege
thy brow, / And dig deep trenches in thy beauty's field"—and while
there are many connections with the sonnets and complaints of Spenser,
the most important relationship between the sonnets and the works of
an English writer is with Sidney's *Astrophil and Stella*. The space available here permits only a brief account of what is a large and inade-
quately studied subject.[42]

As noted above, not only was *Astrophil and Stella* the mark against
which all other sequences would be judged, but also the 1590s saw the
construction of Sidney as the image of the ideal poet. By the end of the
decade, it was common to praise him as immortal, as "ever-living." Such
elevation brought Sidney into the same category as Ovid, whose treatment of time, change, immortality, and the ability of his art to withstand the ravages of time (Book 15 of the *Metamorphoses*) is by far the
most significant single source of the sonnets (see Bate's brilliant account
in *Shakespeare and Ovid*, 87–100).

Sidney's construction of Astrophil as a dramatic voice is followed by Shakespeare in several sonnets. In *Astrophil and Stella* (5), for example, the speaker lists a long series of "truths" according to which he should follow the dictates of reason and virtue and have nothing to do with Stella. The final line, however, dismisses the arguments with the counterargument of desire:

> It is most true, that eyes are form'd to serve
> The inward light: and that the heavenly part
> Ought to be king.

And he concludes:

> True, that true Beautie Vertue is indeed,
> Whereof this Beauty can be but a shade,
> Which elements with mortall mixture breed:
> True, that on earth we are but pilgrims made,
> And should in soule up to our countrey move:
> True, and yet true that I must Stella love.

Both the structure and, suitably modified, the argument of this poem are followed in Shakespeare's 130 ("My mistress' eyes are nothing like the sun") where a list of attributes disqualifying the woman as an object of love is dismissed in the final lines:

> And yet, by heaven, I think my love as rare
> As any she belied with false compare.

In each poem the structure seems designed dramatically to characterize the speaker and furnish him with an inner energy to dismiss the dictates of reason and demonstrate the urgency of his passion. Such demonstrations become grossly physical, as in the two references to erections in Sidney's sequence, "lo, while I do speake, it groweth noone with me" (*AS*, 76) and "I am not I, pitie the tale of me" (*AS*, 45), which are perhaps the ancestors of the phallic display in Shakespeare's 151:

> I do betray
> My nobler part to my gross body's reason;
> My soul doth tell my body that he may
> Triumph in love; flesh stays no farther reason,
> But rising at thy name doth point out thee
> As his triumphant prize.

Astrophil's Stella was a "dark lady," with both a dark complexion and dark eyes that are praised in several sonnets, once in a very early reference to chiaroscuro painting:

> When nature made her chiefe worke, Stella's eyes,
> In colour blacke, why wrapt she beames so bright?
> Would she in beamie blacke, like painter wise,
> Frame daintiest lustre, mixt of shades and light?
> > (*AS* 7; see also 9)

The Arcadian princess Philoclea shared these attributes, as did Lavinia della Rovere, praised by Torquato Tasso in a sonnet first printed in 1581. (Baldwin, *Literary Genetics*, 321–25).

Following Sidney's example, many Elizabethan sonneteers—like writers of prose fiction—conventionally teased their readers with hints of an actuality behind the poems. Sidney had given Astrophil his own coat of arms and had quibbled with the Greek etymology of his own given name, Philip, as "lover of horses" in *Astrophil and Stella* 41, 49, and 53. He had also—and here the private manuscript context of his sonnets is important—made a number of punning references to the married name of the supposed "original" for Stella, Penelope Rich: "Fame / Doth even grow Rich, naming my Stella's name" (35); "Rich fooles there be . . . only in follie rich" (24); "no misfortune, but that Rich she is" (37). Shakespeare's speaker tells his reader unambiguously "My name is Will" (136), and he plays on the multiple senses of his name in the preceding sonnet. In 145 he apparently puns on Anne Hathaway's name ("I hate, from hate away she threw"). But Will is also the heir of Astrophil. And as if in homage, Sidney's punning on "Rich" is echoed in a dozen of the sonnets: thus the young man is "most rich in youth before my sight" (15); the speaker claims "So am I as the rich" (52); and, in what may be a reference to the issue of privacy and secrecy in the sonnet form (102):

> That love is merchandiz'd whose rich esteeming
> The owner's tongue doth publish every where.

There are many other incidental parallels with Sidney's collection. Thus the three equestrian sonnets of *Astrophil and Stella* (41, 49, 53) have their counterparts in 50 and 51, as do Sidney's sonnets dealing with absence (*AS* 38 and 89) in Shakespeare's 27 and 28. And there are several of Shakespeare's poems that seem to be very closely linked to the earlier work. Sidney's 48 is in language and argument highly suggestive of Shakespeare's 139. Sidney's poem ends:

> Yet since my death-wound is already got,
> Deare Killer, spare not thy sweet cruell shot:
> A kind of grace it is to slay with speed.

And Shakespeare's:

> Let me excuse thee: ah, my love well knows
> Her pretty looks have been mine enemies,
> And therefore from my face she turns my foes,
> That they elsewhere might dart their injuries:
> Yet do not so, but since I am near slain,
> Kill me outright with looks, and rid my pain.

Stella, of course, is the Latin for "star." *Astrophil* derives from the Greek for "star-lover." The name was coined in Rabelais's *Gargantua et Pantagruel* in a vaguely comic context (Book IV, chapter 18), where Maistre Astrophile proves an inept navigator: because his eyes are fixed on the stars, he fails to see an impending tempest and the boat almost sinks. This is referred to by Sidney openly—in his *Defense of Poesie*—and obliquely where Astrophil compares himself to "him that both / Lookes to the skies, and in a ditch doth fall " (19).

Shakespeare uses this material in several places. His speaker hopes to gain favor with the "Lord of [his] love" when "whatsoever star that guides my moving / Points me on graciously with fair respect" (26). A more obvious tribute to the Sidney model (and also to Troilus's Petrarchan lament) is in Sonnet 116, where love is defined as

> an ever fixed mark
> That looks on tempests and is never shaken;
> It is the star to every wand'ring bark,
> Whose worth's unknown, although his highth be taken.

The final sonnet in Sidney's collection (*AS* 108) ends :

> So strangely (alas) thy works in me prevaile,
> That in my woes for thee thou art my joy,
> And in my joyes for thee my only annoy.

Earlier it was noted that Shakespeare echoes this rhyme in several places and seems to allude in *Venus and Adonis* and *Lucrece* to the frustrated condition in which Astrophil is left, a frustration encapsulated in the final rhyme twinning "joy" with "annoy." Perhaps Shakespeare's most radical reworking of a Sidney device is the transformation of this rhyme in Sonnet 8, "Music to hear," whose argument for union and procreation seems designed to overcome and replace the image of the forlorn and dejected Petrarchan lover. In the same sonnet, as several commentators have noted, Shakespeare also transforms a speech in favor of marriage by the wicked queen Cecropia in the *New Arcadia* (Book III, chapter 5).[43]

It was Sidney's posthumous descent into print that made his works available to other writers. His works betray no sense of a desire for survival or reputation. Quite the opposite is true:

> In truth I sweare, I wish not there should be
> Graved in mine Epitaph a Poet's name:
>   (*AS* 90)

And Shakespeare's speaker displays an awareness of the potential shame of discovery and disclosure as private writings become public property. Whether or not the volume was authorized, its speaker manifests a marked anxiety about publication, whereby he has made himself "a motley to the view" (110). As he puts it, employing a conspicuously artisan metaphor,

> my name receives a brand,
> And almost thence my nature is subdu'd
> To what it works in, like the dyer's hand.
>
> (111)

But while Shakespeare's speaker may share some attributes with Astrophil, we are never allowed to forget the great social gulf that separates them. Sidney's Astrophil had inhabited a world of court intrigue, chivalry, and international politics, exemplifying the overlap between political and erotic discourse in Elizabethan England. In that milieu, as Arthur Marotti (1982) has shown, a courtier/politician could address the circumstances and frustrations of his public life by writing sonnets about an unattainable and hard-hearted mistress, at whose whim he would live or die. Some professional writers, most notably Spenser, were sufficiently involved with political circles and the mental world of the court that they participated in the same oblique discourses (see Bates, 138–51).

The circumstances of Shakespeare's speaker, in contrast, are not those of a courtier, or of a laureate (like Spenser), or of a professional writing for a patron (like Drayton), but rather those of a male of the upwardly mobile "middling sort."

Especially in the "young man" sonnets, there is a marked class anxiety, as the speaker seeks to define his a role, whether as a friend, tutor, counselor, employee, or sexual rival. Not only are comparisons drawn from the world of the professional theater ("As an unperfect actor on the stage" [23]), but also, almost ubiquitously, from the world of commerce and business. Compared to the prodigal "unthrifty loveliness" (4) of the youth "Making a famine where abundance lies" (1), the speaker inhabits a bourgeois world of debts, loans, mortgages, bonds, contracts, accounts, surpluses, audits, interest, credit, repayment, and usury. To the "dark lady," who is no distant Stella ("My mistress when she walks treads on the ground" [130]), he speaks a similar, though more suggestive, language: "I myself am mortgaged to thy will" (134). In this mental world, marriage is figured as an investment whose dividend is offspring:

> That use is not forbidden usury
> Which happies those that pay the willing loan;
> That's for thyself to breed another thee,
> Or ten times happier be it ten for one.
>
> (6)

Shakespeare would have grown up surrounded by such terms. The many and varied business enterprises of his father included some "forbidden usury," charging interest at a rate higher than 10 percent. He is known to have charged (like many of today's respectable banks) 18 to 20 percent, rates that in those days left him liable to prosecution. Indeed, his fall from town office in Stratford during Shakespeare's teens was probably precipitated by a regional recession that put his debtors out of business (Kay 1995, 3–10). In the sonnet that seems designed to sum up, perhaps say farewell to, the relationship with the young man, the speaker records how he has observed foolish investors growing old and poor by pinning hopes on noble favor (125):

> Have I not seen dwellers on form and favor
> Lose all, and more, by paying too much rent,
> For compound sweet forgoing simple savor,
> Pitiful thrivers, in their gazing spent?

The sonnets' acute awareness of social class does not definitely establish that the speaker is addressing a nobleman, but it does indicate that the relationship is conceived of as crossing a social divide every bit as apparent and potentially scandalous as the sexual divide the poems scout.

There is, however, a context for such a relationship in the discourse of patron-client relationships in the period. At the highest level of the Elizabethan court, courtier-politicians addressed the queen—the fount of all authority and potential patronage—in terms that were often erotically charged. Sir Christopher Hatton, absent from the queen for just two days on account of ill health, wrote to her:

> No death, no, not hell, shall ever win of me my consent so far to wrong myself again as to be absent from you one day . . . I lack that I live by . . . The more I find this lack, the further I go from you . . . My wits are overwrought with thoughts. I find myself amazed. Bear with me, most dear sweet lady. Passion overcometh me. I can write no more. Love me, for I love you . . . Live for ever.

And he signed the letter, as he frequently did, by alluding to her title, E. R. (Elizabetha Regina): "All and EveR yours, your most happy bondman."[44]

Patron-client communications between men were sometimes couched in very similar language. While bureaucratic and legal practices were in some ways formalizing relationships between allies, friends, or business partners, the documentary ties were generally held to be the tip of an iceberg of reciprocal intimacy and trust, which could be overridden by emotional need, obligation, or some other more urgent consideration. Private correspondence and expressions of obligation in the entourages of both Elizabeth and James typically employed an intense and personal style. In a recent study, Lisa Jardine cites an exchange of letters between the lawyer Anthony Bacon and his patron the earl of Essex. Bacon writes:

> My singular good Lord, If God had not sent me the other day so special a defensive of the honour and comfort of your Lordship's presence to fortify my spirits beforehand, they could never have resisted such cruel enemies as have since assailed me without giving any respite or breathing till this morning.

And Essex replies:

> Farewell, worthy Master Bacon, and know that, though I entertain you here with short letters, yet will I send you from sea papers that shall remain as tables of my honest designs and pledges of my love to you from your true and best wishing friend Essex.

In Jardine's analysis, which could also apply to Hatton's letter, "the terms of passionate commitment are virtually indistinguishable from those in a contemporary love sonnet (116-18).[45] And the terms of the letters invite comparison with a sonnet such as 18 ("Shall I compare thee to a summer's day?") where the discourses of love and clientage are inseparable. John Barrell argues that this rhetoric of intense patron-client intimacy is to be found in Sonnet 29, where the speaker is represented as a client (like those waiting fruitlessly in 125) acutely aware of the intense competition for the favor of patrons, grounding his hope in an intimacy that overrides other criteria in selecting recipients of that favor:

> When in disgrace with Fortune and men's eyes
> I all alone beweep my outcast state,
> And trouble deaf heaven with my bootless cries,
> And look upon myself and curse my fate,
> Wishing me like to one more rich in hope,
> Featur'd like him, like him with friends possess'd,
> Desiring this man's art, and that man's scope,

> With what I most enjoy contented least;
> Yet in these thoughts myself almost despising,
> Haply I think on thee, and then my state
> (Like to the lark at break of day arising
> From sullen earth) sings hymns at heaven's gate.
> For thy sweet love rememb'red such wealth brings,
> That then I scorn to change my state with kings.

Emerging from the patron-client discourse in the sonnets is the speaker's concern that he is at a disadvantage for several reasons, some personal and others related to his class and regional origins. The speaker's self-deprecation about his personal qualities, wrapped up in the (probably figurative) term "lameness" in Sonnet 89, may be a version of the aristocratic ease *(sprezzatura)* that was so highly prized in courtly literature.[46] His pose of age, "beated and chopp'd with tann'd antiquity" (62)—

> That time of year thou mayst in me behold
> When yellow leaves, or none, or few, do hang
> Upon those boughs which shake against the cold.
>
> (73)

—may be similarly conventional (especially if it was written by a man in his thirties) and consistent with the tutor-pupil rhetoric of some of Sonnets 1–17. But it may also be possible to detect in the speaker (most obviously, though not only in the "rival poet" sonnets) a consciousness that his middle-class provincial background makes him seem backward and unfashionable in London.[47]

As most commentators have recognized, the sonnet is traditionally a genre of praise, although it can also be used for lament or complaint. As a form of praise, it may fruitfully be related to panegyric or epideictic oratory and traced to the supposedly most ancient roots of poetry (Kerrigan, 18–33). Shakespeare's sonnets are also consistent with patron-client relations in their concentration on praise and on the issues raised by the act of praising. One of the most basic concerns, of course, is how to preserve the value of the currency of praise at a time of panegyric inflation. How, in such circumstances, is individual praise to be believed, and how is it to be effective as praise where exaggeration and hyperbole have become the norm? Many sonnet collections share such a concern, and again the most apparent model is Sidney. Astrophil tells Stella:

> Honour is honourd, that thou doest possesse
> Him as thy slave, and now long needy fame
> Doth even grow rich, naming my *Stella's* name.
> Wit learnes in thee perfection to express,
> Not thou by praise, but praise by thee is raisde:
> It is a praise to praise, when thou art praisde.
>
> (*AS* 35)

But praise and especially the analysis of praise and the relationships that underlie it lead to self-examination and self-definition. In Joel Fineman's influential study, Shakespeare creates a radical internalization of Petrarchism by reordering its dynamic, by directing his—and his readers'— attention to the speaker's subjectivity rather than to the ostensible object of the speaker's devotion: poetry of praise becomes poetry of self-discovery.[48]

Shakespeare's speaker worries about an inability to praise adequately—an inability that harms the subject of his praise but also reveals his own inadequacies, both as a poet and as a human being. Sonnet 1 announces, "From fairest creatures we desire increase," in which Shakespeare uses "increase" in the sense of harvest, new growth, interest, and reproduction. But there is also a conventional panegyric argument at work here, because there is also a sense in which the "fairest creatures" are praised as the source, if not of meaning, then of comparison; and the "increase" they can give a poet is a store of matter, a bounteous *copia* for the journeyman poet to work on.[49] This idea lies behind the poet's advice that other poets seeking to praise the young man should "copy what in you is writ" (84), as well as his own declaration that "I only write of you, / And you and love are still my argument" (76).

But throughout the collection the speaker expresses anxiety at his own lack of eloquence, as in 23 or 80, where he refers to himself as "tongue-tied" (a phrase also used in 85). He complains that he is unable to produce variety and originality:

> Why write I still all one, ever the same,
> And keep invention in a noted weed,

> That every word doth almost tell my name,
> Showing their birth, and where they did proceed?
>
> (76)

One of the arguments to persuade the young man to marry is the poet's inadequacy in duplicating him; reproduction might succeed, he argues, where the poet's metaphors and comparisons have failed (13). The speaker's concerns are focused by the dominant theme of the sonnets: the power of time, usually figured as a destroyer, as the force opposed to life and to the works of human hands.

Sidney's Astrophil, figured as young and willfully reckless, has almost nothing to say about time and memory. In contrast, Spenser's *Amoretti* and *Epithalamion* are carefully structured to immortalize his courtship in the spring of 1594 and his wedding day on June 9 of that year. The treatment of time in Shakespeare's sonnets, however, is much more difficult to characterize, since it includes, for example, the idea that art or love might triumph over time, as well as the opposite position (see, for instance, 15–19, 54, 55, 60).

The subject has attracted a great deal of commentary over the years in a way that probably reflects the variety, complexity, and ambiguity in Shakespeare's text. A reader seeking a context and some broader sense of the conflicting, shifting attitudes that are expressed throughout Shakespeare's volume might profitably consider some of the challenging and ambiguous models that were available to him: examples include Spenser's *Complaints,* Book III of *The Faerie Queene,* and Book XV of Ovid's *Metamorphoses*. In this last text, time is figured as destructive, while the possibility of defeating its power is celebrated by the poet at the conclusion of the work, for which he claims immortality.

There is space here to look only at one brief example of the sonnets' relationships with such texts. In his translation of Book XV of the *Metamorphoses,* Arthur Golding wrote:

> And sith on open sea the wynds do blow my sayles apace,
> In all the world there is not that that standeth at a stay.
> Things eb and flow, and every shape is made too passe away.
> The tyme itself continually is fleeting like a brooke.
> For neyther brooke nor lyghtsomme tyme can tarrye still. But looke
> As every wave dryves other foorth, and that that commes behynd

Both thrusteth and is thrust itself: Even so the tymes by kynd
Doo fly and follow bothe at once, and evermore renew.
For that that was before is left, and streyght there dooth ensew
Anoother that was never erst.

(text from Booth, 552)

Shakespeare's Sonnet 60 follows the words of Golding's translation very closely:

> Like as the waves make towards the pibbled shore,
> So do our minutes hasten to their end,
> Each changing place with that which goes before,
> In sequent toil all forwards do contend.
> Nativity, once in the main of light,
> Crawls to maturity, wherewith being crown'd,
> Crooked eclipses 'gainst his glory fight,
> And Time that gave doth now his gift confound.
> Time doth transfix the flourish set on youth,
> And delves the parallels in beauty's brow,
> Feeds on the rarities of nature's truth,
> And nothing stands but for his scythe to mow:
> And yet to times in hope my verse shall stand,
> Praising thy worth, despite his cruel hand.

It is also instructive to compare this with Spenser's *Amoretti* 75:

> One day I wrote her name upon the strand,
> but came the waves and washed it away:
> agayne I wrote it with a second hand,
> but came the tyde, and made my paynes his pray.
> Vayne man, said she, that doest in vain assay,
> a mortall thing so to immortalize,
> for I my selve shall lyke to this decay,
> and eek my name be wyped out lykewize.
> Not so (quod I) let baser things devize

> to dy in dust, but you shall live by fame:
> my verse your vertues rare shall eternize,
> and in the hevens wryte your glorious name.
> Where whenas death shall all the world subdew,
> our love shall live, and later life renew.[50]

Whereas Spenser promises to inscribe Elizabeth Boyle's name in the heavens, Shakespeare's speaker has the more modest ambition that his own verses might withstand the ravages of time in order to praise the "worth" of his subject. But there are subtler effects at work, too. Perhaps the most striking is that the narrative of human life (the passage beginning, "Nativity, once in the main of light") is an explicit poetic equivalent of the offspring the young man has been urged to produce. In these lines, generated by the poet, is the image of a child, a reproduction of the young man who "crawls to maturity." Second, the opening passage, which closely follows Ovid, might be seen in a somewhat similar light. Finally, by closely imitating Ovid, even though in an unborn state and in an accent yet unknown to the Roman poet, Shakespeare is lending his support to Ovid's claim to poetic immortality expressed in the closing lines of the *Metamorphoses* (reworked in Sonnet 55).

Additional poetic and verbal devices representing resistance to devouring time, censorship, and repression, are ambiguity and polysemy. The complex relationships of the sonnets to the world in which Shakespeare lived is expressed in the ambiguities and puns that are everywhere in the poems.[51] They implicitly, perhaps rebelliously, and in a typically 1590s fashion embody fecundity, vitality, eroticism, and newness—forces that forms, structures, rhyme schemes, narrative, and relationships cannot contain. If we can occasionally view the volume as a reader in Shakespeare's day might have seen it, it will appear that, rather than telling a story in a way that a post-Enlightenment reader might recognize it, the volume moves between a variety of shifting planes, oscillating between certainties and ambiguities, between narrative and drama, between connection and discontinuity.

This section ends with two contrasting sonnets, each representing a distinct kind of utterance in the sequence. The first is perhaps one of the most direct statements in the collection and, as we have seen, was in circulation at an early date. Just as 26 epitomizes the patron-client subject, 144 encapsulates the dynamics of the supposed "love triangle":

Two loves I have of comfort and despair,
Which like two spirits do suggest me still:
The better angel is a man right fair,
The worser spirit a woman color'd ill.
To win me soon to hell, my female evil
Tempteth my better angel from my side,
And would corrupt my saint to be a devil,
Wooing his purity with her foul pride.
And whether that my angel be turn'd fiend
Suspect I may, yet not directly tell,
But being both from me, both to each friend,
I guess one angel in another's hell.
Yet this shall I ne'er know, but live in doubt,
Till my bad angel fire my good one out.

Living "in doubt" is a phrase that might be applied to the speaker's existence represented in many of the sonnets. It is a state that is transferred to the reader in 94, a sonnet whose interlocking ironies, ambiguities, and subtleties continue to challenge commentators and readers alike.

They that have pow'r to hurt, and will do none,
That do not do the thing they most do show,
Who moving others, are themselves as stone,
Unmoved, cold, and to temptation slow,
They rightly do inherit heaven's graces,
And husband nature's riches from expense;
They are the lords and owners of their faces,
Others but stewards of their excellence.
The summer's flow'r is to the summer sweet,
Though to itself it only live and die,
But if that flow'r with base infection meet,
The basest weed outbraves his dignity:
For sweetest things turn sourest by their deeds;
Lilies that fester smell far worse than weeds.[52]

Liberated from the ephemerality of theater performance and from the *I,
me, you, thou, thee* anchors to the sonnet relationship, the poem's words
work on the memory, resonate in the mind. Shakespeare's celebrated
verbal playfulness, the polysemy of his language, here seems to anticipate, indeed to rely upon, publication, whether by circulation or printing. His words acquire currency beyond himself and become the subject
of reading and interpretation. But at the same time and with characteristic doubleness, the linguistic richness also can be seen as an act of social
aspiration, as the appropriation of the ambiguity axiomatically inherent
in courtly speech.

The Sonnets and Their Afterlife

Many of the interpretative and scholarly issues raised by the sonnets are
interconnected in ways that have few parallels in Shakespeare's other
works. The history of the text of the sonnets, for example, is inseparable
both from the history of Shakespeare's reputation and from the tradition
of interpretation.

The sonnets, it is significant to recall, enjoyed nothing of the commercial success of the poems. The most obvious index of this is the fact
that they were not reprinted in Shakespeare's day, appearing only in a
much altered form in Benson's edition of the poems in 1640. Thereafter,
in versions based on Benson's presentation, they appeared in extracts
and anthologies. In the early eighteenth century, neither Pope nor Rowe
included the sonnets in their editions of Shakespeare, relegating them in
each case to a supplementary volume. Malone's 1780 volume was the
first serious critical edition of the sonnets, in which he returned (though
again in a supplement to the main edition) to Thorpe's volume. It is
possible (G. B. Evans, 284) that Malone made use of an unpublished
scholarly edition of the sonnets made by Edward Capell some years earlier. In 1790 Malone included the sonnets in his edition proper, thereby
signaling their inclusion in Shakespeare's canon.[53]

Since then, they have grown to be perhaps his most reprinted work.
As Anthony Hecht observes in his Introduction to the New Cambridge
edition:

> It may be that the single most important fact about Shakespeare's Son-
> nets—at least statistically—is that they regularly outsell everything else
> he wrote. The plays are taught in schools and universities, and a large
> annual sale is thereby guaranteed for *Hamlet, Macbeth, Romeo and Juliet,*

and *A Midsummer* Night's *Dream*. But the Sonnets are still more widely read. (G. B. Evans, 1)

This journey from marginality to ubiquity began with Malone's inclusion of the sonnets in the canon. Such newfound recognition was not achieved without opposition. Rollins cites a reviewer of the 1780s from *The Gentleman's Magazine* who was praising the sonnets of Charlotte Smith. Smith, he wrote, "has undoubtedly conferred honour on a species of poetry which most of her predecessors in this country have disgraced" (Rollins, II.339). More pointedly, George Steevens explained in 1793 why he had continued to exclude Shakespeare's poems and sonnets from reprints of his 1773 edition:

> because the strongest act of Parliament that could be framed would fail to compel readers into their service . . . .Had Shakespeare produced no other works than these his name would have reached us with as little celebrity as time has conferred on that of Thomas Watson, an older and much more elegant sonneteer. (Rollins, II.337)

Given the taste of the times, however, the acceptance of the sonnets was given added impetus, as already suggested, by Malone's analysis of the structure and organization of Thorpe's volume, in particular by his identifying the "I" of the sonnets with Shakespeare and by establishing a distinction between the "young man" sonnets and the "dark lady" sonnets. This distinction, which is usually regarded as a fact rather than an observation, had the effect of opening the way for readings of the *Sonnets* as narrative, as a volume that tells a story. But what kind of story? As Margreta de Grazia has pointed out, "Although the identification of 'Shake-speare' with the 'I' in the Sonnets may seem unexceptional now, it would have been virtually impossible to make in the edition which circulated before Malone" (163). And it is significant that Malone was editing Shakespeare at a time when it was highly—and newly—fashionable to approach works of literature through the study of their authors' lives. It was, after all, the age of Johnson's *Lives of the Poets* (1779–1781) and of Boswell's *Life of Johnson* (1791).[54] The story the sonnets were to tell, then, was the story of Shakespeare's life.

By the end of the eighteenth century, the sonnet—a form that had been neglected for about a century—was itself enjoying a new period of esteem and popularity. The great models for such writers as Gray and Cowper were Spenser and, more crucially, Milton. In Milton's sonnets, even more than in the *Amoretti,* there is frequently a clear autobiographical component, as in, for example, "On His Blindness" ("When I consider how my life is spent"), which echoes Shakespeare's 15 ("When I consider every thing that grows").[55]

As far as writers were concerned, the advent of the Romantic movement led to changes in the way the sonnet as a form was viewed. Whereas to the previous generation it had been a form associated with meditation and reflection, it increasingly came to be conceived of as a window on its author's soul.

As the eighteenth century came to its end, scholars and critics began to look at Shakespeare's sonnets in the same light. In 1797 A. W. von Schlegel declared that "these sonnets paint most unequivocally the actual situation and sentiments of the poet," Wordsworth declared that in these poems "Shakespeare expresses his own feelings in his own person," and George Chalmers claimed to have identified the addressee of the volume.[56]

There have been several studies and surveys of nineteenth-century attitudes to the sonnet, a subject too large to be treated here.[57] Celebrated comments from two major writers, however, encapsulate two very distinct views of the relationship between the sonnets and Shakespeare's life. Wordsworth wrote in "Scorn Not the Sonnet," published in 1827:

> Scorn not the Sonnet; Critic, you have frowned,
> Mindless of its just honours;—with this Key
> Shakespeare unlocked his heart; the melody
> Of this small Lute gave ease to Petrarch's wound;
> A thousand times this Pipe did Tasso sound;
> Camöens soothed it with an Exile's grief;
> The sonnet glittered a gay myrtle Leaf
> Amid the cypress with which Dante crowned
> His visionary brow: a glow-worn Lamp,
> It cheered mild Spenser, called from faery-land
> To struggle through dark ways; and when a damp
> Fell round the path of Milton, in his hand
> The Thing became a trumpet, whence he blew
> Soul-animating strains—alas, too few![58]

The context of the complete poem, so rarely supplied in reference to this remark, makes Wordsworth's position harder to caricature. Clearly he is taking issue with those who, like Steevens, would relegate the sonnet to some lower category of writing and is listing writers who had found a variety of creative and emotional solaces in it. The reference to Shakespeare implies less that the sonnet is confessional, more that the form was one that gave him a special kind of expressive freedom.

Nevertheless, literary history has declared that Wordsworth's sense was the former, an argument with which Robert Browning disagreed. Almost 50 years after the publication of Wordsworth's poem, Browning referred to it in attacking the notion that literature should be decoded to yield the writer's true thoughts, feelings, and nature. In "At the Mermaid," Shakespeare is imagined in the Mermaid Tavern, confronting those who believe they can know him through what he has written. He asks the assembled company,

> Which of you did I enable
> Once to slip inside my breast,
> There to catalogue and label
> What I like least, what I love best,
> Hope and fear, believe and doubt of,
> Seek and shun, respect—deride?
> Who has right to make a rout of
> Rarities he found inside?

Then, in "House," Browning specifically responds to Wordsworth's comments:

> Outside should suffice for evidence:
> And whoso desires to penetrate
> Deeper, must dive by the spirit-sense—
> No optics like yours, at any rate!
> "Hoity toity! A street to explore,
> Your house is no exception! '*With this same key*
> *Shakespeare unlocked his heart,*' once more!"
> Did Shakespeare? If so, the less Shakespeare he![59]

The vehemence of Browning's response testifies to the spread of bio-graphical readings by the 1870s and to the power that biographical criticism had acquired during the century. Even from such a truncated survey as this one, it should be clear that the fashion for biographical speculations about the sonnets may be traced ultimately to Malone's editorial decision to include and present them in such a way as to facili-tate the very interrogation of the text that Browning would deny.

With such thoughts in mind, it may be helpful to recall what Malone was superseding. John Benson has until fairly recently been accorded lit-tle respect by scholars, although he is now acknowledged to have been a reputable and law-abiding publisher. Malone called Benson's edition "illegal" (Rollins, II.22). In fact, Benson's *Poems: Written by Wil. Shake-speare. Gent.* (1640) was part of an attempt to "canonize" Shakespeare, a collection of verses into a handsome quarto that could be sold as a com-panion to the dramatic folio texts ("to be serviceable for the continuance of glory to the deserved Author in these his Poems").

In recent years there has been increasing study of Benson's edition as a distinct literary production in its own right. Benson dropped eight sonnets, provided titles for individual pieces, changed Thorpe's order, conflated sonnets, and incorporated into his volume the whole of the expanded 1612 edition of *The Passionate Pilgrim, The Phoenix and Turtle,* and a collection of poems "by other gentlemen." The sonnets were repackaged into 72 distinct poems (some containing as many as five of the sonnets collected into "stanzas"), each with a title (such as "Immod-erate Passion" or "His praise wounded by her eye") .

Benson's much discussed modification of the text of the sonnets indi-cates at least a certain level of anxiety about who seemed to be doing what to whom and why. Benson retained 20, but dropped 126 ("O thou my lovely boy"), and changed the direct address of 108 ("Nothing, sweet boy") to the neutral "Nothing, sweet love." He grouped together 113, 114, and 115 under the title "Self-flattery of her Beauty," and 122 was headed "Upon the receit of a Table Booke from his Mistriss" (de Grazia, 164). Consequently the orientation of the volume seems to be much more unambiguously heterosexual. But many modern accounts overstate the degree of the gender modification. It has recently been argued that Benson seems to have been much more concerned about modifying the "dark lady" sonnets, because of their threatening implica-tions for family structure and the social order.[60] His grouping of sonnets into longer units perhaps further suggests that the form had come to appear unfamiliar, possibly somewhat primitive, to midcentury eyes.

His attitude to authorship, on the other hand, may have had much in common with the manuscript culture that was close to its end by 1640, but from which the sonnets had come (*Shakespeare Verbatim,* 169).

Benson's attempt, just before England was convulsed by civil war, to make fashionable verses of the 1590s palatable to the taste of 1640 achieved little success. The vogue for sonnets was long over. But his volume repays study today, partly because it enables us to see behind the monumentally institutionalized, post-Malone Shakespeare industry in ways that may help to uncover some of the more striking and challenging qualities of the sonnets. One of the most significant trends in modern criticism of the sonnets has been to consider them—whether or not they were authorized—not as narrative but as meditations, some linked, some not, some exploring a speaker's psyche, some not; another trend has been to resist Malone's assumption that the collection has two distinct sections.[61]

We have already seen how the sonnets became "literature" in time for the heyday of the Romantic poets and in the midst of the new vogue for literary biography. Thereafter, they were assumed to be highly personal writings. The Romantic compulsion to read the sonnets as autobiography inspired attempts to rearrange them to tell their "story" more clearly (Ingram and Redpath, xxiv–xxxiii). It also led to attempts to relate them to what was known or could be surmised about Shakespeare's life. Some commentators speculated that the publication of the sonnets was the result of a conspiracy by Shakespeare's jealous rivals or enemies, seeking to embarrass him by publishing love poems apparently addressed to a man rather than to the conventional sonnet-mistress. The five appendices to H. E. Rollins's New Variorum edition document the first century of such endeavors, and Samuel Schoenbaum's *Shakespeare's Lives* subjects them to vigorous, often scathing scrutiny. Attention was directed towards "problems," such as the identity of "Mr. W. H.," the "young man," the "rival poet" and the "dark lady" (not, incidentally, a phrase Shakespeare ever uses in the sonnets).

There has been a great deal of criticism of the sonnets in the generations after Rollins. The major editions, by Booth, Kerrigan, G. B. Evans, and the Arden, are of necessity deeply grounded in the traditions of commentary, and their accounts are generally helpful guides to what has been written. Of anthologies of criticism, the three most valuable to students are probably those by Edward Hubler (1962), Hilton Landry (1976), and Peter Jones (1977).[62] More recent studies are well summarized by Heather Dubrow (Riverside, 48–50).

As is to be expected in the case of a text that is widely read, there is a steady market for good editions—whether for reading or study—and

single-volume commentaries. Arden, and the editions by Kerrigan and
G. B. Evans, are especially to be recommended in this regard, and
Booth's edition has many remarkable and unique qualities. Of single-
volume studies, those by Booth, J. B. Leishman and Georgio Melchiori
have proved particularly influential. The tradition continues in Helen
Vendler's commentary-edition, *The Art of Shakespeare's Sonnets,* which
includes (1–43) a trenchant critique of modern critical approaches.[63]

A Lover's Complaint

The consequences of love, the pain of rejection, desertion, and loss of
reputation are powerful elements in the poem that follows the sequence.
Despite Thorpe's unambiguous attribution of the piece to Shakespeare,
A Lover's Complaint was rejected from the canon on distinctly flimsy
grounds until quite recently.

There has been a great deal of investigation to establish the poem's
authenticity and date. It is now generally accepted as Shakespearean
and dated at some point between 1600 and 1609, possibly revised from
a first version of 1600 for publication in Thorpe's volume. Forceful arguments for its authenticity were crowned by Kerrigan's edition (see especially 389–94), which has played a valuable role in restoring its visibility, as did numerological studies such as those of Alastair Fowler and
Thomas Roche. Drawing heavily on Spenser and Daniel, it is the complaint of a wronged woman at the duplicity of a man (see Kerrigan's
Motives of Woe). It is in some sense as much a companion to *Lucrece* and to
All's Well That Ends Well as to the sonnets

Its connections with the narrative poems, the plays, and the genre of
female complaint have begun to be revealed in recent scholarship. The
woman is a city (176) besieged by an eloquent wooer ("how deceits were
gilded in his smiling" [173]), whose essence is dissimulation ("his passion, but an art of craft" [245]). There has been a growing tendency to
relate the poem to its immediate context in Thorpe's sonnets volume,
and to find it a reflection (or gloss or critique) of the preceding sequence
(see Arden, 86–95).

The poem consists of 329 lines, disposed into 47 seven-line rhyme-
royal stanzas. It is in four sections. In the first, the unidentified "I" of the
poem encounters a distressed woman, "Storming her world with sorrow's wind and rain" (7), throwing love tokens into a river (36–42); as
she rips love letters to shreds, she cries out:

> O false blood, thou register of lies,
> What unapproved witness dost thou bear!
> Ink would have seem'd more black and damned here!
>
> (52–55)

As the observer watches, an old man, a former courtier "that the ruffle knew / Of court, of city" (58–59), approaches and politely asks the woman to tell "In brief the grounds and motives of her woe" (62–63). Reluctant at first, she is persuaded by the old man's gentility and reserve as he sits "comely distant" from her.

After what has been essentially a prologue, she embarks on her story, which occupies the rest of the poem, which is in three sections. In the first passage, of just over 100 lines (71–176), she tells of her predicament—"Woe is me, too early I attended / A youthful suit" (78–79) and explains something of its situation. In the second, of almost identical length (177–280), she recounts the wooing to which she succumbed: "thus he gan besiege me." In the final section (281–329), she resumes the lament, doubtless the same lament she had been crying out before the poem began and before either the old man or the "I" had encountered her. Neither of these figures responds to her.

As *Lucrece* is framed by the words "without beginning" (Dedication) and "everlasting" (1855), *A Lover's Complaint* ends as it begins—with a weeping woman. It also concludes in an open-ended fashion, as the woman poses a question to the "father" (as she refers to him at 71 and 288) to whom she has, in effect, made her confession. She asks for opinions, but knows they will not be unanimous:

> Thus merely with the garment of a Grace
> The naked and concealed fiend he cover'd,
> That th' unexperient gave the tempter place,
> Which like a cherubin above them hover'd.
> Who, young and simple, would not be so lover'd?,
> Ay me, I fell, and yet do question make
> What should I do again for such a sake.
>
> (316–22)

Her predicament embodies two related and typically gendered stereotypes: the deserted victim of a sexual predator and a self divided between desire and reason. In this case they are combined in the same person. More than that, of course, the ending shows a person trapped and doomed, like the figures in Spenser's Cave of Mammon (*FQ,* II.vii), to endless repetition of the mistake or fault that has brought them to that miserable place.

In her description of her seducer she lists his admired attributes, some of which have a distinctly Sidneian ring:

> Well could he ride, and often men would say.
> That horse his mettle from his rider takes;
> Proud of subjection, noble by the sway,
> What rounds, what bounds, what course, what stop he makes!
> (106–9)

He is well stocked with eloquent arguments ("on the tip of his subduing tongue" [120]) and empowered with every grace of body and mind. In language that echoes the sonnets, *All's Well That Ends Well,* and *Hamlet,* she tells the old man:

> That he did in the general bosom reign
> Of young, of old, and sexes both enchanted,
> To dwell with him in thoughts, or to remain
> In personal duty, following where he haunted.
> Consents bewitch'd, ere he desire, have granted,
> And dialogu'd for him what he would say,
> Ask'd their own wills and made their wills obey.
> (127–33)

The man's reputation as a seducer does not deter her ("who ever shunned by precedent . . . ?" she asks [155]) since she tells the old man she is not governed by reason but by appetite (166–68). She is also flattered by the lover's speeches, in which he argues that he has remained untouched—mentally and spiritually—by his previous sexual encounters. He tells her,

> All my offenses that abroad you see
> Are errors of the blood, none of the mind;
> Love made them not.
> (183–85)

He then shows the woman a bundle of trophies from his lovers, demonstrating not only their worthlessness but also making clear that he has been the pursued, not the pursuer. The litany concludes with an account of how, as he puts it, "My parts had pow'r to charm a sacred nun" (260), and he tells of a nun who had given up her vows and celibate life to follow him. Finally he makes his major request: she has the power to rescue him and all those who are devoted to him from the intolerable pressures under which they all live. It is those other women who are begging her to sleep with him:

> Now all these hearts that do on mine depend,
> Feeling it break, with bleeding groans they pine,
> And supplicant their sighs to you extend
> To leave the batt'ry that you make 'gainst mine.
>   (274–77)

All of which, she rapidly discovers, is false. Experience teaches her that

> Against the thing he sought he would exclaim:
> When he most burnt in heart-wish'd luxury,
> He preach'd pure maid, and prais'd cold chastity.
>   (313–15)

The poem is, as noted earlier, closely related to other female complaints (see the lists in Kerrigan, Roe, 61–63, and Bates, 139). Unlike some lamenting female speakers, the woman is not dead and not a ghost, although the fact that she is first heard as an echo and that her final stanza begins five of its lines with "O" may be designed to suggest that her endless woe is resounding incessantly, perhaps eternally.

The relationship of this poem to the sonnets is probably best approached by analogy with other poems connected with groups of sonnets (as in Daniel, Spenser, and others). Another approach is through dating, and the indications are that the poem was composed at the turn of the century and perhaps revised shortly before Thorpe's publication: hence its echoes of *All's Well* and *Cymbeline*. An additional approach is through intertextuality, setting the poem in relation to Chaucer's Franklin's Tale, Spenser's *Complaints,* and other works. Critics are only beginning to explore this text.

In the context of our study, the debt that is most relevant is to Spenser's poem *The Ruines of Time* (Kerrigan cites some parallel passages, 390–91). Spenser's poem is dense, multiple, and various, including meditations on history, an encounter with the spirit of the Roman-British city of Verulam by the banks of the river, and laments and praise for Sir Philip Sidney.

Spenser imposes a variety of interlocking structural patterns on the flux of history and the brevity of human life and accomplishment, using multiples of seven, for example, to structure his elegy on Sidney. Perhaps in acknowledgment, the woman's final speech in Shakespeare's poem is 7 seven-line stanzas, or 49 lines; but the thrust of Shakespeare's poem seems to be away from the idea of art or form as a consolation amid the vicissitudes of life. The two poems repay study together.

But there may be another, more immediate connection with Spenser and his poem. His *Ruines* was written shortly after the death of Sidney, and one of its subjects is poetic immortality, pointedly contrasted with the towers and monuments of cities, such as the now ruined Verulam. As we have noted, in 1598 Sidney's immortality was announced by the publication of his collected works. Then at Christmas of that year Spenser came home destitute and broken hearted from Ireland, and died shortly afterwards. In one of his later poems, *Prothalamion,* he had represented himself walking on the meadows along the south bank of the Thames. I have suggested earlier, on the basis of the publication of Shakespeare's works at that time, that these events in 1598 and 1599 led to a transformation in Shakespeare's sense of himself and his visibility in the literary marketplace. In addition, at the time Spenser was being given his laureate funeral, Shakespeare and his company began to move the timbers of their theater across the river to the new site where the Globe would be built in the spring of 1599. From that site, the most visible structure to the east was the Tower of London, which the Elizabethans erroneously believed was Roman and built by Julius Caesar. In *Richard II,* the Queen says to her ladies, "This way the King will come, this is the way / To Julius Caesar's ill-erected Tower" (5.2.1–2). As the Globe's wooden structure took shape, with "upon her head a platted hive of straw" (8), there could have been no better place in England than the "weeping margent" of the Thames from which to contemplate the broad shapes of history and meditate on the relationship between the gilded monuments of princes and the powerful rhymes of poets.

Conclusion

The sonnets occupy a distinct, marginal space between social classes, between public and private, narrative and dramatic forms. And they proceed not through inverting categories but rather through interrogating them. Variations are played on Elizabethan conventions of erotic discourse —love without sex, sex without love, a "master-mistress" who is "prick'd . . . out for women's pleasure" as the ultimate in the unattainable ("to my purpose nothing" [20]). Like Spenser's *Amoretti*, Shakespeare's collection meditates on the relationships among love, art, time, and immortality. But it remains a meditation, even when it seems most decided. Thus the young man is conventionally told, "So long as men can breathe or eyes can see, / So long lives this, and this gives life to thee" (18). Although the verses have survived, the young man's name has not.

Part of the concerns shared with *Venus and Adonis* and *Lucrece* is the sense of the fatal consequences of desire that crossed boundaries and burst out of limits. As was noted earlier, such transgressiveness, not always treated so tragically, was a staple of the literature of the 1590s. At the end of his career, Shakespeare would return to the theme, showing in *The Two Noble Kinsmen* the madness and despair that overcome the jailer's daughter when she falls in love with a prince to whom, because of her social class, she is all but invisible. In contrast, the sonnets, no less than the plays, are the products of a writer who—as a poet, a writer for the stage, an actor, and a prosperous businessman with a coat of arms— possessed a remarkable degree of freedom to cross physical, social, and linguistic boundaries.

The unique, marginal position of the stage, together with Shakespeare's own unique situation, meant that he could draw upon both city and court styles and languages in order to show, for instance, Eastcheap or the Inns of Court to the nobility at Whitehall, and stage kings and queens amid the taverns and brothels of the south bank of the Thames. Frequently the values of these different worlds are shown in competition, and more often than not the competition ends with an ambiguous resolution, completed in the mind of the audience—as indicated by such titles as *As You Like It* and *Twelfth Night, or What You Will*.

An instructive example is *The Merry Wives of Windsor*. This play, although set in the bourgeois world of townsfolk, is one of Shakespeare's most obviously "courtly" plays, not only because it was allegedly commissioned by the queen, who wanted to see Falstaff in love, but also because of its many allusions to court and political events and personalities. It may indeed have been written for a specific court occasion.

The court and bourgeois worlds collide in a curiously ambivalent and ambiguous way. On the surface, the plot is a piece of bourgeois triumphalism. In the course of the play and in a way that might recall aspects of *Venus and Adonis, Lucrece,* and the sonnets, the respectable female townsfolk find themselves prey to the errant, questing sexual urges of the gentleman Fenton and of Sir John Falstaff. Fenton is an exemplary courtly wooer, but for much of the play his intentions, like those of Lyly's heroes, are left ambiguous. Courtly wooing did not necessarily end in marriage (any more than Hatton's highly charged letters to the queen were to be taken literally as those of a lover), but bourgeois wooing was supposed to do so.[64] At the end of the *Merry Wives,* it is the power of bourgeois marriage—what we would today call family values—that subdues the phallic energies of both Falstaff and Fenton. What we see on stage is a young middle-class girl marrying into, and supposedly taming the sexuality of, the gentry. Shakespeare's own granddaughter was to marry into this class and, after her husband was knighted, she died as Lady Bernard. After Page has given his final blessing to the union, with the kind of proverbial nostrum associated with his class ("what cannot be eschew'd must be embrac'd"), his wife gathers the company—including the humiliated Falstaff—together:

> Well, I will muse no further. Master Fenton,
> Heaven give you many, many merry days!
> Good husband, let us every one go home,
> And laugh this sport o'er by a country fire—
> Sir John and all.
> (5.5.237–43; Riverside, 356)

But the context—perhaps the occasion and setting—of this "victory" is wholly courtly, and the subject is derived from that paradigmatic courtly stimulus, a queen's desire for a story. Even removed from that immediate setting, the context of the final episode is the impending arrival of the Queen of Fairies, announced by Mistress Quickly (5.5.55–76). At an even more fundamental level, a play about wives and weddings is, to say the least, an intriguing contribution to the queen's cult of unchanging virginity.

The ambiguity of the *Merry Wives* seems calculated, designed to make definitive interpretation—the decoding of the "truth" behind the play or the deciphering of its meaning—impossible. As such, it may, perhaps surprisingly, be seen to operate in ways that are analogous to the sonnets. Montaigne has left an account of the value of such ambiguity in cultivating in its readers the disposition for which he strove throughout his life, and it presents a tantalizing picture of the kind of reader Shakespeare might have wished for:

> No generous spirit stayes and relies upon himselfe. . . . His nourishment is admiration, questing [Fr. *la chasse*, i.e. the hunt] and ambiguity: Which Apollo declared sufficiently, alwayes speaking ambiguously, obscurely and obliquely unto us; not feeding, but busying and amusing us. It is an irregular, uncertaine motion, perpetuall, patternlesse and without end. His inventions enflame, follow and enter-produce one another. . . . There's more adoe to enterpret interpretations, than to interpret things: and more bookes upon bookes, then upon any other subject. we doe but enter-glose our selves. (III.xiii,. "Of Experience," tr. Florio, 326–27)[65]

However marginal their position in professional criticism and in the classroom, Shakespeare's sonnets are works that possess an astonishing continuing appeal, and the poems were by far his most renowned and successful publications in his own lifetime. These considerations were the starting points of the present study. I have tried, as far as possible in a short volume, to show what it was about these works that made them so appealing to Shakespeare's contemporaries. One conclusion to be drawn from the account offered here is that the contrasting reputations of Shakespeare's sonnets and poems since their author's death serve as an index of broader cultural and historical developments, just as much as they testify to changes in taste and fashion over four centuries. Another conclusion, however, is that the study of these works shows (to adapt Ben Jonson's phrase) that Shakespeare's standing as a writer "for all time" is inseparable from his being so emphatically the poet of his own astonishing age. It has been my aim to relate the poems and sonnets generally to the culture of the 1590s and specifically to other English writers of that time, in order to help modern readers recover some sense of the novelty, innovation, and bravado of these works, and to encourage more "well-wishing adventurers" as they set forth to explore these products of a crucial period in Shakespeare's development as an artist.

Notes and References

Chapter One

1. See also the chapters "Elizabethan" and "Shakespeare's Career" in my companion volume to the present study: Dennis Kay, *William Shakespeare: His Life and Times* (New York: Twayne, 1995), 106–18, 138–52.

2. Emrys Jones, ed., *The New Oxford Book of Sixteenth Century Verse* (Oxford: Oxford University Press, 1991).

3. Michael Drayton, "To My Most Dearely-loved Friend Henery Reynolds Esquire. Of Poets and Poesie," lines 17–30, in *Michael Drayton: Poems,* ed. John Buxton (London: Routledge, 1953), 1.151.

4. E. A. J. Honigmann, *Shakespeare's Impact on his Contemporaries* (Manchester: Manchester University Press, 1982), 1–24; Dennis Kay, *William Shakespeare: His Life, Work, and Era* (New York: Morrow, 1992), 162–67.

5. Alfred Harbage, Samuel Schoenbaum, and Sylvia Stoler Wagonheim, *Annals of English Drama, 975–1700,* 3rd ed. (New York: Routledge, 1989). In the discussion of the statistics I am indebted to Andrew Gurr, *The Shakespearean Playing Companies* (Oxford: Clarendon Press, 1996).

6. See Gerald Eades Bentley, *The Profession of Dramatist in Shakespeare's Time, 1590–1642* (Princeton: Princeton University Press, 1971).

7. See H. R. Woudhuysen, *Sir Philip Sidney and the Circulation of Manuscripts 1558–1640* (Oxford: Clarendon Press, 1997).

8. Michael G. Brennan, *Literary Patronage in the Renaissance: The Pembroke Family* (London: Routledge, 1988), 55–65.

9. For an account of Sidney's reputation, see Dennis Kay, "Introduction. Sidney—A Critical Heritage" in *Sir Philip Sidney: An Anthology of Modern Criticism,* ed. Dennis Kay (Oxford: Oxford University Press, 1987), 3–41.

10. See Kay, *Sidney,* 18–20.

11. Louis Adrian Montrose, "The Elizabethan Subject and the Spenserian Text," in *Literary Theory/Renaissance Texts,* ed. P. Parker and D. Quint (Baltimore: Johns Hopkins University Press, 1986), 303–40.

12. See David Norbrook, *Poetry and Politics in the English Renaissance* (London: Routledge, 1984), chaps. 5 and 8.

13. From the translation of Camden's *Annales* by Thomas Browne, *The Historie of the Life and Reigne of that Famous Princesse, Elizabeth* (1629), 231–32. See R. M. Cummings, *Edmund Spenser: The Critical Heritage* (London: Routledge, 1971), 315–16.

14. See Richard Helgerson, *Self-Crowned Laureates: Spenser, Jonson, Milton and the Literary System* (Berkeley: University of California Press, 1983).

15. Lorna Hutson, *Thomas Nashe In Context* (Oxford: Oxford University Press, 1989), 11.

16. Stephen May, *The Elizabethan Courtier Poets: The Poems and their Contexts* (Columbia: University of Missouri Press, 1991).

17. See, for example, two studies by Louis Adrian Montrose: "Of Gentlemen and Shepherds: The Politics of Elizabethan Pastoral Form," *ELH* 50 (1983), 415–59; and "Celebration and Insinuation: Sir Philip Sidney and the Motives of Elizabethan Courtship," *Renaissance Drama* 8 (1977), 3–35. See also Dennis Kay, " 'She Was A Queen, And Therefore Beautiful': Sidney, His Mother, and Queen Elizabeth," *Review of English Studies,* n.s., 43 (1992), 17–39.

18. Kay, *Shakespeare* (1995), 106–18.

19. George Puttenham, *The Arte of English Poesie,* ed. G. D. Willcock and Alice Walker (Cambridge: Cambridge University Press, 1936), 299–300, 186.

20. Catherine Bates, *The Rhetoric of Courtship in Elizabethan Language and Literature* (Cambridge: Cambridge University Press, 1992), 83–88: see also chaps. 1 and 2.

21. Helen Hackett, *Virgin Mother, Maiden Queen: Elizabeth I and the Cult of the Virgin Mary* (London: Macmillan, 1995), chap. 6.

22. Arthur Marotti, " 'Love Is Not Love': Elizabethan Sonnet Sequences and the Social Order," *ELH* 49 (1982), 396–428; Peter Stallybrass and Ann Rosalind Jones, "The Politics of *Astrophil and Stella,*" *Studies in English Literature* 24 (1984), 53–68.

23. Thomas Wilson, *The Arte of Rhetorique (1553),* ed. Robert Hood Bowers (Gainesville: University of Florida Press, 1962), 201.

24. See Douglas Bruster, *Drama and the Market in the Age of Shakespare* (Cambridge: Cambridge University Press, 1992).

25. See Lawrence Manley, ed., *London in the Age of Shakespeare: An Anthology* (London: Croom Helm, 1986), and Gail K. Paster, *The Idea of the City in the Age of Shakespeare* (Athens: University of Georgia Press, 1985).

26. Emrys Jones, "London in the Early Seventeenth century: An Ecological Approach," *The London Journal* 6 (1980), 123–33, esp.126.

27. Peter Stallybrass and Allon White, *The Politics and Poetics of Transgression* (Ithaca, N.Y.: Cornell University Press, 1986).

28. Richard Helgerson, *The Elizabethan Prodigals* (Berkeley: University of California Press, 1976); see also Arthur F. Kinney's excellent *Humanist Poetics: Thought, Rhetoric, and Fiction in Sixteenth-Century England* (Amherst: University of Massachusetts Press, 1986).

29. The clearest short introduction is still Elizabeth Story Donno, "The Epyllion," in *English Poetry and Prose 1540–1674,* ed. Christopher Ricks (London: Sphere, 1970). Her anthology, *Elizabethan Minor Epics* (London: Routledge, 1963), contains an excellent selection.

30. Sandra Clark, ed., *Amorous Rites: Elizabethan Erotic Verse* (London: Dent, 1994) contains texts by Lodge, Beaumont and Marston, along with Shakespeare and Marlowe.

31. The classic study is Stephen Greenblatt, *Renaissance Self-Fashioning: More to Shakespeare* (Chicago: University of Chicago Press, 1980).

32. Steven Mullaney, *The Place of the Stage: License, Play, and Power in Renaissance England* (Chicago: University of Chicago Press, 1986).

33. Richard Helgerson, *Forms of Nationhood: The Elizabethan Writing of England* (Chicago: University of Chicago Press, 1992),14–15, 301.

Chapter Two

1. There are several facsimiles. I have used William Shakespeare, *Venus and Adonis* (1593) (Menston: Scolar, 1969). Most editions reproduce the preliminary material.

2. G. P. V. Akrigg, *Shakespeare and the Earl of Southampton* (London: Methuen, 1968).

3. See "Clapham's *Narcissus:* A Pre-Text for Shakespeare's *Venus and Adonis?* (text, translation, and commentary)," ed. Charles Martindale and Colin Burrow, *English Literary Renaissance* 22 (1992), 147–76.

4. Mark Eccles, *Shakespeare in Warwickshire* (Madison: University of Wisconsin Press, 1961); A. E. M. Kirkwood, "Richard Field, Printer, 1589–1624," *The Library,* 4th ser., 12 (1931), 1–39.

5. Michael G. Brennan, *Literary Patronage in the English Renaissance: The Pembroke Family* (London: Routledge, 1988), 55–58; Arden, 53–69.

6. Text from *Christopher Marlowe: The Complete Poems and Translations,* ed. Stephen Orgel (Harmondsworth: Penguin, 1971), 135.

7. Ovid's poem, which is a response to those who belittle the idea of poetic immortality, concludes with a ringing series of assertions of the triumph or art over mortality and the superiority of literary monuments over physical structures. The passage (lines 31–42) is reworked in Shakespeare's Sonnet 55.

8. Geoffrey Bullough, *Narrative and Dramatic Sources of Shakespeare,* vol. I (1957), 161–78.

9. See Jonathan Bate, *Shakespeare and Ovid* (Oxford: Clarendon Press, 1993), 50–58.

10. *Hero and Leander,* 1.91–93 in *Marlowe Poems,* ed. Orgel, 33.

11. Marlowe's Aurora, in contrast, is "red for anger" that her lover stayed so long with her (*Hero and Leander,* 2.89).

12. All quotations from Edmund Spenser, *The Faerie Queene,* ed. A. C. Hamilton (London: Longman, 1977).

13. For a succinct account of Spenser's relation to the tradition of the epyllion, see James Nohrnberg, *The Analogy of "The Faerie Queene"* (Princeton: Princeton University Press, 1978), 590–92.

14. Text from *The Riverside Chaucer,* 3rd ed., ed. Larry D. Benson (Boston: Houghton Mifflin, 1987), 473.

15. All references to Sidney's verse are to W. R. Ringler, ed., *The Poems of Sir Philip Sidney* (Oxford: Oxford University Press, 1962).

16.   Heather Dubrow, *Echoes of Desire:. Petrarchism and Its Counterdiscourse* (Ithaca, N.Y.: Cornell University Press, 1995).

17.   Sidney is a notable exception. For a study of relations between his writings and his distinctly problematic dealings with Queen Elizabeth, see Kay, "She was a Queen," cited in chapter 1.

18.   See Lucy Gent, *Picture and Poetry 1560–1620* (Leamington Spa: James Hall, 1981), 38–78. For books on art and perspective purchased by Southampton, see her catalogue, 81–86.

19.   See the survey of criticism in Donald G. Watson, "The Contrarieties of Venus and Adonis," *Studies in Philology* 75 (1978), 32–63.

20.   H. E. Rollins, *Shakespeare: The Poems, New Variorum Edition* (Philadelphia: Lippincott, 1938).

21.   Text from Brian Vickers, *Shakespeare: The Critical Heritage, 1623–1801,* (London: Routledge, 1974–1981), 5:314.

22.   R. A. Foakes, ed., *Coleridge on Shakespeare: The Text of the Lectures of 1811–12* (London: Routledge, 1971), 131.

23.   Keats enthusiastically cites *Venus and Adonis* 1033–38, as well as passages from Sonnet 17 in a letter to J. H. Reynolds: see *John Keats,* The Oxford Authors, ed. Elizabeth Cook (Oxford: Oxford University Press, 1990), 367–68.

24.   C. S. Lewis, *English Literature in the Sixteenth Century Excluding Drama* (Oxford: Clarendon Press, 1954), 498–99. For a similarly "anti-Venus" view, see Don Cameron Allen, "On *Venus and Adonis,*" *Elizabethan and Jacobean Studies: Presented to F. P. Wilson* (Oxford: Oxford University Press, 1959), 100–111.

25.   For Maxwell, see J. C. Maxwell, ed., *The Poems,* The New Shakespeare (Cambridge: Cambridge University Press, 1966).

26.   Robert Ellrodt, "Shakespeare the Non-dramatic Poet," in *The Cambridge Companion to Shakespeare Studies,* ed. Stanley Wells (Cambridge: Cambridge University Press, 1986), 45.

27.   Richard A. Lanham, *The Motives of Eloquence: Literary Rhetoric in the Renaissance* (New Haven: Yale University Press, 1976). See also Lucy Gent, " 'Venus and Adonis': the Triumph of Rhetoric," *Modern Language Review* 69 (1974), 721–29.

28.   William Keach, *Elizabethan Erotic Narratives* (New Brunswick, N. J.: Rutgers University Press, 1977) and Clark Hulse, *Metamorphic Verse: The Elizabethan Minor Epic* (Princeton: Princeton University Press, 1981).

29.   See, for example, Heather Asals, "*Venus and Adonis*: The Education of a Goddess," *Studies in English Literature* 13 (1973), 31–51; and Lennet Daigle, "*Venus and Adonis*: Some Traditional Contexts," *Shakespeare Studies* 13 (1980), 31–46.

30.   Heather Dubrow, *Captive Victors: Shakespeare's Narrative Poems and Sonnets* (Ithaca, N.Y.: Cornell University Press, 1987); Jonathan Bate, *Shakespeare and Ovid* (Oxford: Oxford University Press, 1993). See also Dubrow's *Echoes of Desire.*

31. See, for example, Lauren Silberman, "The Hermaphrodite and the Metamorphosis of Spenserian Allegory," *English Literary Renaissance* 17 (1987), 207–23; Gayle Whittier, "The Sublime Androgyne Motif in Three Shakespearean Works," *Journal of Medieval and Renaissance Studies* 19 (1989), 185–210; and Catherine Belsey, "Love as Trompe-l'oeil: Taxonomies of Desire in *Venus and Adonis,*" *Shakespeare Quarterly* 46 (1995), 257–300.

32. See Katherine Duncan-Jones, " 'Much Ado with Red and White': The Earliest Readers of Shakespeare's *Venus and Adonis* (1593)," *Review of English Studies,* n.s., 44 (1993), 479–501.

Chapter Three

1. My text throughout is the Riverside, although I refer occasionally to a copy of the 1594 quarto (Q1), several facsimiles of which are available, such as William Shakespeare, *Lucrece* (1594) (Menston: Scolar Press, 1968).

2. It is possible that Nashe was emboldened by the apparent relish of Southampton for erotic verse to dedicate to the young nobleman his semi-pornographic poem *A Choise of Valentines,* as well as his dazzling work of prose fiction *The Unfortunate Traveller* (1594). These seem to have been speculative dedications.

3. The arguments are conveniently summarized in Roe, *Poems,* 289–92.

4. See the text provided in E. K. Chambers, 1930, II.192, and in the edition by B. N. de Luna cited below.

5. For accounts of the sources, see Bullough, *Narrative and Dramatic Sources,* vol. 1 (London: Routledge and Kegan Paul,1957), 179–202; and Baldwin, *On the Literary Genetics of Shakespere's Poems* (Urbana: University of Illinois Press, 1950).

6. Bullough, *Sources,* 179–83.

7. Bate, *Shakespeare and Ovid,* 65–66, 104–6.

8. The standard modern study of Renaissance copiousness is Terence Cave, *The Cornucopian Text: Problems of Writing in the French Renaissance* (Oxford: Oxford University Press, 1978).

9. See Baldwin, *Literary Genetics,* 108–12, and Prince's Arden edition, 65.

10. The most important and substantial political reading of *Lucrece* is in Annabel Patterson, *Reading Between the Lines* (1993).

11. The passage also contains a tantalizing reference to Essex's literary tastes.

12. All references to Sidney's verse are to Ringler, *Poems.*

13. This list of "contents" from the 1616 quarto (Sig. A3v)? is in Prince's Arden edition, xvii.

14. See Sonnet 24, which begins "Mine eye hath play'd the painter and hath stell'd / Thy beauty's form in table of my heart."

15. At the numerical center (line 372) of Daniels's *Complaint of Rosamund,* she receives a casket from the king. She meditates on the intricate work of art and finds in it "the presage of my fall."

16. Emrys Jones, *Scenic Form in Shakespeare* (Oxford: Oxford University Press, 1971).

17. A point made definitively by Heather Dubrow in *Captive Victors,* 80–142.

18. For Paridell's rape of Hellenore, see *FQ,* III.x.

19. It seems Shakespeare remembered these lines; see the Prince's words at the end of *Romeo and Juliet*:

> A glooming peace this morning with it brings.
> The sun, for sorrow, will not show his head.
> Go hence, to have more talk of these sad things;
> Some shall be pardon'd, and some punished.
> For never was a story of more woe
> Than this of Juliet and her Romeo.
>
> (5.3.306–10)

20. Linda Woodbridge, "Palisading the Body Politic," in *True Rites and Maimed Rites,* ed. Linda Woodbridge and Edward Berry (Urbana: University of Illinois Press, 1992), 27–98.

21. "Prey" is editorial. Q1 has "pray" at lines 342 ("That for his pray to pray he doth begin"), 421, 677, and "praie" at 697.

22. Sir Philip Sidney, *An Apology for Poetry,* ed. Geoffrey Shepherd (Manchester: Manchester University Press, 1973), 102.

23. Ian Donaldson, *The Rapes of Lucretia: A Myth and its Transformations* (Oxford: Oxford University Press, 1982), and Stephanie H. Jed, *Chaste Thinking: The Rape of Lucretia and the Birth of Humanism* (Bloomington: Indiana University Press, 1989).

24. Augustine, *Concerning the City of God Against the Pagans,* trans. Henry Bettenson, introduction by Dom D. Knowles (London: Penguin, 1972), bk. I, chap. 19, 28–31. In these paragraphs I paraphrase Augustine's argument except where quotation is indicated.

25. See A. C. Hamilton, *The Early Shakespeare* (San Marino, Cal.: Huntington Library Publications, 1967).

26. See R. Thomas Simone, *Shakespeare and "Lucrece": A Study of the Poem in Relation to the Plays* (Salzburg: Salzburg Studies in English Literature, 1974).

27. See the new Arden edition of *Titus Andronicus* by Jonathan Bate (London: Routledge, 1995), and the references in his *Shakespeare and Ovid.* See also references to Philomel and to Lucrece in *Edward III* 2.1.106–111 and 3.1.194–6 (Riverside, 1741–2, 1749).

28. See Harriet Hawkins, "The Poetic and Critical *Rape of Lucrece*," in *The Devil's Party: Critical Counter-Interpretations of Shakespearean Drama* (Oxford: Oxford University Press, 1985).

29. In addition to Donaldson (1982) and Jeb (1989), see also Robert S. Miola, *Shakespeare's Rome* (Cambridge: Cambridge University Press, 1983).

30. Don Cameron Allen, "*The Rape of Lucrece*," in *Image and Meaning* (Baltimore: Johns Hopkins University Press, 1968), 58–76.

31. Richard Levin, "The Ironic Reading of *The Rape of Lucrece*," *Shakespeare Survey* 34 (1981), 85–92.

32. John Kerrigan, *Motives of Woe: Shakespeare and the "Female Complaint"* (Oxford: Oxford University Press, 1991). See also Thomas P. Roche Jr., *Petrarch and the English Sonnet Sequences* (New York: AMS Press, 1989), chap. 7.

33. Lanham, *Motives of Eloquence,* 109.

34. Katharine Eisaman Maus, "Taking Tropes Seriously: Language and Violence in Shakespeare's *Rape of Lucrece*," *Shakespeare Quarterly* 37 (1986), 66–82.

35. Joel Fineman, "Shakespeare's Will: The Temporality of Rape," *Representations* 20 (1987), 25–76.

36. An example is Michael Platt, "*The Rape of Lucrece* and the Republic for Which It Stands," *Critical Review* 19 (1975), 59–79.

37. Coppelia Kahn, "The Rape of Shakespeare's Lucrece," *Shakespeare Studies* 9 (1976), 45–72. See also Catherine R. Stimpson, "Shakespeare and the Soil of Rape," in *The Woman's Part: Feminist Criticism of Shakespeare,* ed. Carolyn Ruth Lenz, Gayle Green, and Carol Thomas Neely (Urbana: University of Illinois Press, 1980), 56–64.

38. Nancy Vickers, " 'The Blazon of Sweet Beauty's Best': Shakespeare's *Lucrece*," in *Shakespeare and the Question of Theory,* ed. Patricia Parker and Geoffrey Hartman (London: Methuen, 1985), 95–115.

Chapter Four

1. *The Complete Works of Shakespeare,* ed. David M. Bevington, updated 4th ed. (New York: Longman, 1997).

2. Carleton Brown, ed., *Poems by Sir John Salusbury and Robert Chester,* EETS ES 113 (1914).

3. William H. Matchett, "*The Phoenix and the Turtle": Shakespeare's Poem and Chester's "Loues Martyr"* (The Hague: Mouton 1965).

4. John Buxton, "Two Dead Birds," in *English Renaissance Studies Presented to Dame Helen Gardner,* ed. John Carey (Oxford: Oxford University Press, 1981), 44–55.

5. Marie Axton, *The Queen's Two Bodies: Drama and the Elizabethan Succession* (London: Royal Historical Society, 1978), 118–20. See also Anthea Hume, "*Love's Martyr,* 'The Phoenix and the Turtle', and the Aftermath of the Essex Rebellion," *Review of English Studies,* n.s., 40 (1989), 48–71.

6. E. A. J. Honigmann, *Shakespeare: The "Lost" Years* (Manchester: Manchester University Press, 1985), 90–113.

7. See the concise summary in Andrew Gurr, *The Shakespearean Playing Companies* (Oxford: Clarendon Press, 1996), 257–62.

8.   For the coat of arms, see Schoenbaum, 228–32.

9.   Dennis Kay, *Melodious Tears: The English Funeral Elegy from Spenser to Milton* (Oxford: Oxford University Press, 1990), 64–66.

10.   Baldwin, *Literary Genetics,* 368; Peter Dronke, "The Phoenix and the Turtle," *Orbis Litterarium* 23 (1968), esp. 208.

11.   See Dronke and Robert Ellrodt, "An Anatomy of *The Phoenix and the Turtle*," *Shakespeare Survey* 15 (1962), 99–110.

12.   For example, William Empson, "*The Phoenix and the Turtle*," *Essays in Criticism* 16 (1966), 147–53.

13.   J. Middleton Murry, *Discoveries* (1924), cited in Rollins, *Poems,* 565–66.

14.   G. Wilson Knight, *The Mutual Flame: On Shakespeare's Sonnets and "The Phoenix and the Turtle"* (London: 1955).

15.   C. S. Lewis (1954), 509.

16.   An exception is Marjorie Garber, "Two Birds With One Stone: Lapidary Re-Inscription in *The Phoenix and Turtle*," *The Upstart Crow* 5 (1984), 5–19.

17.   Schoenbaum, 67, and Kay, *Shakespeare* (1992), 41–42.

18.   Text from Nicholas Rowe, "Some Account of the Life &c of Mr. William Shakespear," in Shakespeare, *Works,* ed. Rowe (1709), vol. 1, xxxvi.

19.   For a transcript, see Chambers, 1930, II.246: for a modernized text, see Evans, 183.

20.   Ibid.

21.   Some transcriptions of this worn inscription read "BLESE" in line three.

22.   Honigmann, *The "Lost" Years,* 77–79.

23.   Gary Taylor, "A New Shakespeare Poem? The Evidence . . . ," *Times Literary Supplement* 20 December 1985, 1447.

24.   For accounts of the controversy, see Roe, 2, Evans, 62–66, and Donald W. Foster, " 'Shall I die?' Post Mortem: Defining Shakespeare," *Shakespeare Quarterly* 38 (1987), 58–77. Arguments for Shakespeare's authorship are conveniently summarized in Stanley Wells and Gary Taylor, with John Jowett and William Montgomery, *William Shakespeare: A Textual Companion* (Oxford: Oxford University Press, 1987), 450–55.

25.   The most substantial recent contribution to an understanding of the idea and practice of authorship within manuscript culture is H. R. Woudhuysen, *Sir Philip Sidney and the Circulation of Manuscripts 1558–1640* (Oxford: Clarendon Press, 1997).

26.   Foster's first substantial effort was the book *Elegy by W. S.: A Study in Attribution* (Newark: University of Delaware Press, 1989). He returned to the subject in "*A Funeral Elegy:* W[illiam] S[hakespeare]'s 'Best-Speaking Witnesses'," *PMLA* 111 (1996), 1080–105.

Chapter Five

1.   See Thomas Roche's survey, "Shakespeare and the Sonnet Sequence," in *English Poetry and Prose, 1540–1674,* ed. Christopher Ricks (Lon-

don: Sphere, 1970), 101–18; also J. W. Lever, *The Elizabethan Love Sonnet* (London: Methuen, 1956); and Michael R. G. Spiller, *The Development of the Sonnet: An Introduction* (London: Routledge, 1992).

2.   Kay, *Shakespeare* (1995), 59.

3.   Kerrigan (33–46) analogously argues that the preoccupation with time in the sequence is related not only to the technological developments in making more, and more widely available timepieces, but also to the related development of the so-called Protestant work ethic.

4.   Thomas P. Roche Jr., *Petrarch and the English Sonnet Sequences* (New York: AMS Press, 1989) 1.

5.   Mark Musa, *Dante's "Vita Nuova": A Translation and an Essay* (Bloomington: Indiana University Press, 1973), 96. Subsequent parenthetical references are to this edition.

6.   Leonard Forster, *The Icy Fire: Five Studies in European Petrarchism* (Cambridge: Cambridge University Press, 1969).

7.   Text from *Petrarch's Lyric Poems,* ed. R. M. Durling (Cambridge, Mass.: Harvard University Press, 1976), 272–73. The literal translation is mine.

8.   Text from Sir Thomas Wyatt, *The Complete English Poems,* ed. R. A. Rebholz (London: Penguin, 1978), 80.

9.   The standard edition is H. E. Rollins, ed., *Tottel's Miscellany (1557–1587),* 2nd ed., 2 vols. (Cambridge, Mass.: Harvard University Press, 1965).

10.   See Arthur F. Marotti, *John Donne: Coterie Poet* (Madison: University of Wisconsin Press, 1986), 3–24.

11.   Patricia Fumerton, *Cultural Aesthetics: Literature and the Practice of Social Ornament* (Chicago: University of Chicago Press, 1991).

12.   Rosalie Colie, *The Resources of Kind: Genre-Theory in the Renaissance* (Berkeley: University of California Press, 1973), and her *Shakespeare's Living Art* (Princeton: Princeton University Press, 1974), 31–134. See also Arden, 101–2.

13.   In what follows, quotations are taken from the Riverside, but I have also used the facsimile published by the Scolar Press (Menston, 1968). Stephen Booth's edition contains a reproduction of the 1609 edition, but omits *A Lover's Complaint.*

14.   All quotations from Sidney are taken from Ringler, *Poems.* On Sidney's reputation, see chapter 1.

15.   Ingram and Redpath, 3–4; Kerrigan, 168; G. B. Evans, 115.

16.   Rollins provides an exhaustive catalogue: II.171–232.

17.   Gurr, *Shakespearean Playing Companies,* 142–44 ; Leeds Barroll, *Politics, Plague, and Shakespeare's Theater* (Ithaca, N.Y.: Cornell University Press, 1991), 38–41.

18.   See Rollins, II.480 for a list of candidates. Also S. Schoenbaum, "Shakespeare's Dark Lady: A Question of Identity," in Philip Edwards, ed., *Shakespeare's Styles* (Liverpool: Liverpool University Press, 1980), 221–39.

19.   See Chambers, 1930, 1.569–71 and, for a text together with an attempt to decode the poem's allegorical sense, B. N. de Luna, *The Queen Declined: An Interpretation of "Willobie His Avisa"* (Oxford: Oxford University Press, 1970).

20. Katherine Duncan-Jones, "Was the 1609 *Shake-speares Sonnets* Really Unauthorized?" *Review of English Studies,* n.s., 34 (1983), 151–71; Arden, 86–95.

21. See Peter Beal, *Index of English Literary Manuscripts, 1450–1625,* vol. 1 (London: Mansell Bowker, 1980), pt. II, 452–54.

22. Mary Hobbs, "Shakespeare's Sonnet II—'A Sugred Sonnet'?" *Notes and Queries* 224 (1979), 112–13; Gary Taylor, "Some Manuscripts of Shakespeare's Sonnets," *Bulletin of the John Rylands Library* 68 (1985–1986), 210–46.

23. *Shakespeare's Sonnets* and *A Lover's Complaint,* ed. Stanley Wells (Oxford: Oxford University Press, 1985), 186. A text is also provided in Kerrigan, 444. For a skeptical view, see Arden, 453–62.

24. See Arthur F. Marotti, "Shakespeare's Sonnets as Literary Property," in *Soliciting Interpretation: Literary Theory and Seventeenth-Century English Poetry,* ed. Elizabeth D. Harvey and Katharine Eisaman Maus (Chicago: University of Chicago Press, 1990), 143–73. Disagreeing with Duncan-Jones, Marotti argues for much less Shakespearean involvement in the organization of the volume.

25. Andrew Gurr, "Shakespeare's First Poem: Sonnet 145," *Essays in Criticism* 21 (1971), 221–26.

26. See G. B. Evans, 113, and the detailed study by A. K. Heiatt, C. W. Heiatt, and A. L. Prescott, "When Did Shakespeare Write Sonnets 1609?" *Studies in Philology* 88 (1991), 69–109; also Arden, 13–28.

27. See Grace Ioppolo, *Revising Shakespeare* (Cambridge, Mass.: Harvard University Press, 1991).

28. In what follows I have drawn on the important studies by MacD. P. Jackson, "Punctuation and the Compositors of Shakespeare's *Sonnets,* 1609," *The Library,* 5th Series (1975), 1–24; Randall McLeod, "A Technique of Headline Analysis, with Application to *Shakespeares Sonnets,* 1609," *Studies in Bibliography* 32 (1979), 197–210; *Textual Companion* to the Wells and Taylor Oxford edition; and G. B. Evans.

29. G. B. Evans concludes that "the weight of evidence . . . makes it next to impossible to suppose that Shakespeare himself had any in-house connection with the printing of Q," in G. B. Evans, 279.

30. Katharine M. Wilson, *Shakespeare's Sugared Sonnets* (London: George Allen & Unwin, 1974), 146–71.

31. Philip Edwards, *Shakespeare and the Confines of Art* (London: Methuen, 1968), 31.

32. The two most important numerological readings are Alastair Fowler, *Triumphal Forms: Structural Patterns in Elizabethan Poetry* (Cambridge: Cambridge University Press, 1970), and Roche, *Petrarch and the English Sonnet Sequences.* See also Arden, 97–102

33. See Jonathan Goldberg, *Sodometries: Renaissance Texts, Modern Sexualities* (Stanford: Stanford University Press, 1992), and Gregory W. Bredbeck, *Sodomy and Interpretation: Marlowe to Milton* (Ithaca, N.Y.: Cornell University Press, 1991).

34. For a fuller account, see Alan Bray, *Homosexuality in Renaissance England* (London: Gay Men's Press, 1982), esp. 48–70.

35. James M. Saslow, *Ganymede in the Renaissance: Homosexuality in Art and Society* (New Haven: Yale University Press, 1986).

36. The standard account is Bruce R. Smith, *Homosexual Desire in Shakespeare's England: A Cultural Poetics* (Chicago: University of Chicago Press, 1991).

37. Laura Levine, *Men in Women's Clothing: Anti-theatricality and Effeminization, 1579–1642* (Cambridge: Cambridge University Press, 1994), 139.

38. Some particularly important studies are Jean E. Howard, "Crossdressing, the Theatre, and Gender Struggle in Early Modern England," *Shakespeare Quarterly* 39 (1988), 418–40; Kate McLuskie, "The Act, the Role, and the Actor: Boy Actresses on the Elizabethan Stage," *New Theatre Quarterly* 3 (1987), 120–30; Richmond Barbour, " 'When I Acted Young Antinous': Boy Actors and the Erotics of Jonsonian Theatre," *PMLA* 110 (1995), 1006–22; and Stephen Orgel, *Impersonations* (Cambridge: Cambridge University Press, 1996).

39. Helen Hackett, *Virgin Mother, Maiden Queen: Elizabeth I and the Cult of the Virgin Mary* (London: Macmillan, 1995), 164–70.

40. See the lengthy blazon of Pyrocles in female attire in the 1590 edition of *The Countess of Pembroke's Arcadia,* ed. M. Evans (London: Penguin, 1977), bk. I, chap. 12, 130–32.)

41. Joseph Pequigney, *Such Is My Love: A Study of Shakespeare's Sonnets* (Chicago: University of Chicago Press, 1985), argues for a much less ambiguous homoeroticism in the poems.

42. G. B. Evans, in his edition, notes about 15 connections; Anne Ferry, *The Inward Language* (Chicago: University of Chicago Press, 1981), 160–67, is an excellent short guide to the relationship.

43. In the 1590 edition, the chapter is entitled, "*Suttle Cecropia visites sad Philoclea. The shamelesse Aunts shrewd temptations to loue and mariage. The modest neeces maidenly resistance*" (259v). See M. Evans, *Arcadia,* 457–62. Several of Sonnets 1–17 draw on this chapter, in which the wicked queen tries to persuade the virtuous Philoclea (who is love with Pyrocles—who is cross-dressed as an Amazon) to consider marriage to her tragically doomed son Amphialus.

44. A letter of 1573, cited in Anne Somerset, *Elizabeth I* (London: Fontana, 1992), 334–35.

45. References are to the chapter "Companionate Marriage Versus Male Friendship," in Lisa Jardine, *Reading Shakespeare Historically* (London: Routledge, 1996).

46. See Frank Whigham, *Ambition and Privilege: The Social Tropes of Elizabethan Courtesy Theory* (Berkeley: University of California Press, 1984), chap. 4.

47. Shakespeare's language would have seemed provincial, retaining some obsolete forms and some rustic vocabulary (like the Warwickshire dialect word "mobled" in *Hamlet*) when compared to the vocabulary and verb forms of writers such as Jonson and Nashe. See N. F. Blake, *Shakespeare's Language: An*

Introduction (London: Macmillan, 1983), and S. S. Hussey, *The Literary Language of Shakespeare* (London: Longman, 1982).

48. Joel Fineman, *Shakespeare's Perjured Eye: The Invention of Poetic Subjectivity in the Sonnets* (Berkeley: University of California Press, 1986).

49. Kerrigan, 27–30, makes a similar point.

50. William A. Oram et al., *The Yale Edition of the Shorter Poems of Edmund Spenser* (New Haven: Yale University Press, 1989), 645.

51. See Howard Felperin, *The Uses of the Canon: Elizabethan Literature and Contemporary Theory* (Oxford: Oxford University Press, 1989), chap. 4.

52. See Georgio Melchiori, *Shakespeare's Dramatic Meditations: An Experiment in Criticism* (Oxford: Oxford University Press, 1976), for a dazzling account of the ambiguities in this sonnet and for a study of ambiguity in several other sonnets. For additional samples of the massive commentary, see Kerrigan, 290-94, G. B. Evans, 201-3, and Booth, 305-9.

53. See the two important studies, Arthur Marotti, "Shakespeare's Sonnets as Literary Property," cited above, and Margreta de Grazia, *Shakespeare Verbatim* (Oxford: Oxford University Press, 1991), esp. 162–75.

54. See Gary Taylor's trenchant account in *Reinventing Shakespeare: A Cultural History from the Restoration to the Present* (London: Hogarth, 1990), 154–57.

55. See E. A. J. Honigmann, ed., *Milton's Sonnets* (London: Macmillan, 1966).

56. A. W. von Schlegel, *A Course of Lectures on Dramatic Art and Literature* (1808); Wordsworth, "Essay, supplementary to the Preface" (1815); Chalmers, *An Apology for Believers in the Shakspeare-Papers* (1797). Fuller references are in Taylor, *Reinventing Shakespeare*, 427, and see the note to Gill's edition of Wordsworth below.

57. Apart from the comments collected by Rollins, see Kenneth Muir, *Shakespeare's Sonnets* (London: Allen and Unwin, 1979), chap. 8, and S. Schoenbaum, *Shakespeare's Lives* (Oxford: Oxford University Press, 1970).

58. *William Wordsworth,* ed. Stephen Gill (Oxford: Oxford University Press, 1984), 356–57; for Wordsworth's comments on Steevens and the sonnets, see 647.

59. "At the Mermaid" and "House," in *The Poems of Robert Browning,* selected by Sir Humphrey Milford (Oxford: Oxford University Press, 1949), 569, 573.

60. Margreta de Grazia, "The Scandal of Shakespeare's Sonnets," *Shakespeare Survey* 46 (1993), 35–49.

61. See two studies by Heather Dubrow: *Captive Victors* and " 'Incertainties Now Crown Themselves Assur'd': The Politics of Plotting Shakespeare's Sonnets," *Shakespeare Quarterly* 47 (1996), 291–305.

62. Edward Hubler et al., eds., *The Riddle of Shakespeare's Sonnets* (New York: Basic Books, 1962); Hilton Landry, *New Essays on Shakespeare's Sonnets*

(New York: A.M.S., 1976); and Peter Jones, ed., *Shakespeare: The Sonnets* (London: Macmillan, 1977).

63.   Stephen Booth, *An Essay on Shakespeare's Sonnets* (New Haven: Yale University Press, 1969); J. B. Leishman, *Themes and Variations in Shakespeare's Sonnets* (London: Hutchinson, 1961); Georgio Melchiori, *Shakespeare's Dramatic Meditations: An Experiment in Criticism* (Oxford: Oxford University Press, 1976); Helen Vendler, *The Art of Shakespeare's Sonnets* (Cambridge, Mass.: Harvard University Press, 1997).

64.   See Bates, *Rhetoric of Courtship,* chaps. 1, 2, and 4.

65.   I have used the three-volume edition of *Montaigne's Essays,* trans. John Florio (1603), (London: Dent, 1910), 3.326–27.

Selected Bibliography

PRIMARY WORKS

Shakespeare

The Narrative Poems. Edited by Maurice Evans. The New Penguin Shakespeare. London: Penguin, 1989.

The Poems. Edited by F. T. Prince. The Arden Shakespeare. London: Methuen, 1960.

The Poems. Edited by John Roe. The New Cambridge Shakespeare. Cambridge: Cambridge University Press, 1992.

The Riverside Shakespeare. 2nd ed. Edited by G. Blakemore Evans, with the assistance of J. J. M. Tobin. Boston: Houghton Mifflin, 1997.

Shakepeare's Sonnets. Edited by Katherine Duncan-Jones. The Arden Shakespeare. Third series. New York: Thomas Nelson and Sons Ltd., 1997

Shakespeare's Sonnets. Edited by W. G. Ingram and Theodore Redpath. London: University of London Press, 1964.

Shakespeare's Sonnets. Edited with analytic commentary by Stephen Booth. New Haven: Yale University Press, 1977.

Shakespeare's Sonnets and A Lover's Complaint. Edited by Stanley Wells. Oxford: Oxford University Press, 1985.

Shakespeare: The Poems. Edited by H. E. Rollins. New Variorum Edition, 2 vols. Philadelphia: Lippincott, 1938.

The Sonnets. Edited by. H. E. Rollins. New Variorum Edition, 2 vols. Philadelphia: Lippincott, 1944.

The Sonnets. Edited by G. Blakemore Evans, with an introduction by Anthony Hecht. The New Cambridge Shakespeare. Cambridge: Cambridge University Press, 1996.

The Sonnets and A Lover's Complaint. Edited by John Kerrigan. New Penguin Shakespeare. London: Penguin, 1986.

Wells, Stanley, and Gary Taylor, with John Jowett and William Montgomery. *William Shakespeare: A Textual Companion*. Oxford: Oxford University Press, 1987.

Works. Edited by Stanley Wells and Gary Taylor. Oxford: Oxford University Press, 1986.

Other

Augustine. *Concerning the City of God Against the Pagans*. Translated by Henry Bettenson with an introduction by Dom D. Knowles. London: Penguin, 1972.

Brown, Carleton, ed. *Poems by Sir John Salusbury and Robert Chester*. London: Early English Texts Society, Early Series 113 (1914).

166

Chaucer, Geoffrey. *The Riverside Chaucer,* 3rd ed. Edited by Larry D. Benson. Boston: Houghton Mifflin, 1987.

Donno, Elizabeth Story, ed. *Elizabethan Minor Epics.* London: Routledge, 1963.

Marlowe, Christopher. *Christopher Marlowe: The Complete Poems and Translations.* Edited by Stephen Orgel. Harmondsworth: Penguin, 1971.

Musa, Mark. *Dante's "Vita Nuova": A Translation and an Essay.* Bloomington: Indiana University Press, 1973.

Petrarch. *Petrarch's Lyric Poems.* Edited by R. M. Durling. Cambridge, Mass.: Harvard University Press, 1976.

Puttenham, George. *The Arte of English Poesie.* Edited by G. D. Willcock and Alice Walker. Cambridge: Cambridge University Press, 1936.

Sidney, Sir Philip. *The Poems of Sir Philip Sidney.* Edited by William A. Ringler Jr. Oxford: Oxford University Press, 1962.

————. *An Apology for Poetry.* Edited by Geoffrey Shepherd. Manchester: Manchester University Press, 1973.

————. *The Countess of Pembroke's Arcadia.* Edited by Maurice Evans. Harmondsworth: Penguin, 1977.

Spenser, Edmund. *The Faerie Queene.* Edited by A. C. Hamilton. London: Longman, 1977.

————. *The Yale Edition of the Shorter Poems of Edmund Spenser.* Edited by William A. Oram et al . New Haven: Yale University Press, 1989.

Tottel's Miscellany (1557-1587), 2nd ed. 2 vols. Edited by H. E. Rollins. Cambridge, Mass.: Harvard University Press, 1965.

Wyatt, Sir Thomas. *The Complete English Poems.* Edited by R. A. Rebholz. London: Penguin, 1978.

SECONDARY WORKS

Books

Akrigg, G. P. V. *Shakespeare and the Earl of Southampton.* London: Methuen, 1968.

Allen, Don Cameron. *Image and Meaning.* Baltimore: Johns Hopkins University Press, 1968.

Axton, Marie. *The Queen's Two Bodies: Drama and the Elizabethan Succession.* London: Royal Historical Society, 1978.

Baldwin, T. W. *On the Literary Genetics of Shakespere's Poems.* Urbana: University of Illinois Press, 1950.

Bate, Jonathan. *Shakespeare and Ovid.* Oxford: Clarendon Press, 1993.

Bates, Catherine. *The Rhetoric of Courtship in Elizabethan Language and Literature.* Cambridge: Cambridge University Press, 1992.

Bentley, Gerald Eades. *The Profession of Dramatist in Shakespeare's Time, 1590–1642.* Princeton: Princeton University Press, 1971.

Booth, Stephen. *An Essay on Shakespeare's Sonnets.* New Haven: Yale University Press, 1969.

Bray, Alan. *Homosexuality in Renaissance England.* London: Gay Men's Press, 1982.

Bredbeck, Gregory W. *Sodomy and Interpretation: Marlowe to Milton.* Ithaca, N.Y.: Cornell University Press, 1991.

Brennan, Michael G. *Literary Patronage in the English Renaissance: The Pembroke Family.* London: Routledge, 1988.

Bruster, Douglas. *Drama and the Market in the Age of Shakespeare.* Cambridge: Cambridge University Press, 1992.

Bullough, Geoffrey. *Narrative and Dramatic Sources of Shakespeare.* Vol. 1. London: Routledge and Kegan Paul, 1957.

Cave, Terence. *The Cornucopian Text: Problems of Writing in the French Renaissance.* Oxford: Oxford University Press, 1978.

Chambers, E. K. *William Shakespeare: A Study of Facts and Problems.* 2 vols. Oxford: Oxford University Press, 1930.

Clark, Sandra, ed. *Amorous Rites: Elizabethan Erotic Verse.* London: Dent, 1994.

Colie, Rosalie. *The Resources of Kind: Genre-Theory in the Renaissance.* Berkeley: University of California Press, 1973.

———. *Shakespeare's Living Art.* Princeton: Princeton University Press, 1974.

de Grazia, Margreta. *Shakespeare Verbatim.* Oxford: Oxford University Press, 1991.

de Luna, B. N. *The Queen Declined: An Interpretation of "Willobie His Avisa."* Oxford: Oxford University Press, 1970.

Donaldson, Ian. *The Rapes of Lucretia: A Myth and Its Transformations.* Oxford: Oxford University Press, 1982.

Dubrow, Heather. *Captive Victors: Shakespeare's Narrative Poems and Sonnets.* Ithaca: Cornell University Press, 1987.

———. *Echoes of Desire: Petrarchism and Its Counterdiscourse.* Ithaca, N.Y.: Cornell University Press, 1995.

Eccles, Mark. *Shakespeare in Warwickshire.* Madison: University of Wisconsin Press, 1961.

Edwards, Philip. *Shakespeare and the Confines of Art.* London: Methuen, 1968.

Felperin, Howard. *The Uses of the Canon: Elizabethan Literature and Contemporary Theory.* Oxford: Oxford University Press, 1989.

Fineman, Joel. *Shakespeare's Perjured Eye: The Invention of Poetic Subjectivity in the Sonnets.* Berkeley: University of California Press, 1986.

Ferry, Anne. *The Inward Language.* Chicago: University of Chicago Press, 1981.

Foster, Donald W. *Elegy by W. S.: A Study in Attribution.* Newark: University of Delaware Press, 1989).

Forster, Leonard. *The Icy Fire: Five Studies in European Petrarchism.* Cambridge: Cambridge University Press, 1969.

Fowler, Alastair. *Triumphal Forms: Structural Patterns in Elizabethan Poetry.* Cambridge: Cambridge University Press, 1970.

Fumerton, Patricia. *Cultural Aesthetics: Literature and the Practice of Social Ornament.* Chicago: University of Chicago Press, 1991.

Gent, Lucy. *Picture and Poetry, 1560–1620*. Leamington Spa: James Hall, 1981.

Goldberg, Jonathan. *Sodometries: Renaissance Texts, Modern Sexualities*. Stanford: Stanford University Press, 1992.

Greenblatt, Stephen. *Renaissance Self-Fashioning: More to Shakespeare*. Chicago: University of Chicago Press, 1980.

Gurr Andrew. *The Shakespearean Playing Companies*. Oxford: Clarendon Press, 1996.

Hackett, Helen. *Virgin Mother, Maiden Queen: Elizabeth I and the Cult of the Virgin Mary*. London: Macmillan, 1995.

Hawkins, Harriet. *The Devil's Party: Critical Counter-Interpretations of Shakespearean Drama*. Oxford: Oxford University Press, 1985.

Helgerson, Richard. *The Elizabethan Prodigals*. Berkeley: University of California Press, 1976.

————. *Self-Crowned Laureates: Spenser, Jonson, Milton and the Literary System*. Berkeley: University of California Press, 1983.

————. *Forms of Nationhood: The Elizabethan Writing of England*. Chicago: University of Chicago Press, 1992.

Honigmann, E. A. J. *Shakespeare's Impact on His Contemporaries*. Manchester: Manchester University Press, 1982.

————. *Shakespeare: The "Lost" Years*. Manchester: Manchester University Press, 1985.

Hulse, Clark. *Metamorphic Verse: The Elizabethan Minor Epic*. Princeton: Princeton University Press, 1981.

Hutson, Lorna. *Thomas Nashe in Context*. Oxford: Oxford University Press, 1989.

Ioppolo, Grace. *Revising Shakespeare*. Cambridge: Harvard University Press, 1991.

Jardine, Lisa. *Reading Shakespeare Historically*. London: Routledge, 1996.

Jed, Stephanie H. *Chaste Thinking. The Rape of Lucretia and the Birth of Humanism*. Bloomington: Indiana University Press, 1989.

Jones, Emrys, ed. *The New Oxford Book of Sixteenth-Century Verse*. Oxford: Oxford University Press, 1991.

Jones, Peter, ed. *Shakespeare: The Sonnets: A Casebook*. London: Macmillan, 1977.

Kay, Dennis. *William Shakespeare: His Life, Work and Era*. New York: Morrow, 1992.

————. *William Shakespeare: His Life and Times*. New York: Twayne, 1995.

Keach, William. *Elizabethan Erotic Narratives*. New Brunswick, N.J.: Rutgers University Press, 1977.

Kerrigan, John. *Motives of Woe: Shakespeare and the "Female Complaint."* Oxford: Oxford University Press, 1991.

Kinney, Arthur F. *Humanist Poetics: Thought, Rhetoric, and Fiction in Sixteenth-Century England*. Amherst: University of Massachusetts Press, 1986.

Lanham, Richard A. *The Motives of Eloquence: Literary Rhetoric in the Renaissance*. New Haven: Yale University Press, 1976.

Leishman, J. B. *Themes and Variations in Shakespeare's Sonnets*. London: Hutchinson, 1961.

Lever, J. W. *The Elizabethan Love Sonnet.* London: Methuen, 1956.

Levine, Laura. *Men in Women's Clothing: Anti-theatricality and Effeminization, 1579–1642.* Cambridge: Cambridge University Press, 1994.

Lewis, C. S. *English Literature in the Sixteenth Century Excluding Drama.* Oxford: Clarendon Press, 1954.

Manley, Lawrence, ed. *London in the Age of Shakespeare: An Anthology.* London: Croom Helm, 1986.

Marotti, Arthur F. *John Donne: Coterie Poet.* Madison: University of Wisconsin Press, 1986.

Matchett, William H. *"The Phoenix and the Turtle": Shakespeare's Poem and Chester's "Loues Martyr."* The Hague: Mouton, 1965.

May, Stephen. *The Elizabethan Courtier Poets: The Poems and Their Contexts.* Columbia: University of Missouri Press, 1991.

Melchiori, Georgio. *Shakespeare's Dramatic Meditations: An Experiment in Criticism.* Oxford: Oxford University Press, 1976.

Miola, Robert S. *Shakespeare's Rome.* Cambridge: Cambridge University Press, 1983.

Muir, Kenneth. *Shakespeare's Sonnets.* London: Allen and Unwin, 1979.

Mullaney, Steven. *The Place of the Stage: License, Play, and Power in Renaissance England.* Chicago: University of Chicago Press, 1986.

Norbrook, David. *Poetry and Politics in the English Renaissance.* London: Routledge, 1984.

Orgel, Stephen. *Impersonations.* Cambridge: Cambridge University Press, 1996.

Paster, Gail K. *The Idea of the City in the Age of Shakespeare.* Athens: University of Georgia Press, 1985.

Patterson, Annabel. *Reading Between the Lines.* Madison: University of Wisconsin Press, 1993.

Pequigney, Joseph. *Such Is My Love: A Study of Shakespeare's Sonnets.* Chicago: University of Chicago Press, 1985.

Roche, Thomas P., Jr. *Petrarch and the English Sonnet Sequences.* New York: AMS Press, 1989.

Saslow, James M. *Ganymede in the Renaissance: Homosexuality in Art and Society.* New Haven: Yale University Press, 1986.

Schoenbaum, S. *Shakespeare's Lives.* Oxford: Oxford University Press, 1970.

———. *Shakespeare: A Compact Documentary Life.* Oxford: Oxford University Press, 1977.

Simone, R. Thomas. *Shakespeare and "Lucrece": A Study of the Poem in Relation to the Plays.* Salzburg: Salzburg Studies in English Literature, 1974.

Smith, Bruce R. *Homosexual Desire in Shakespeare's England: A Cultural Poetics.* Chicago: University of Chicago Press, 1991.

Spiller, Michael. *The Development of the Sonnet: An Introduction.* London: Routledge, 1992.

Stallybrass, Peter, and Allon White. *The Politics and Poetics of Transgression.* Ithaca, N.Y.: Cornell University Press, 1986.

Taylor, Gary. *Reinventing Shakespeare: A Cultural History from the Restoration to the Present*. London: Hogarth, 1990.

Vendler, Helen. *The Art of Shakespeare's Sonnets*. Cambridge, Mass.: Harvard University Press, 1997.

Vickers, Brian. *Shakespeare: The Critical Heritage, 1623–1801*. 6 vols. London: Routledge, 1974–1981.

Whigham, Frank. *Ambition and Privilege: The Social Tropes of Elizabethan Courtesy Theory*. Berkeley: University of California Press, 1984.

Wilson, Katharine M. *Shakespeare's Sugared Sonnets*. London: Allen & Unwin, 1974.

Woudhuysen, H. R. *Sir Philip Sidney and the Circulation of Manuscripts, 1558–1640*. Oxford: Clarendon Press, 1997.

Articles

Barbour, Richmond. " 'When I Acted Young Antinous': Boy Actors and the Erotics of Jonsonian Theatre." *PMLA* 110 (1995): 1006–22.

Belsey, Catherine. "Love as Trompe-l'oeil: Taxonomies of Desire in *Venus and Adonis*." *Shakespeare Quarterly* 46 (1995): 257–300.

Buxton, John. "Two Dead Birds." In *English Renaissance Studies Presented to Dame Helen Gardner*, edited by John Carey, 44–55. Oxford: Oxford University Press, 1981.

de Grazia, Margreta. "The Scandal of Shakespeare's Sonnets." *Shakespeare Survey* 46 (1993): 35–49.

Donno, Elizabeth Story. "The Epyllion." In *English Poetry and Prose, 1540–1674*, edited by Christopher Ricks. London: Sphere, 1970.

Dronke, Peter. "*The Phoenix and the Turtle*." *Orbis Litterarium* 23 (1968), esp. 208.

Dubrow, Heather. " 'Incertainties Now Crown Themselves Assur'd': The Politics of Plotting Shakespeare's Sonnets." *Shakespeare Quarterly* 47 (1996): 291–305.

Duncan-Jones, Katherine. "Was the 1609 *Shake-speares Sonnets* Really Unauthorized?" *Review of English Studies*, n.s., 34 (1983): 151–71.

———. " 'Much Ado with Red and White': The Earliest Readers of Shakespeare's *Venus and Adonis* (1593)." *Review of English Studies*, n.s., 44 (1993): 479–501.

Ellrodt, Robert. "An Anatomy of *The Phoenix and the Turtle*." *Shakespeare Survey* 15 (1962): 99–110.

Empson, William. "*The Phoenix and the Turtle*." *Essays in Criticism* 16 (1966): 147–53.

Fineman, Joel. "Shakespeare's Will: The Temporality of Rape." *Representations* 20 (1987): 25–76.

Foster, Donald W. " 'Shall I die?' Post Mortem: Defining Shakespeare." *Shakespeare Quarterly* 38 (1987): 58–77.

————. "*A Funeral Elegy:* W[illiam] S[hakespeare]'s 'Best-Speaking Witnesses.' " *PMLA* 111 (1996): 1080–105.

Garber, Marjorie, "Two Birds With One Stone: Lapidary Re-Inscription in *The Pheonix and Turtle,*" *The Upstart Crow* 5 (1984), 5–19.

Heiatt, A. K., C. W. Heiatt, and A. L. Prescott. "When Did Shakespeare Write Sonnets 1609?" *Studies in Philology* 88 (1991): 69–109.

Howard, Jean E. "Crossdressing, the Theatre, and Gender Struggle in Early Modern England." *Shakespeare Quarterly* 39 (1988): 418–40.

Jackson, MacD. P. "Punctuation and the Compositors of Shakespeare's *Sonnets,* 1609." *The Library,* 5th Series (1975): 1–24.

Jones, Emrys. "London in the Early Seventeenth Century: An Ecological Approach." *The London Journal* 6 (1980): 123–33.

Kahn, Coppelia. "The Rape of Shakespeare's Lucrece." *Shakespeare Studies* 9 (1976): 45–72.

Levin, Richard. "The Ironic Reading of *The Rape of Lucrece.*" *Shakespeare Survey* 34 (1981): 85–92.

Marotti, Arthur F. " 'Love Is Not Love': Elizabethan Sonnet Sequences and the Social Order." *ELH* 49 (1982): 396–428.

Marotti, Arthur F. "Shakespeare's Sonnets as Literary Property." In *Soliciting Interpretation: Literary Theory and Seventeenth-Century English Poetry,* edited by Elizabeth D. Harvey and Katharine Eisaman Maus. Chicago: University of Chicago Press, 1990, 143–73.

Martindale, Charles, and Colin Burrow, eds. "Clapham's *Narcissus*: A Pre-Text for Shakespeare's *Venus and Adonis*? (text, translation, and commentary)." *English Literary Renaissance* 22 (1992): 147–76.

Maus, Katharine Eisaman. "Taking Tropes Seriously: Language and Violence in Shakespeare's *Rape of Lucrece.*" *Shakespeare Quarterly* 37 (1986): 66–82.

McLeod, Randall. "A Technique of Headline Analysis, with Application to *Shakespeares Sonnets,* 1609." *Studies in Bibliography* 32 (1979): 197–210.

McLuskie, Kate. "The Act, the Role, and the Actor: Boy Actresses on the Elizabethan Stage." *New Theatre Quarterly* 3 (1987): 120–30.

Montrose, Louis Adrian. "Of Gentlemen and Shepherds: The Politics of Elizabethan Pastoral Form." *ELH* 50 (1983): 415–59.

————. "The Elizabethan Subject and the Spenserian Text." In *Literary Theory/Renaissance Texts,* edited by P. Parker and D. Quint, 303-40. Baltimore: Johns Hopkins University Press, 1986.

Roche, Thomas P. "Shakespeare and the Sonnet Sequence." In *English Poetry and Prose, 1540–1674,* edited by Christopher Ricks, 101-18. London: Sphere, 1970.

Schoenbaum, S. "Shakespeare's Dark Lady: A Question of Identity." In *Shakespeare's Styles,* edited by Philip Edwards. Liverpool: Liverpool University Press, 1980.

Stimpson, Catherine R. "Shakespeare and the Soil of Rape." In *The Woman's Part: Feminist Criticism of Shakespeare,* edited by Carolyn Ruth Lenz, Gayle

Green, and Carol Thomas Neely, 56–64. Urbana: University of Illinois Press, 1980.

Taylor, Gary. "A New Shakespeare Poem? The Evidence . . ." *Times Literary Supplement,* 20 December 1985, 1447.

Taylor, Gary. "Some Manuscripts of Shakespeare's Sonnets," *Bulletin of the John Rylands Library* 68 (1985–1986): 210–46.

Vickers, Nancy. " 'The Blazon of Sweet Beauty's Best': Shakespeare's *Lucrece.*" In *Shakespeare and the Question of Theory,* edited by Patricia Parker and Geoffrey Hartman, 95–115. London: Methuen, 1985.

Woodbridge, Linda. "Palisading the Body Politic." In *True Rites and Maimed Rites,* edited by Linda Woodbridge and Edward Berry, 27–98. Urbana: University of Illinois Press, 1992.

Index

The Author

Dennis Kay was Fellow and Tutor in English at Lincoln College, Oxford, and University Lecturer in English at Oxford University from 1980 to 1995, and served for eight years as General Supervisor of the M.Phil Program in Shakespeare and the Drama to 1640 at Oxford. He has held visiting positions at the Henry E. Huntington Library and at George Washington University, and has taught at the Bread Loaf School of English since 1979. His books include *Sir Philip Sidney: An Anthology of Modern Criticism* (1987), *Melodious Tears: The English Funeral Elegy from Spenser to Milton* (1990), *William Shakespeare: His Life, Works, and Era* (1992), and *William Shakespeare: His Life and Times* (1995). In 1995 Professor Kay became the inaugural holder of the Russell M. Robinson II Distinguished Chair of Shakespeare at the University of North Carolina at Charlotte.

The Editor

Arthur F. Kinney is the Thomas W. Copeland Professor of Literary History at the University of Massachusetts, Amherst, and the director of the Center for Renaissance Studies there; he is also an adjunct professor of English at New York University. He has written several books in the field, including *Humanist Poetics, Continental Humanist Poetics, John Skelton: Priest as Poet,* and the forthcoming *Lies Like the Truth: "Macbeth" and the Cultural Moment.* He is the founding editor of the journal *English Literary Renaissance* and editor of the book series Massachusetts Studies in Early Modern Culture.